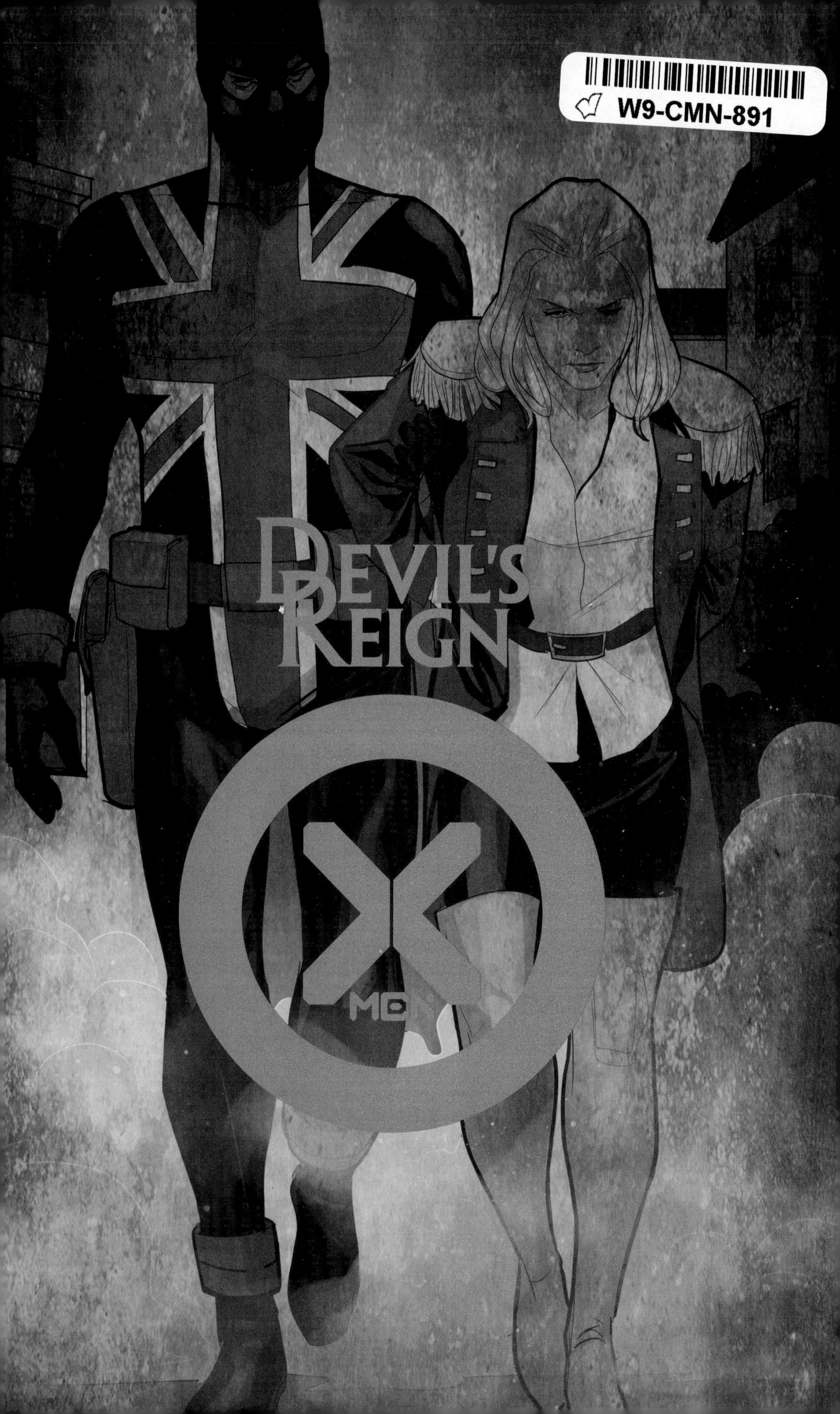
DEVIL'S
REIGN

DEVIL'S REIGN

DEVIL'S REIGN: X-MEN #1-3

WRITER **GERRY DUGGAN** | ARTIST **PHIL NOTO**

LETTERERS **VC's CORY PETIT** (#1-3) &
CLAYTON COWLES (#2) WITH **JOE CARAMAGNA** (#3)

COVER ART **PHIL NOTO** | ASSISTANT EDITOR **LAUREN AMARO**

EDITOR **JORDAN D. WHITE**

DEVIL'S REIGN: WINTER SOLDIER

WRITERS **JACKSON LANZING** & **COLLIN KELLY** | ARTIST **NICO LEON**

COLOR ARTIST **FELIPE SOBREIRO** | LETTERER **VC's JOE CARAMAGNA**

COVER ART **FELIPE MASSAFERA** | ASSISTANT EDITOR **KAITLYN LINDTVEDT**

EDITOR **ALANNA SMITH**

X-MEN CREATED BY **STAN LEE** & **JACK KIRBY**

COLLECTION EDITOR **JENNIFER GRÜNWALD**
ASSISTANT EDITOR **DANIEL KIRCHHOFFER**
ASSISTANT MANAGING EDITOR **MAIA LOY**
ASSOCIATE MANAGER, TALENT RELATIONS
LISA MONTALBANO

VP PRODUCTION & SPECIAL PROJECTS
JEFF YOUNGQUIST
BOOK DESIGNER **JAY BOWEN**
SVP PRINT, SALES & MARKETING **DAVID GABRIEL**
EDITOR IN CHIEF **C.B. CEBULSKI**

DEVIL'S REIGN: X-MEN. Contains material originally published in magazine form as DEVIL'S REIGN: X-MEN (2022) #1-3 and DEVIL'S REIGN: WINTER SOLDIER (2022) #1. First printing 2022. ISBN 978-1-302-93459-0. Published by MARVEL WORLDWIDE, INC., a subsidiary of MARVEL ENTERTAINMENT, LLC. OFFICE OF PUBLICATION: 1290 Avenue of the Americas, New York, NY 10104. © 2022 MARVEL No similarity between any of the names, characters, persons, and/or institutions in this book with those of any living or dead person or institution is intended, and any such similarity which may exist is purely coincidental. **Printed in Canada.** KEVIN FEIGE, Chief Creative Officer; DAN BUCKLEY, President, Marvel Entertainment; JOE QUESADA, EVP & Creative Director; DAVID BOGART, Associate Publisher & SVP of Talent Affairs; TOM BREVOORT, VP, Executive Editor; NICK LOWE, Executive Editor, VP of Content, Digital Publishing; DAVID GABRIEL, VP of Print & Digital Publishing; MARK ANNUNZIATO, VP of Planning & Forecasting; JEFF YOUNGQUIST, VP of Production & Special Projects; ALEX MORALES, Director of Publishing Operations; DAN EDINGTON, Director of Editorial Operations; RICKEY PURDIN, Director of Talent Relations; JENNIFER GRUNWALD, Director of Production & Special Projects; SUSAN CRESPI, Production Manager; STAN LEE, Chairman Emeritus. For information regarding advertising in Marvel Comics or on Marvel.com, please contact Vit DeBellis, Custom Solutions & Integrated Advertising Manager, at vdebellis@marvel.com. For Marvel subscription inquiries, please call 888-511-5480. **Manufactured between 6/17/2022 and 7/19/2022 by SOLISCO PRINTERS, SCOTT, QC, CANADA.**

10 9 8 7 6 5 4 3 2 1

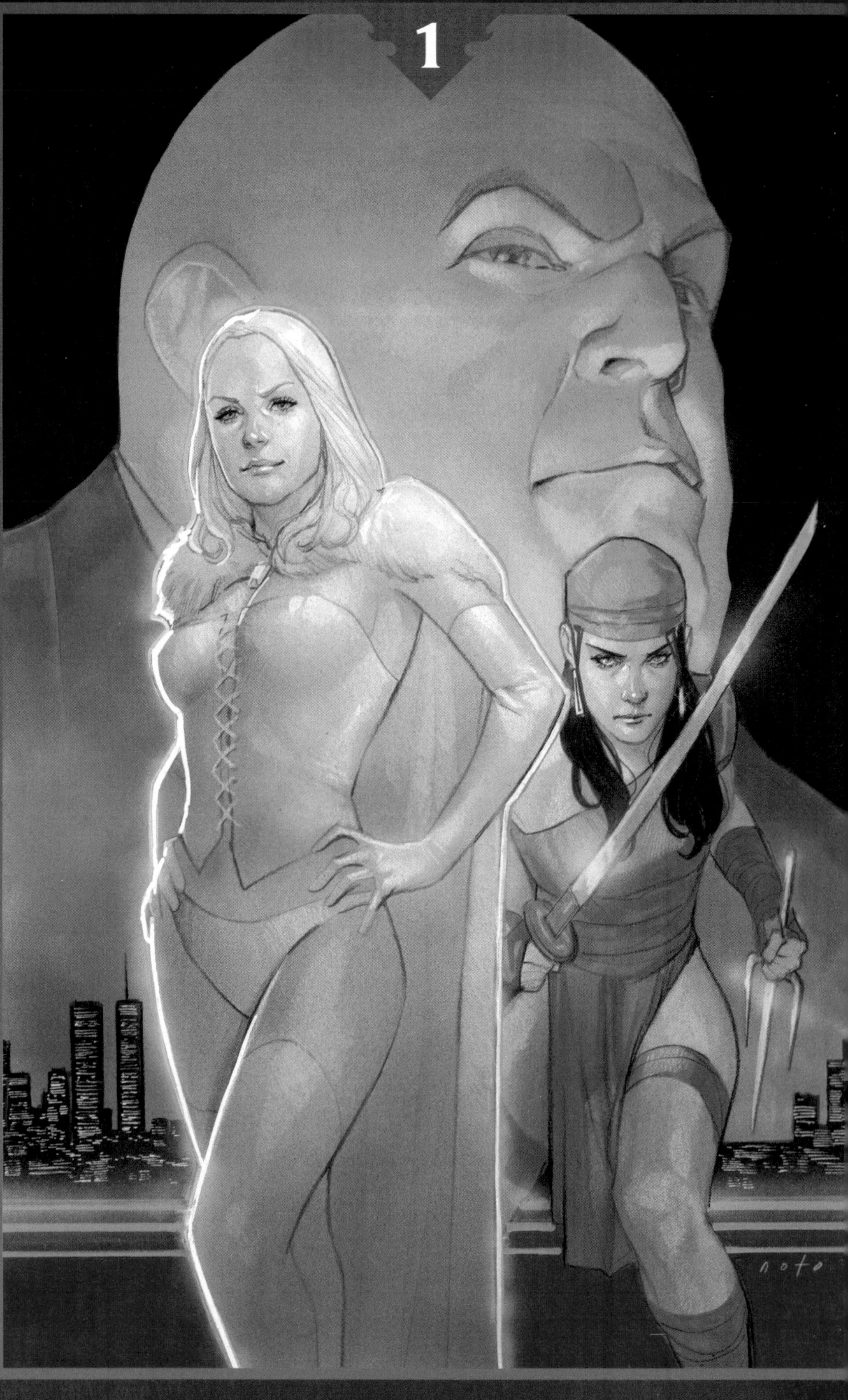
1
noto

[devilsre....[0.1]
[ignxmen.....[0.1]

"Wilson Fisk ruled this city by fear...
but it wasn't his only weapon. He
had his fat fingers into everything,
and when fear wasn't enough, there
were whispers of invisible women that
made sure the men and institutions
bent to his will. And it worked. He's
the most powerful man in the most
important city in the world. "

-- AN UNNAMED REPORTER
ABOUT TOWN

[devilsre....[0.1]
[ignxmen.....[0.1]

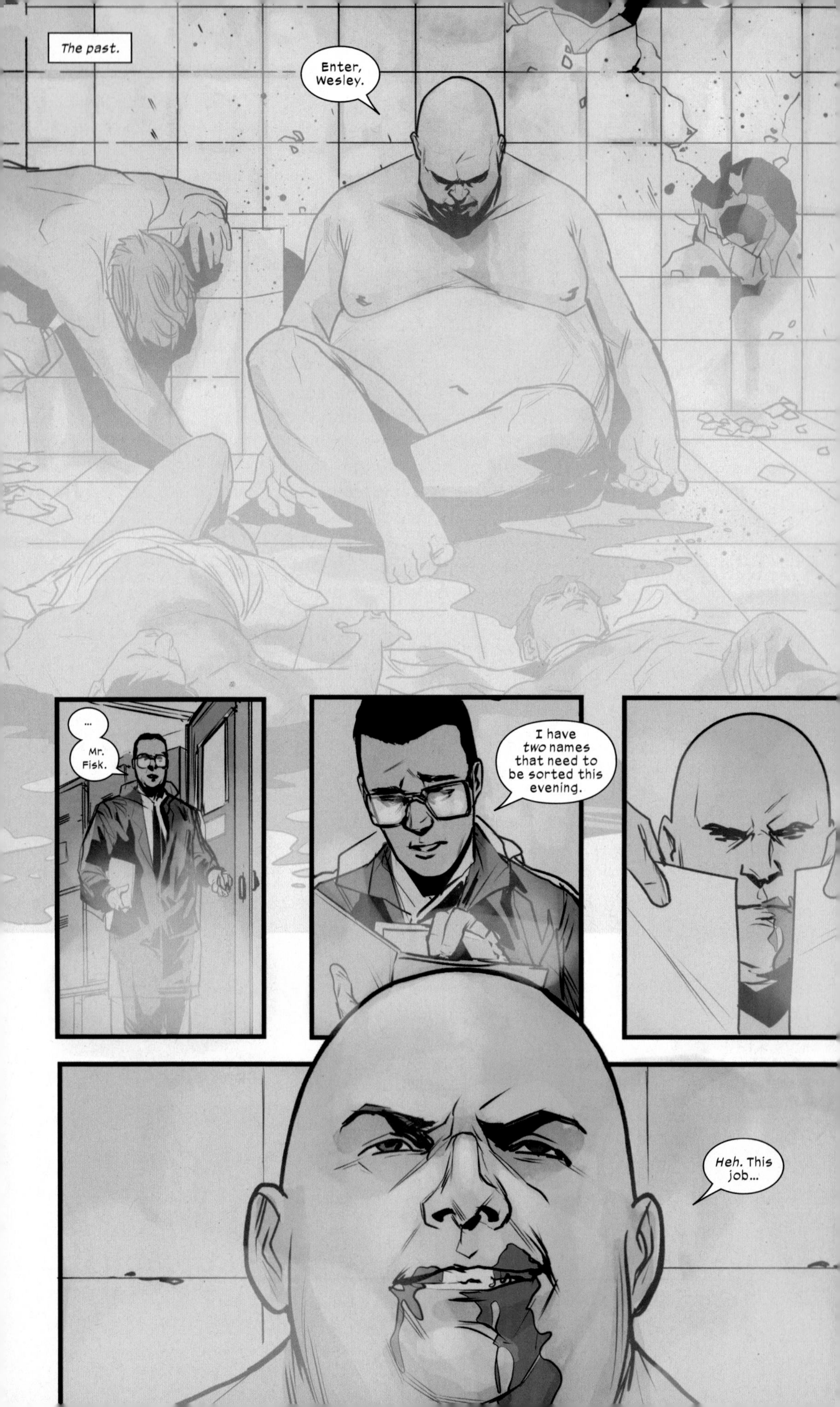
The past.
Enter, Wesley.
...
Mr. Fisk.
I have *two* names that need to be sorted this evening.
Heh. This job...

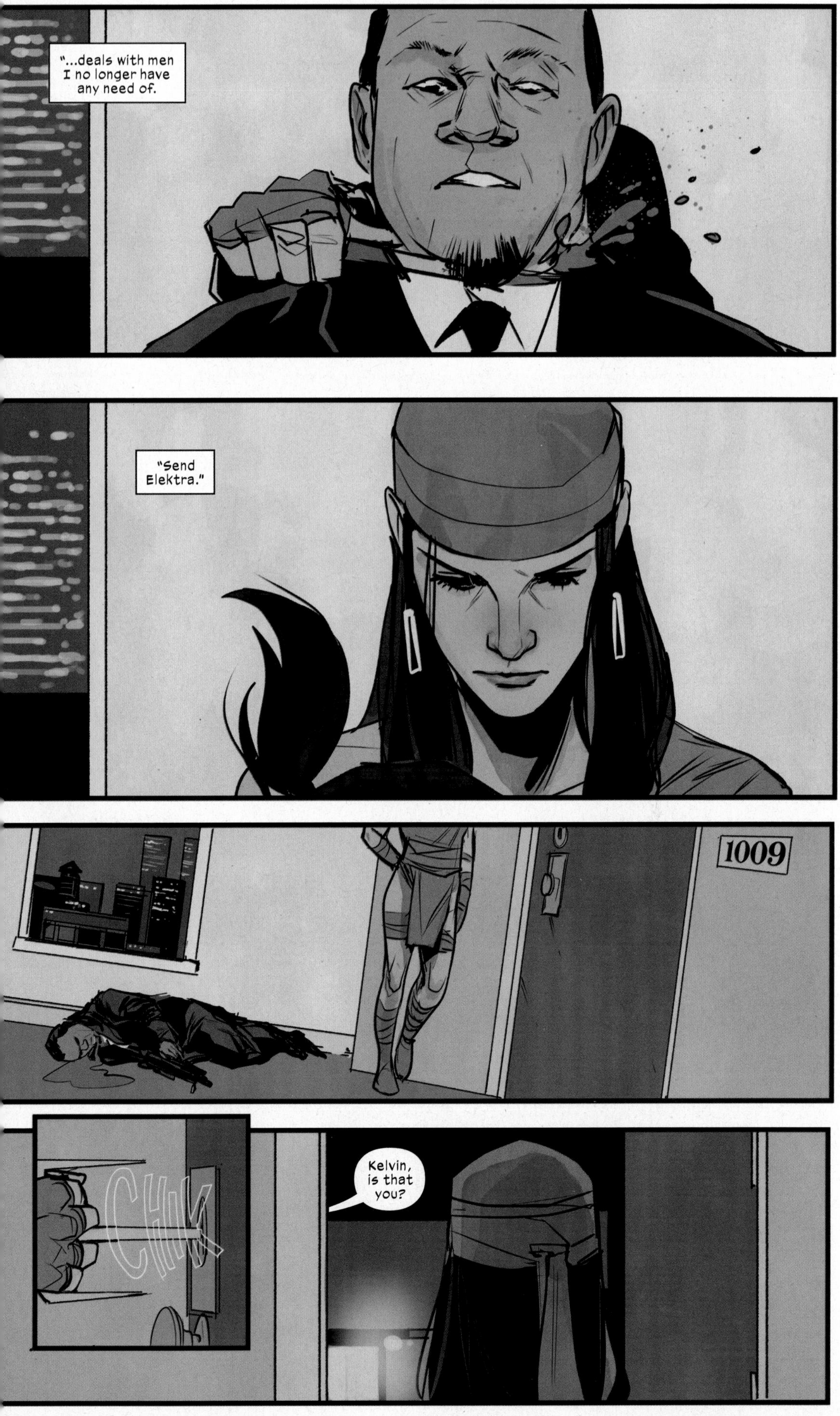
"...deals with men I no longer have any need of.
"Send Elektra."
1009
CHK
Kelvin, is that you?

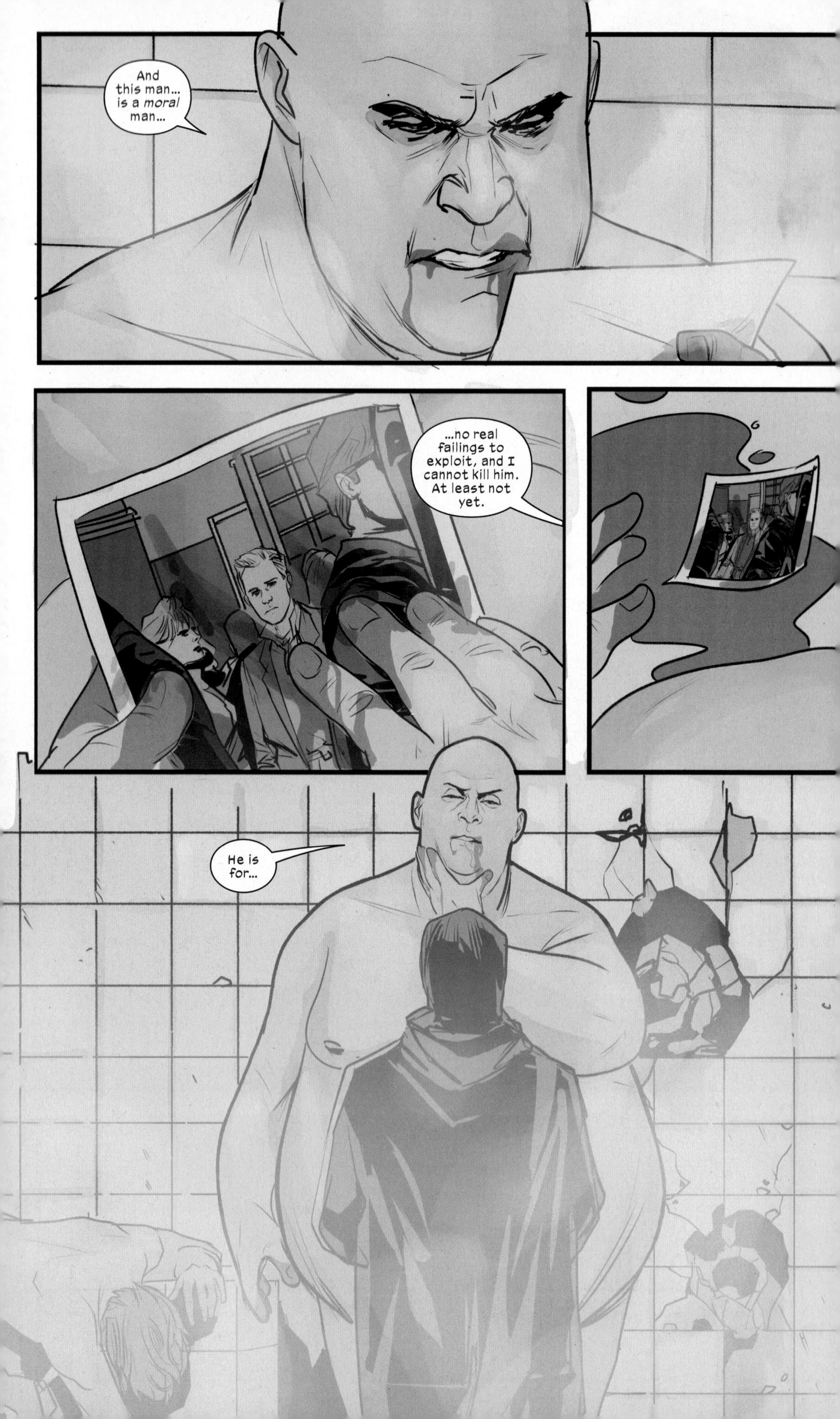
And this man... is a *moral* man...
...no real failings to exploit, and I cannot kill him. At least not yet.
He is for...

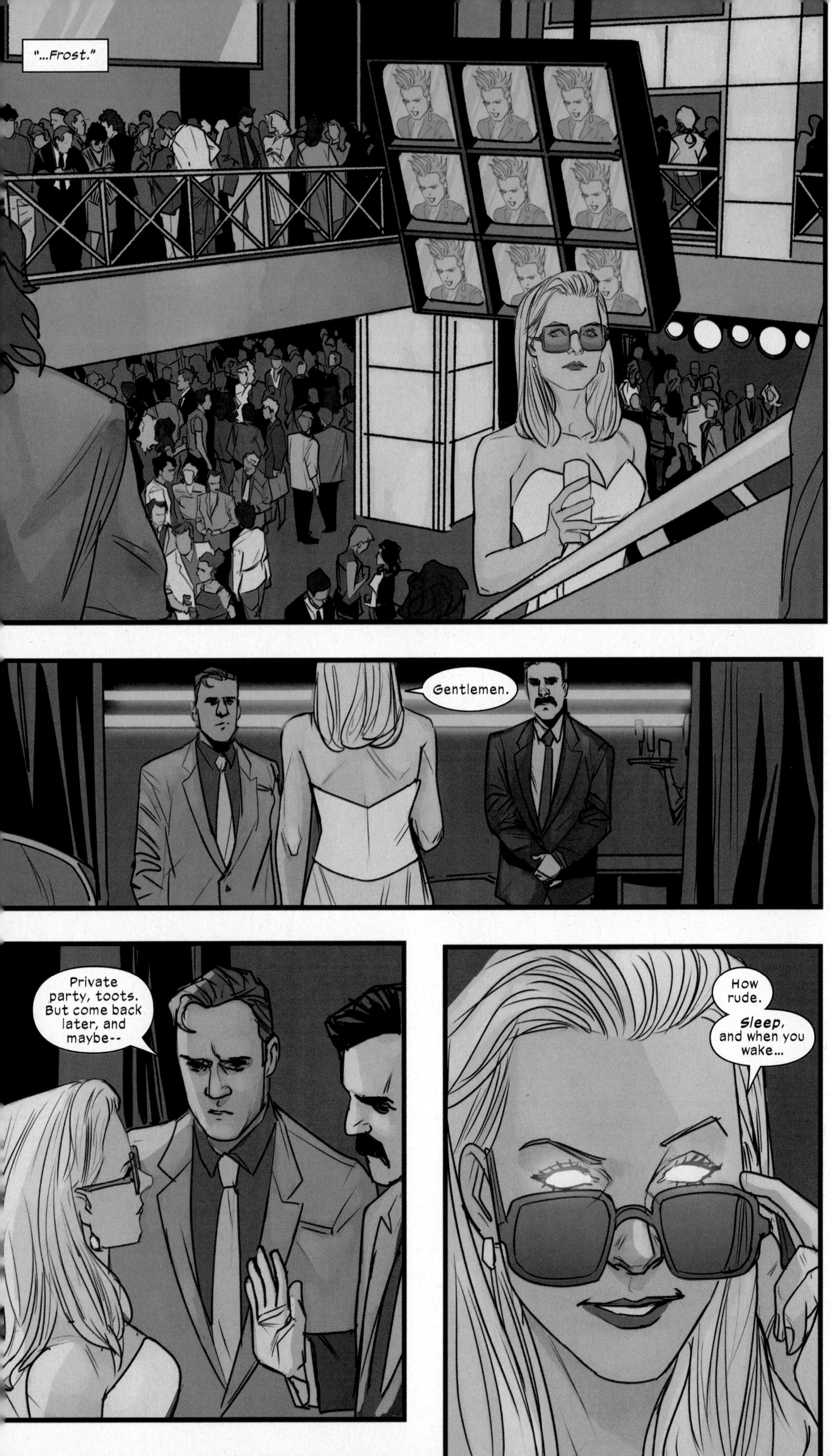
"...Frost."
Gentlemen.
Private party, toots. But come back later, and maybe--
How rude.
Sleep, and when you wake...

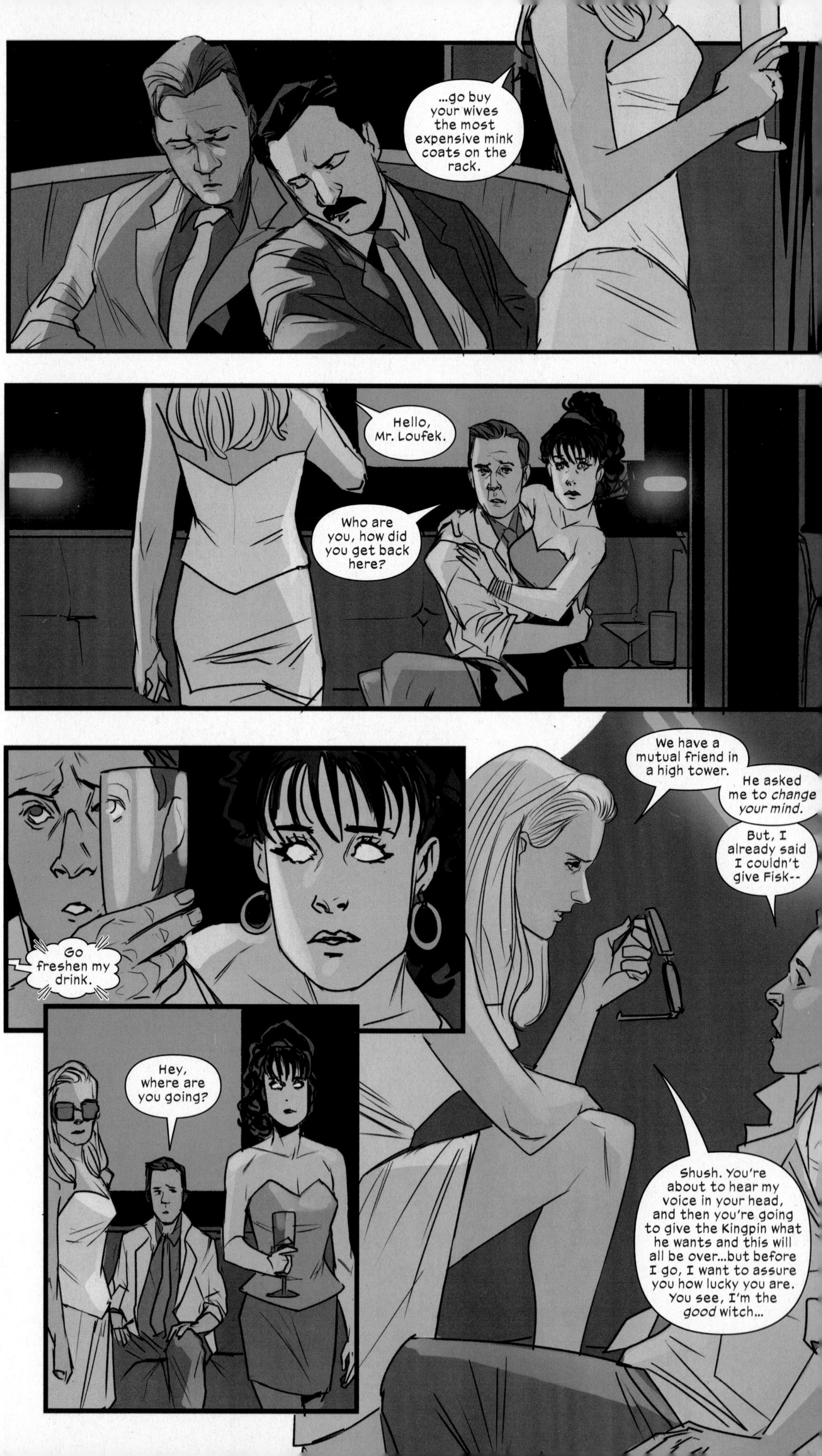

...go buy your wives the most expensive mink coats on the rack.
Hello, Mr. Loufek.
Who are you, how did you get back here?
Go freshen my drink.
We have a mutual friend in a high tower.
He asked me to *change your mind.*
But, I already said I couldn't give Fisk--
Hey, where are you going?
Shush. You're about to hear my voice in your head, and then you're going to give the Kingpin what he wants and this will all be over...but before I go, I want to assure you how lucky you are. You see, I'm the *good* witch...

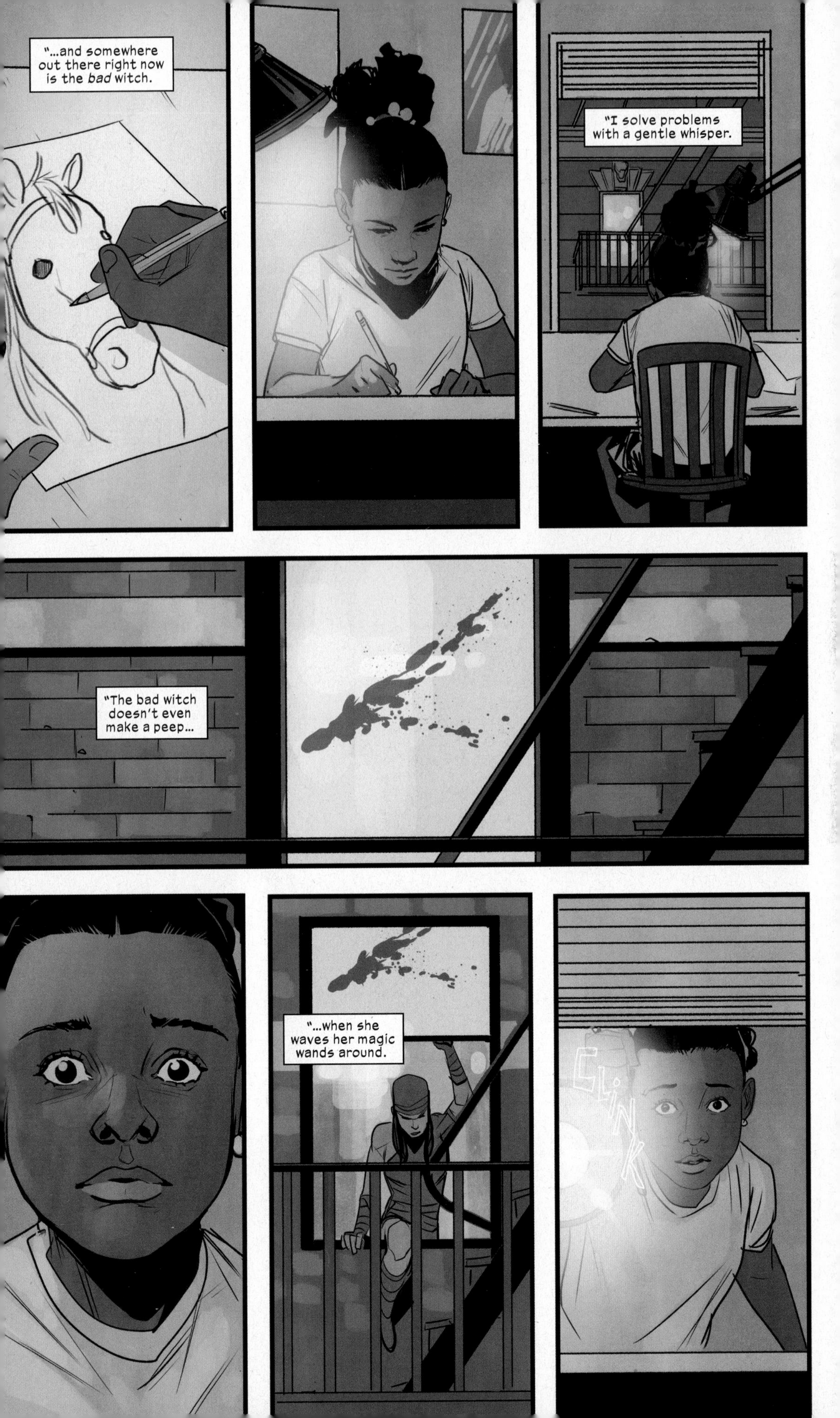
"...and somewhere out there right now is the *bad* witch.
"I solve problems with a gentle whisper.
"The bad witch doesn't even make a peep...
"...when she waves her magic wands around.
CLINK

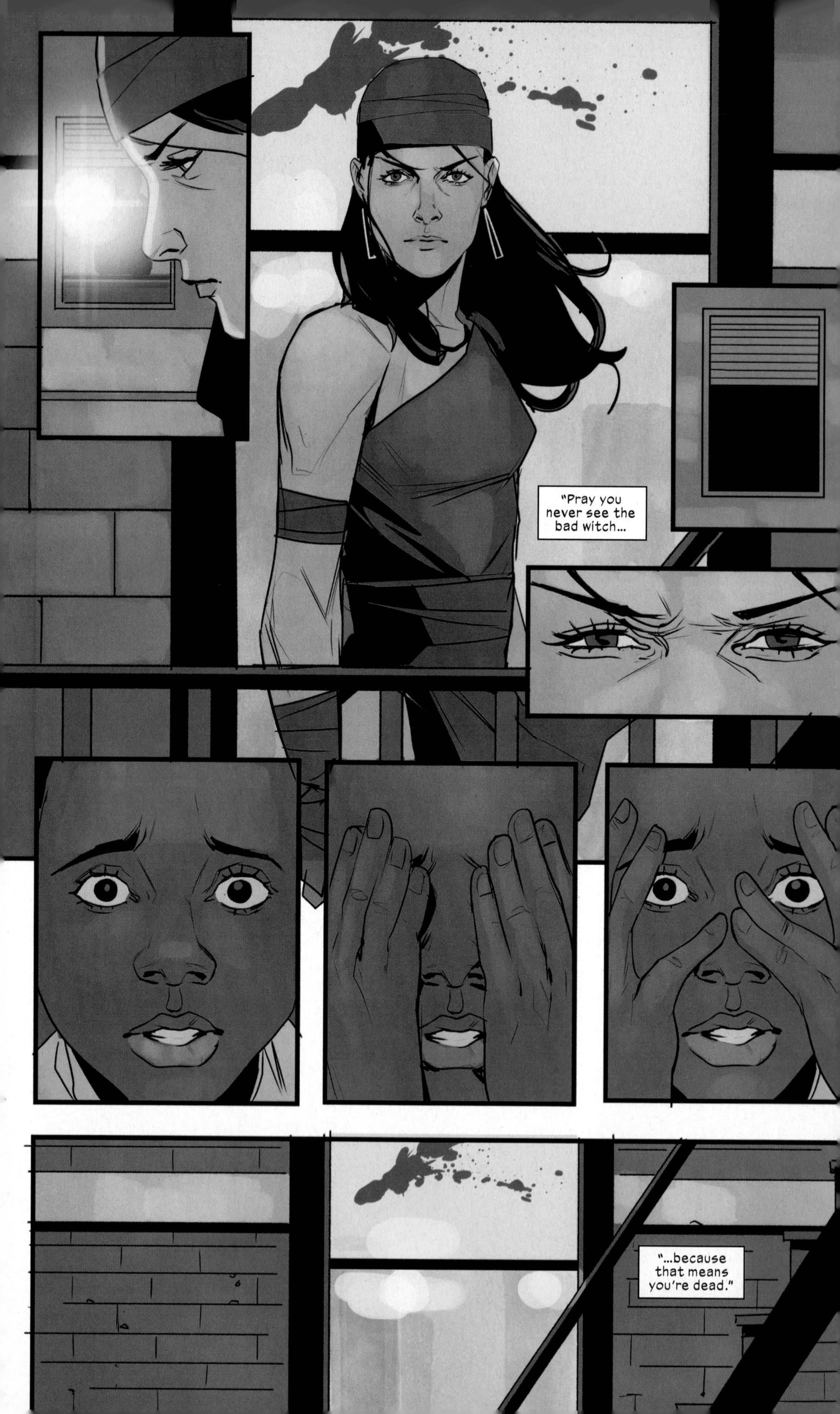
"Pray you never see the bad witch...
"...because that means you're dead."

SECRETS OF THE PAST

No outlaw has evaded more justice than Wilson Fisk, former kingpin of a vast criminal empire and now the duly elected mayor of New York. Fisk has failed to wash his hands of his old life and has set his ire upon the city and every costume vigilante in it -- including the newly elected X-Men, who have just publically lost their leader, Cyclops, while responding to a rampage in Manhattan. Needing to protect the truth about mutant resurrection, Cyclops has taken on the persona of Captain Krakoa and returned to the public eye to lead the X-Men, currently operating out of a Krakoa-grown base known as the Treehouse.

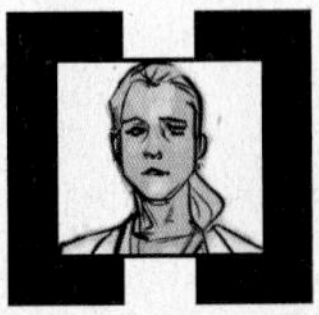
Emma Frost

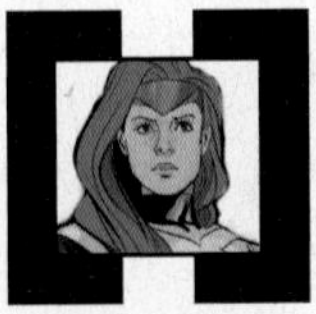
Jean Grey

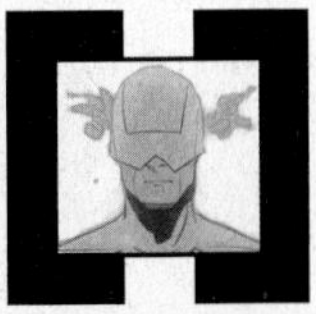
Captain Krakoa

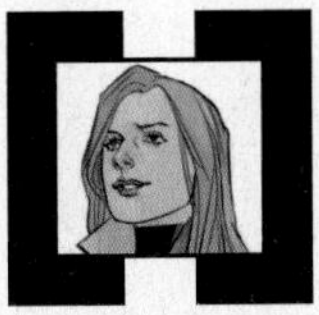
Polaris

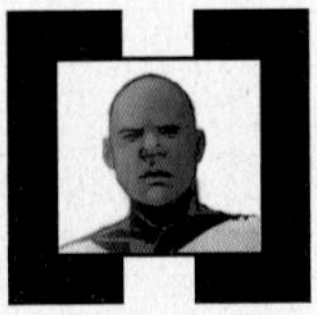
Synch

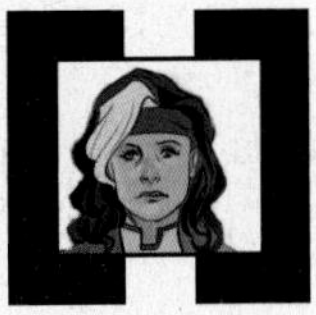
Rogue

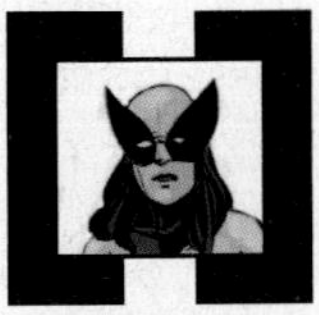
Wolverine

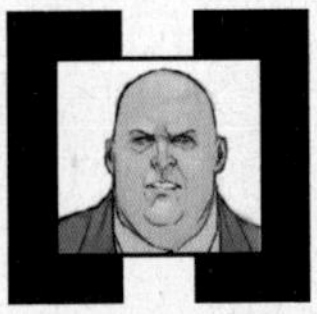
Kingpin

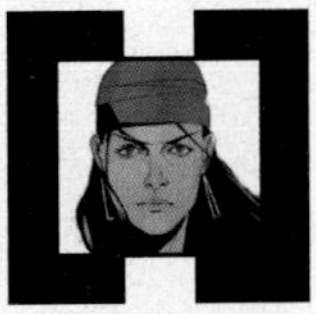
Elektra

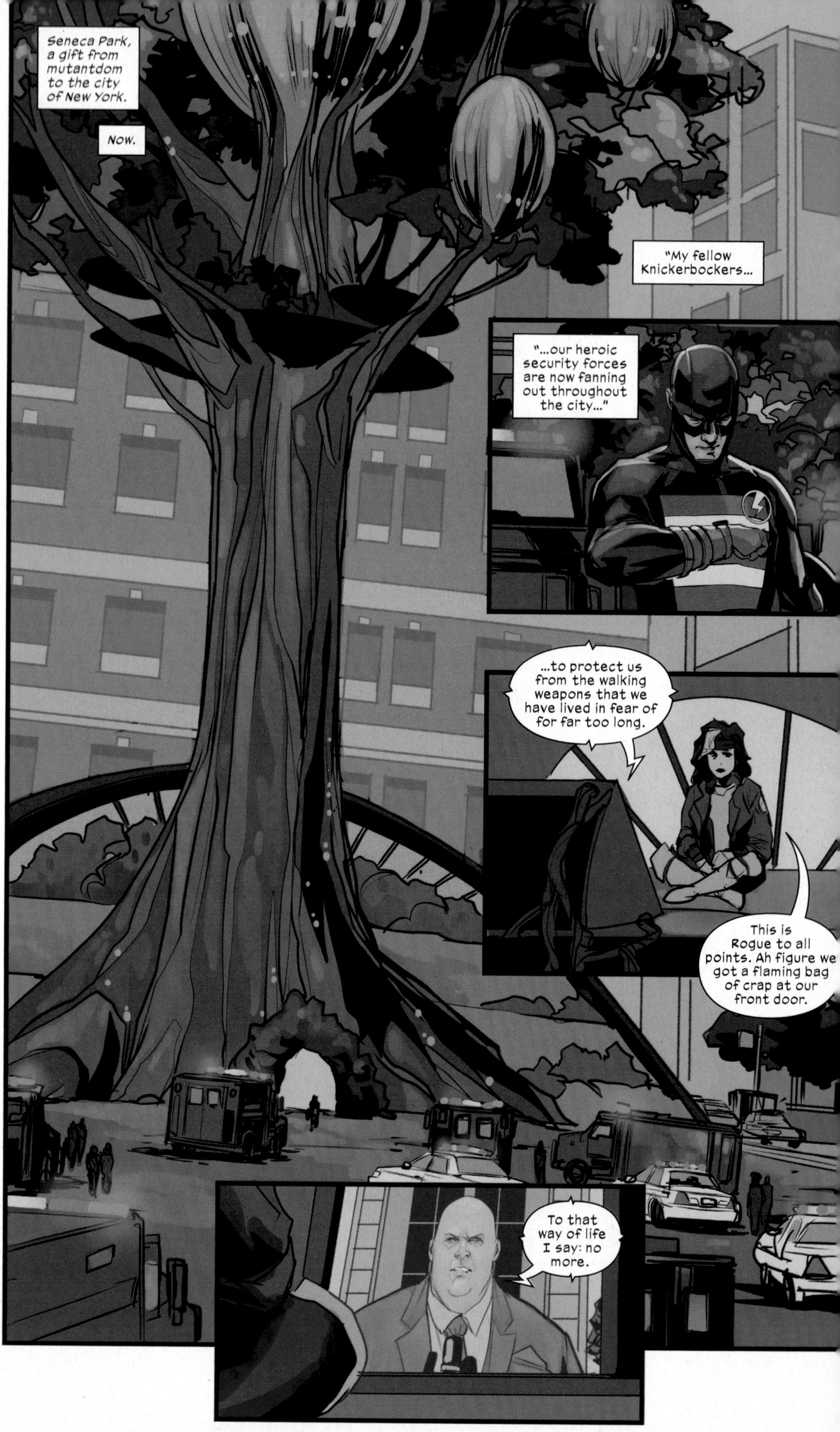

Seneca Park, a gift from mutantdom to the city of New York.
Now.
"My fellow Knickerbockers...
"...our heroic security forces are now fanning out throughout the city..."
...to protect us from the walking weapons that we have lived in fear of for far too long.
This is Rogue to all points. Ah figure we got a flaming bag of crap at our front door.
To that way of life I say: no more.

Our beloved city has suffered too much at the hands of the vigilantes.

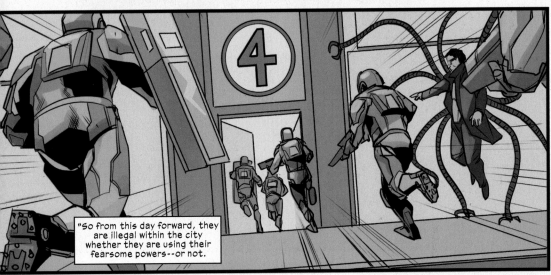

"So from this day forward, they are illegal within the city whether they are using their fearsome powers--or not.

"We want to return to to simpler days. And we want that ridiculous and dangerous tree removed from Midtown Manhattan."

Time's up, X-Men!

Across town at the United Nations.

Mister Leland, are you aware of what's transpiring at the Treehouse?

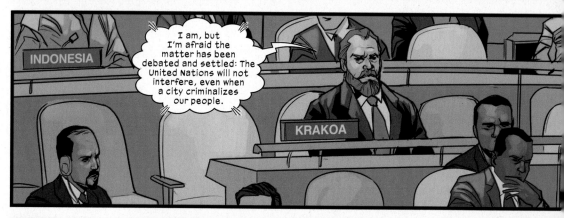

INDONESIA

I am, but I'm afraid the matter has been debated and settled: The United Nations will not interfere, even when a city criminalizes our people.

KRAKOA

Ordinarily, I would tell Cyclops to move across the river to New Jersey, but I have no love for the current Mayor of New York City, and if I can embarrass him, it would bring me great pleasure. Plus, I paid a fortune for the real estate.

Here is what I propose.

Ah. Ha. Yes, I would think that would do the trick.

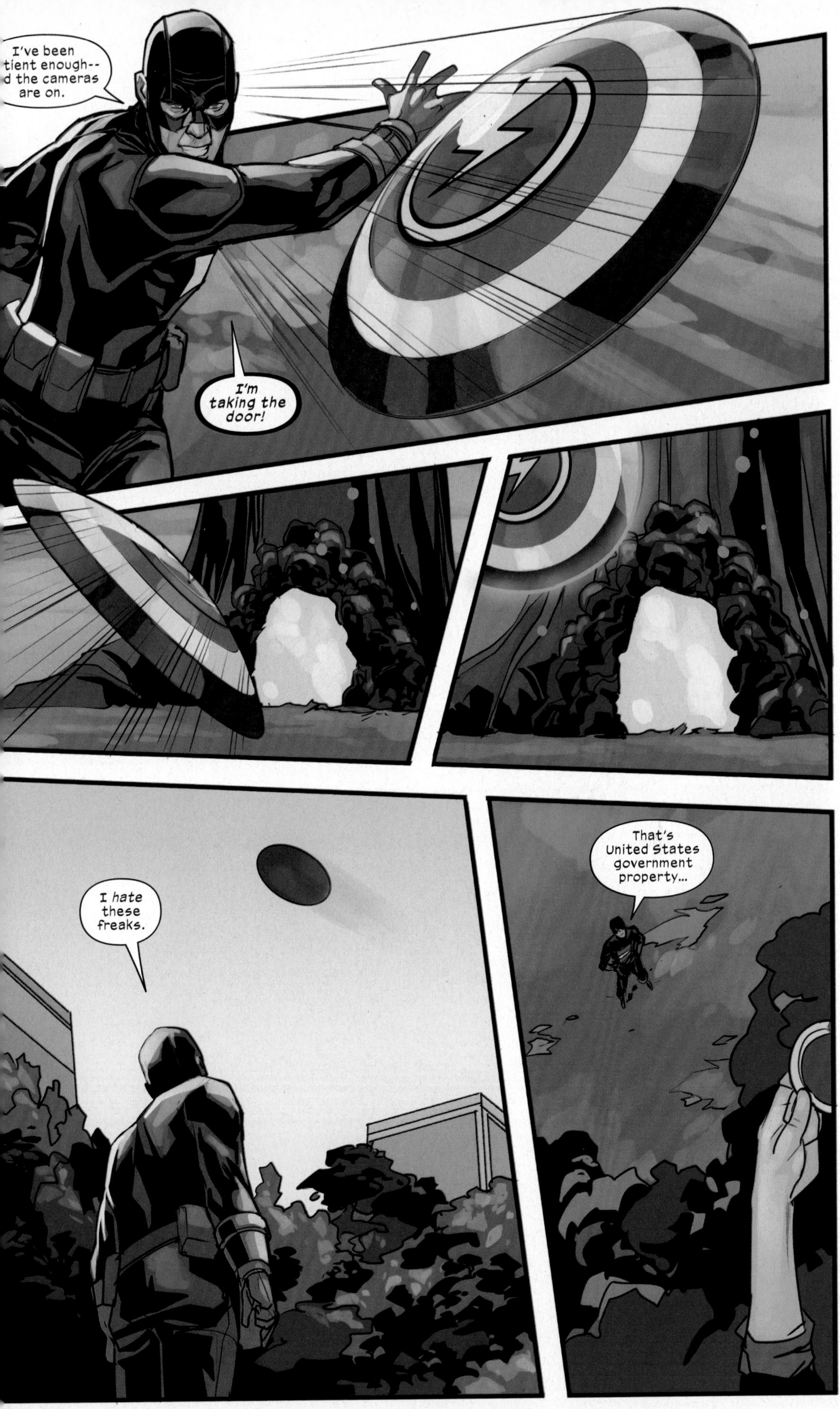

I've been
tient enough--
d the cameras
are on.
I'm taking the door!
I *hate* these freaks.
That's United States government property...

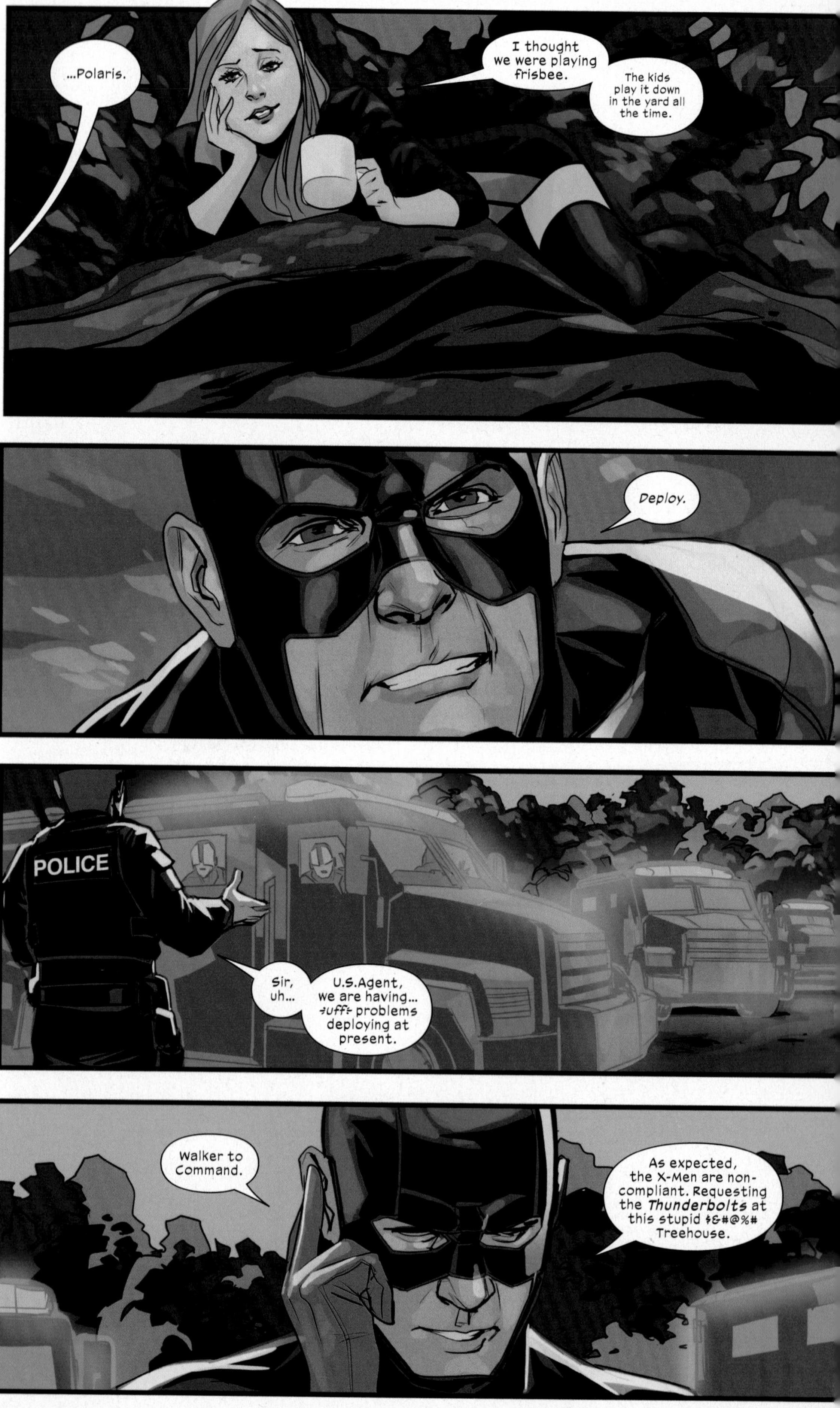
...Polaris.
I thought we were playing frisbee.
The kids play it down in the yard all the time.
Deploy.
Sir, uh...
U.S.Agent, we are having... *uff* problems deploying at present.
POLICE
Walker to Command.
As expected, the X-Men are non-compliant. Requesting the *Thunderbolts* at this stupid $&#@%# Treehouse.

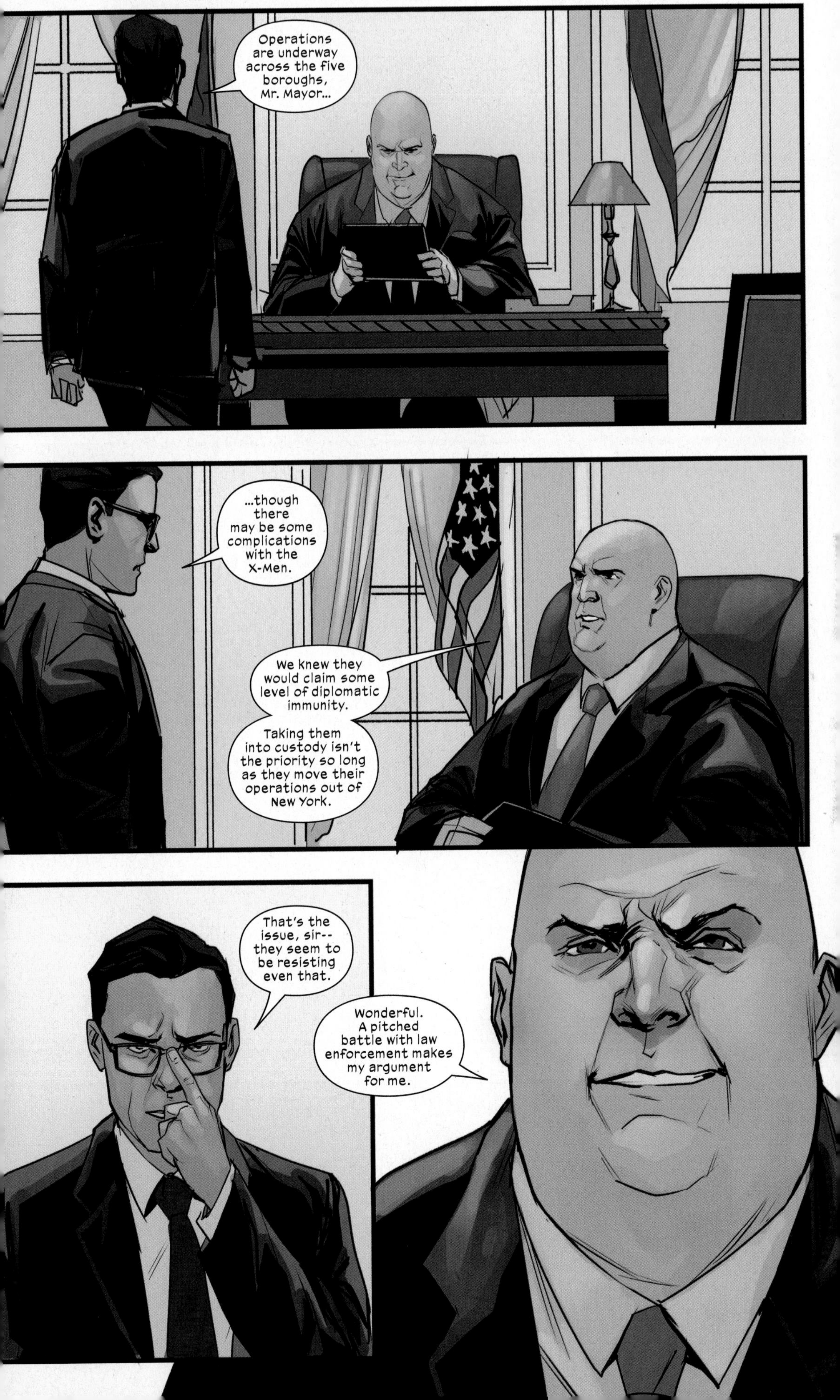
Operations are underway across the five boroughs, Mr. Mayor...
...though there may be some complications with the X-Men.
We knew they would claim some level of diplomatic immunity.
Taking them into custody isn't the priority so long as they move their operations out of New York.
That's the issue, sir-- they seem to be resisting even that.
Wonderful. A pitched battle with law enforcement makes my argument for me.

You do realize if we're filmed fighting his cops that we're doing the Kingpin's work for him?

Please, Scott. Let's accord him the honor of his position. It's-- *Mayor* Kingpin.

Polaris, stall for a few moments more.

We can be X-Men, we may just have to give up Seneca Gardens. It seems to be a point of pride for Mayor Fisk that he's going to make it illegal for us to operate in New York City... and I'd rather pick my battles.

So what happens to the Treehouse?

It becomes Emma's new Airbnb?

How about we open the first homeless shelter on Central Park West?

I second that.

Let's table the Treehouse for now...and go face the music.

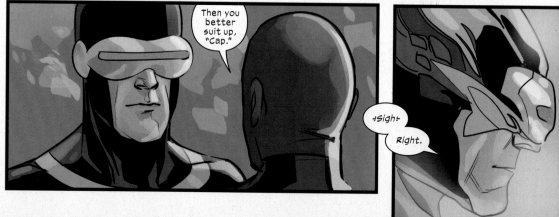

Then you better suit up, "Cap."

‡Sigh‡

Right.

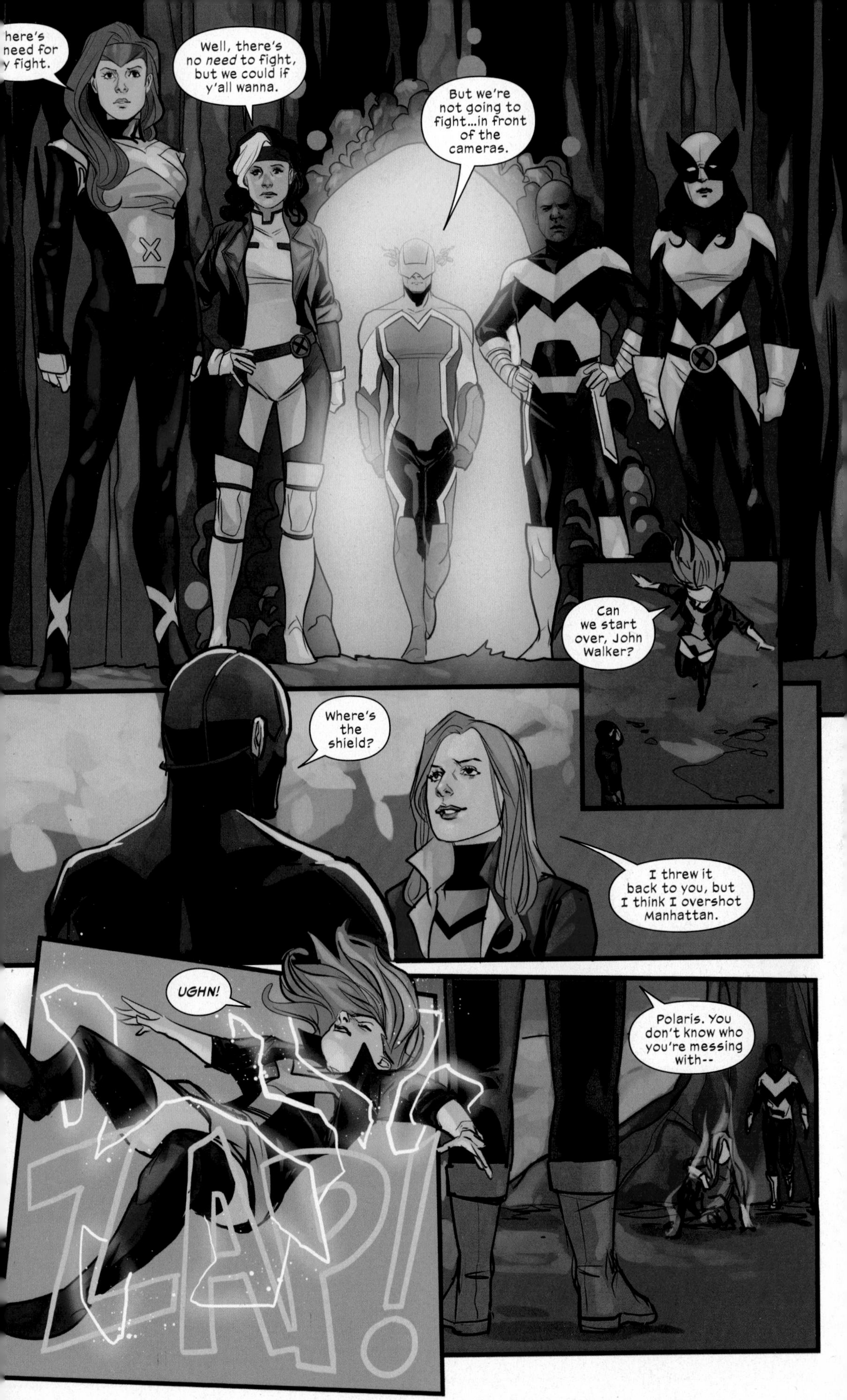
here's
need for
y fight.
Well, there's no *need* to fight, but we could if y'all wanna.
But we're not going to fight...in front of the cameras.
Can we start over, John Walker?
Where's the shield?
I threw it back to you, but I think I overshot Manhattan.
UGHN!
ZAP!
Polaris. You don't know who you're messing with--

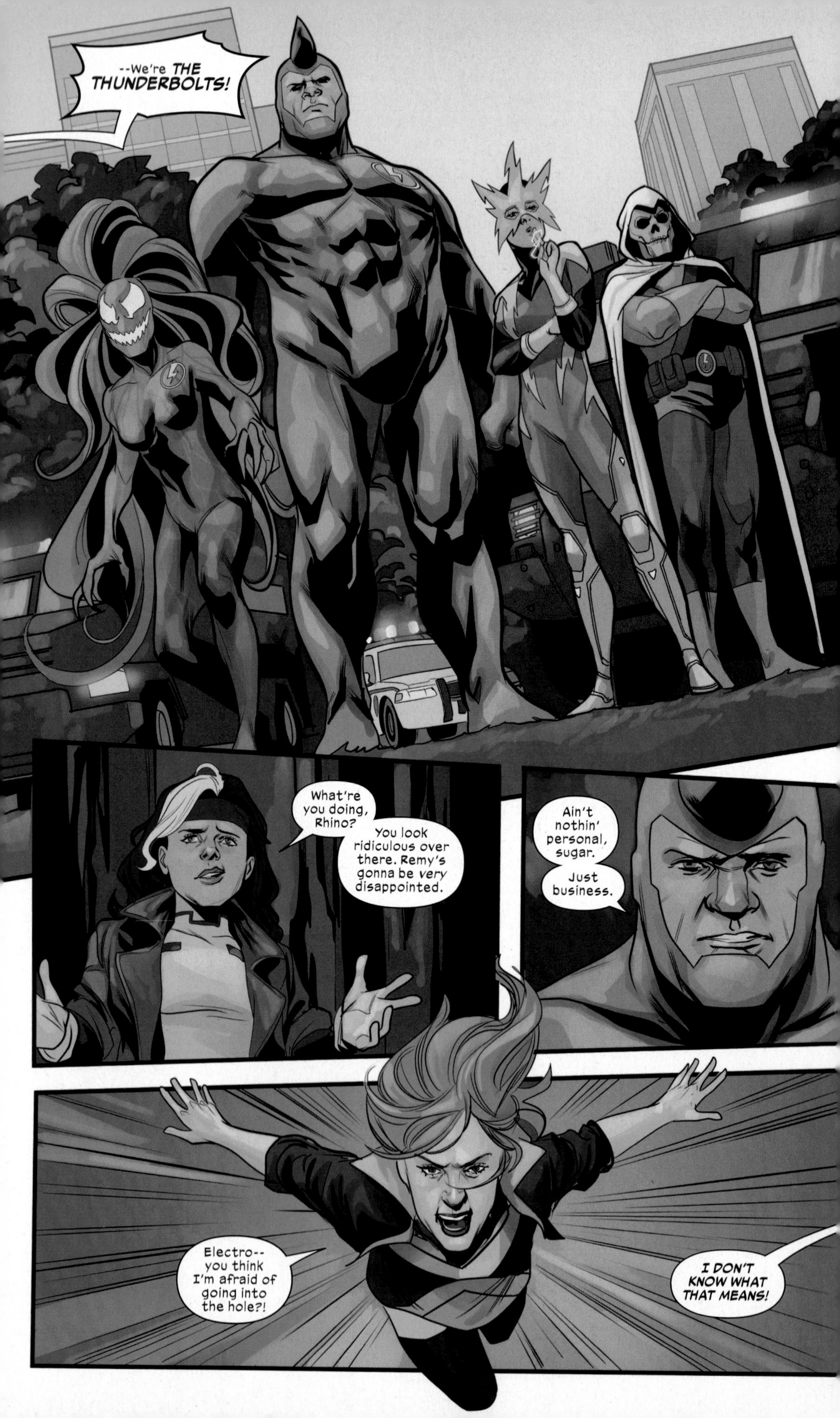
--We're THE THUNDERBOLTS!
What're you doing, Rhino?
You look ridiculous over there. Remy's gonna be very disappointed.
Ain't nothin' personal, sugar.
Just business.
Electro-- you think I'm afraid of going into the hole?!
I DON'T KNOW WHAT THAT MEANS!

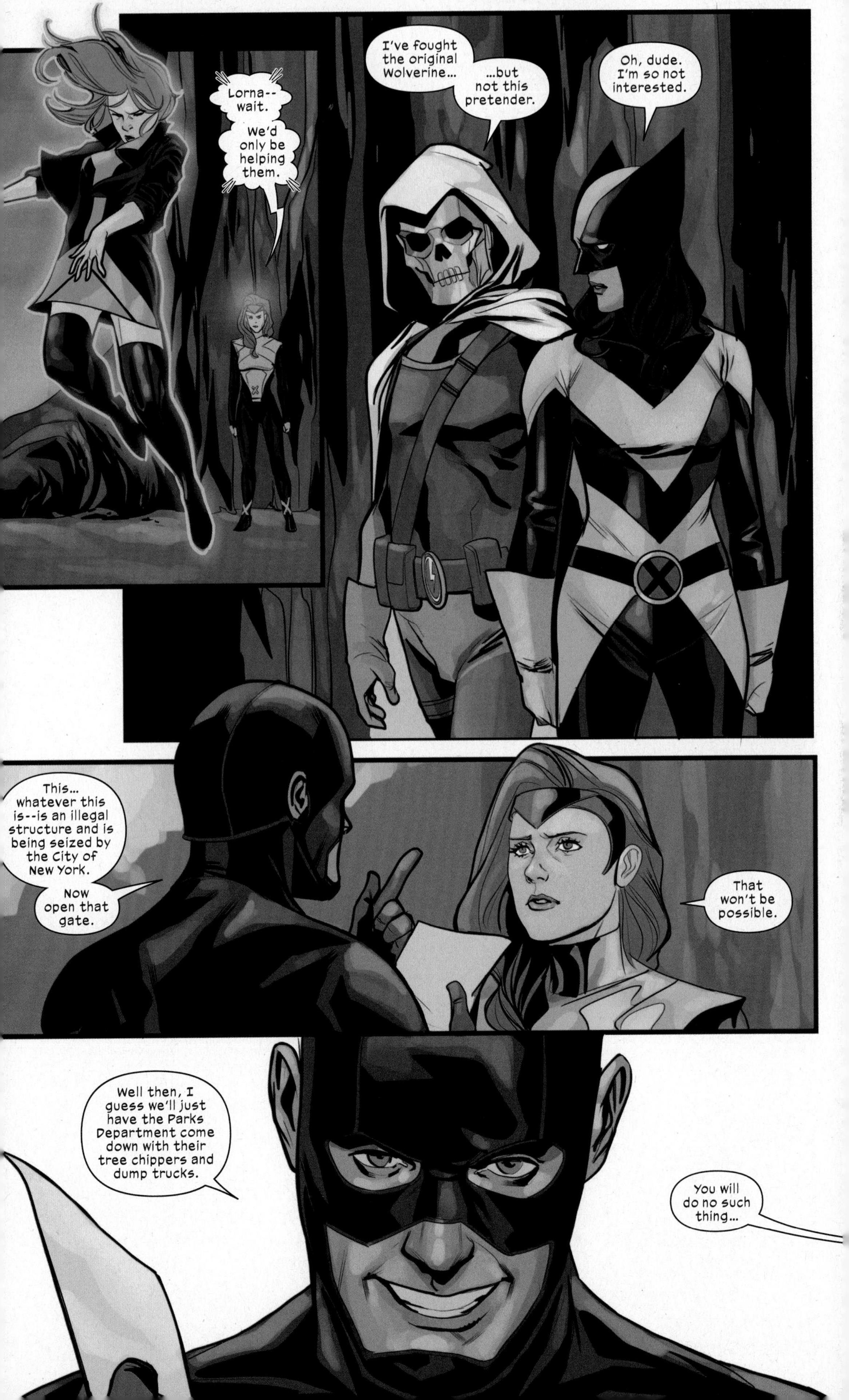
Lorna--
wait.
We'd only be helping them.
I've fought the original Wolverine...
...but not this pretender.
Oh, dude. I'm so not interested.
This... whatever this is--is an illegal structure and is being seized by the City of New York.
Now open that gate.
That won't be possible.
Well then, I guess we'll just have the Parks Department come down with their tree chippers and dump trucks.
You will do no such thing...

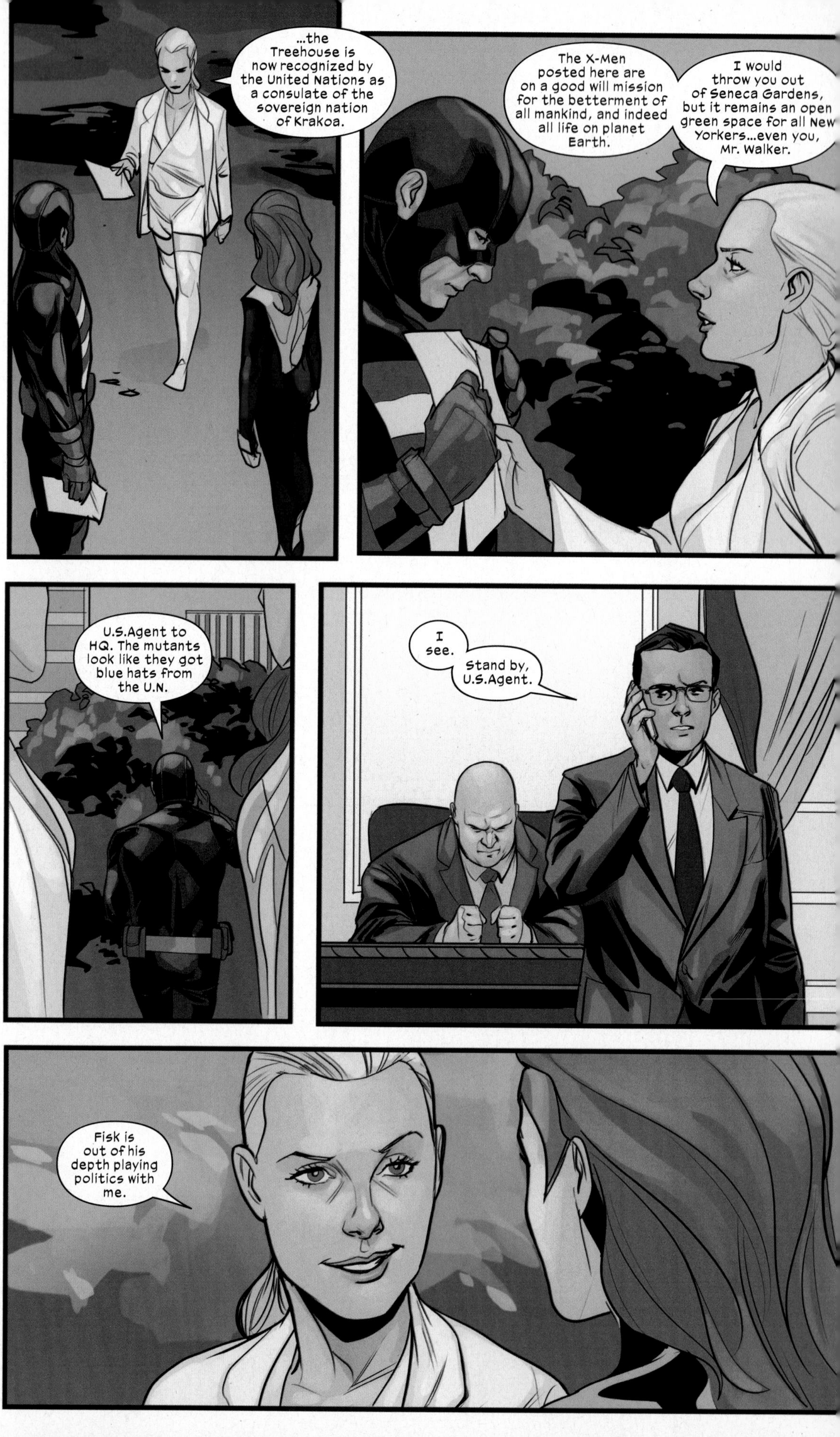
...the Treehouse is now recognized by the United Nations as a consulate of the sovereign nation of Krakoa.
The X-Men posted here are on a good will mission for the betterment of all mankind, and indeed all life on planet Earth.
I would throw you out of Seneca Gardens, but it remains an open green space for all New Yorkers...even you, Mr. Walker.
U.S.Agent to HQ. The mutants look like they got blue hats from the U.N.
I see.
Stand by, U.S.Agent.
Fisk is out of his depth playing politics with me.

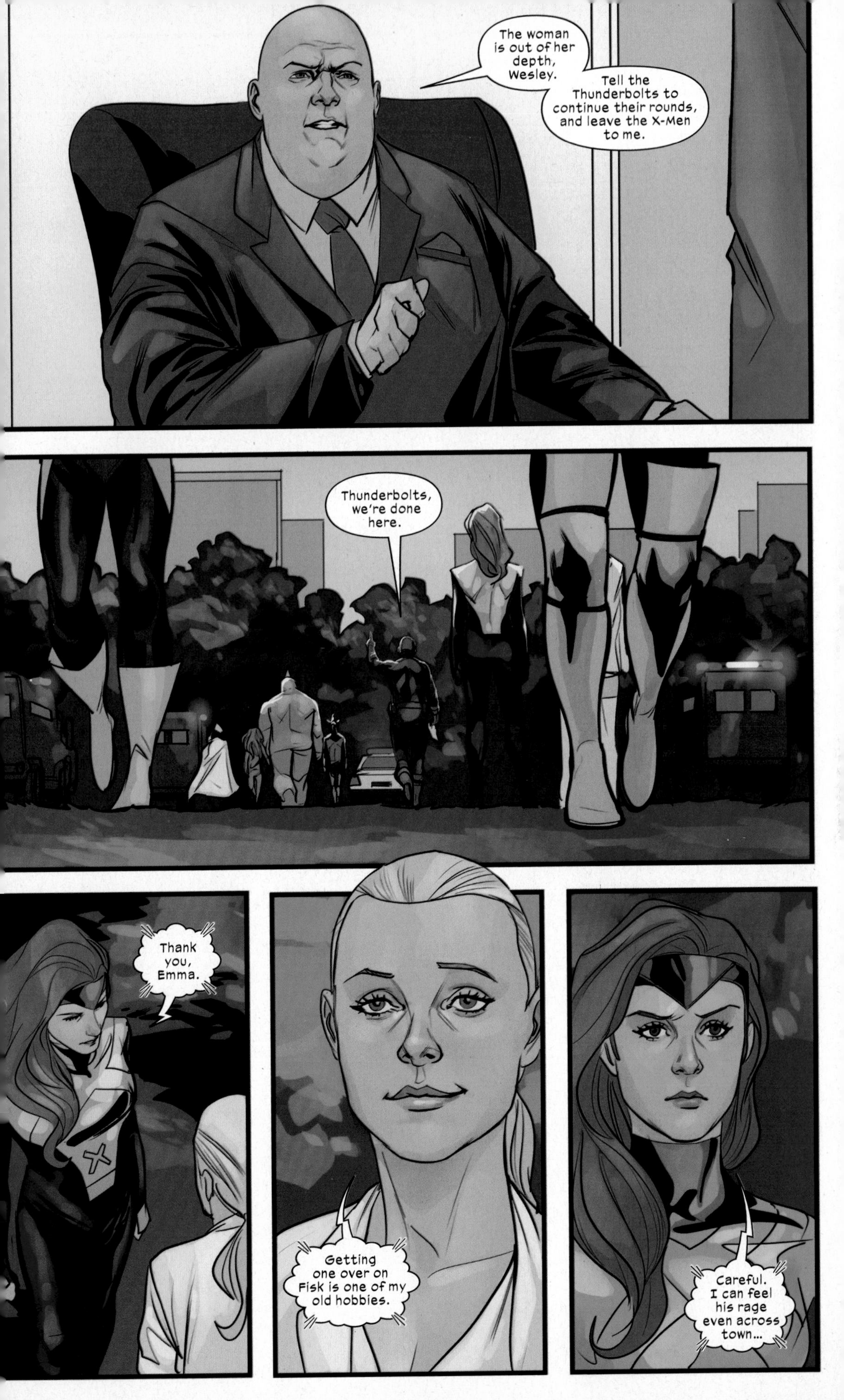
The woman is out of her depth, Wesley.
Tell the Thunderbolts to continue their rounds, and leave the X-Men to me.
Thunderbolts, we're done here.
Thank you, Emma.
Getting one over on Fisk is one of my old hobbies.
Careful. I can feel his rage even across town...

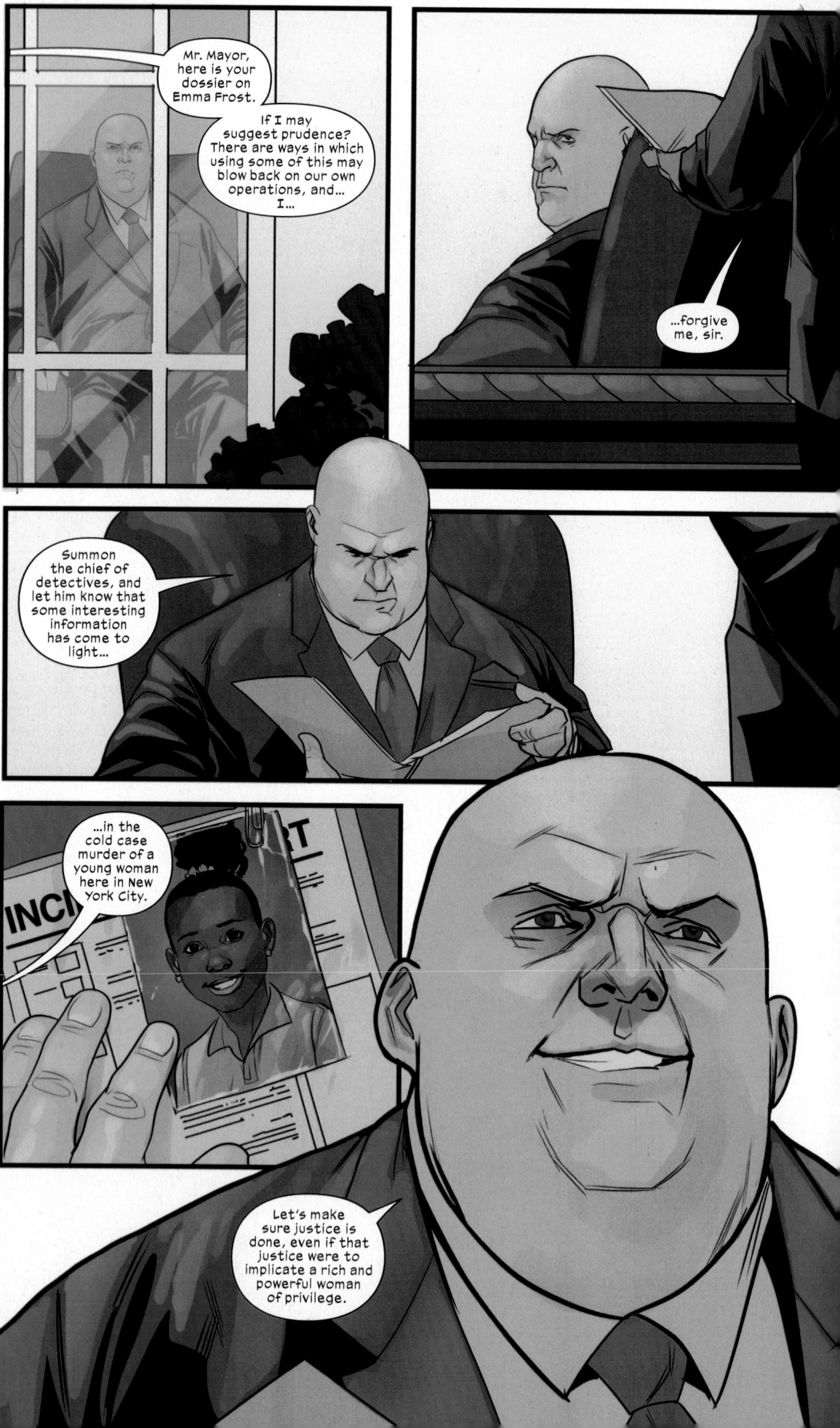

Mr. Mayor, here is your dossier on Emma Frost.
If I may suggest prudence? There are ways in which using some of this may blow back on our own operations, and... I...
...forgive me, sir.
Summon the chief of detectives, and let him know that some interesting information has come to light...
...in the cold case murder of a young woman here in New York City.
Let's make sure justice is done, even if that justice were to implicate a rich and powerful woman of privilege.

[devilsre....[0.1]
[ignxmen.....[0.1]

"When you push to change the world,
it pushes back."

-- EMMA FROST

[devilsre....[0.1]
[ignxmen.....[0.1]

2

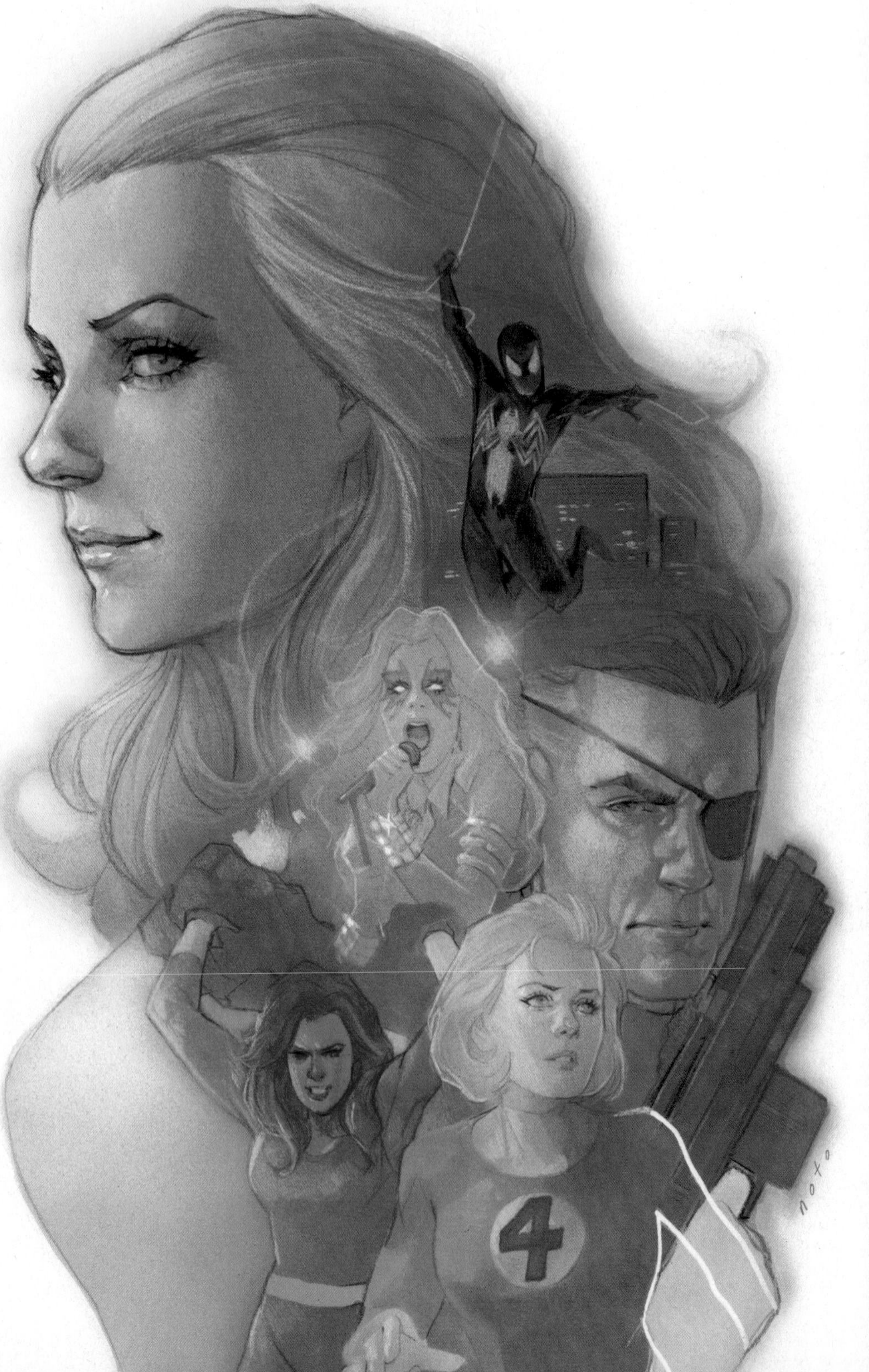
noto

[devilsre....[0.2]
[ignxmen.....[0.2]

"When observing Frost, make sure the photographer has the absolute minimum of information, and the longest lens available. Distance will serve us well, Mr. Wesley."

-- WILSON FISK

[devilsre....[0.2]
[ignxmen.....[0.2]

[devilsreignxmen_02]

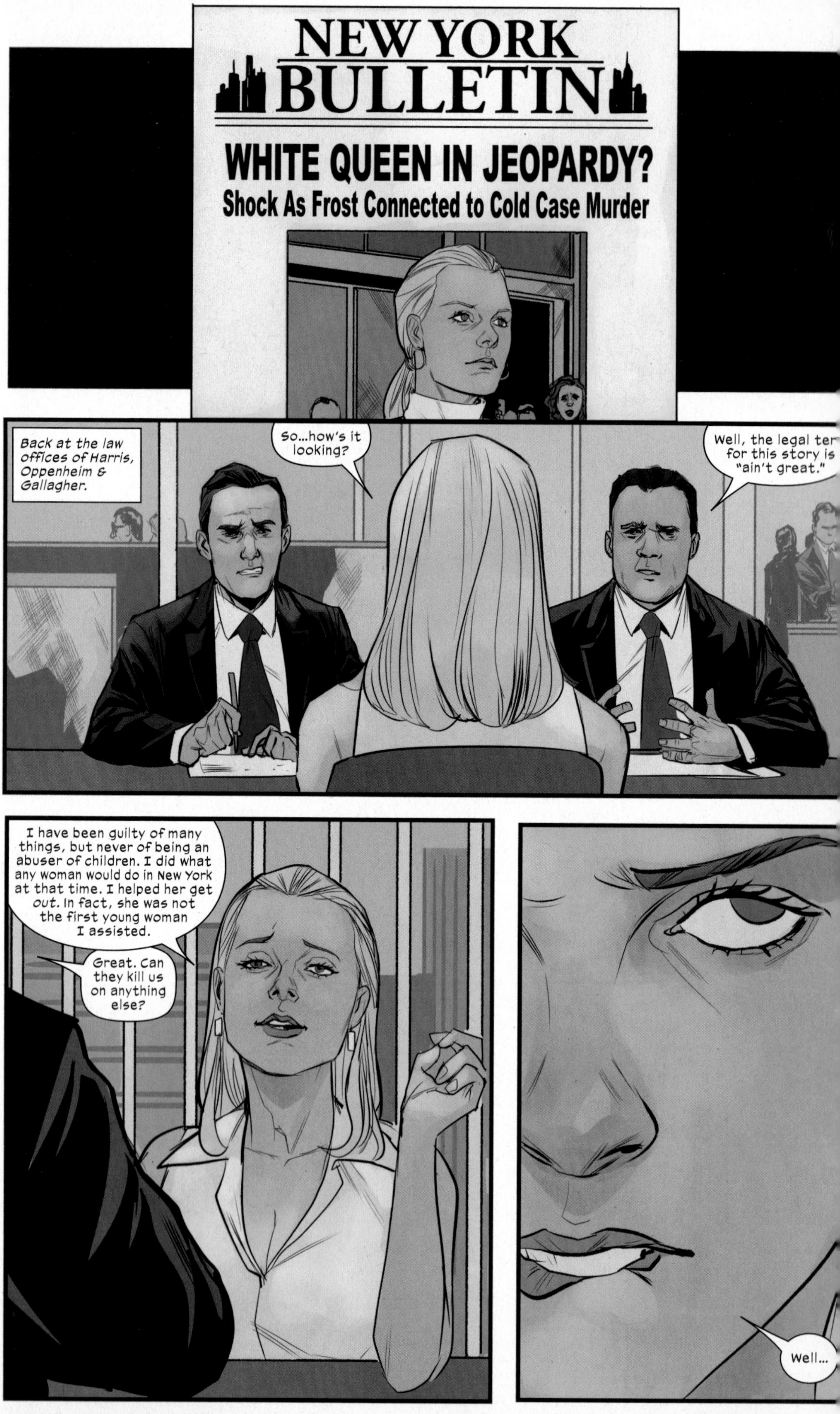
NEW YORK BULLETIN
WHITE QUEEN IN JEOPARDY?
Shock As Frost Connected to Cold Case Murder
Back at the law offices of Harris, Oppenheim & Gallagher.
So...how's it looking?
Well, the legal ter for this story is "ain't great."
I have been guilty of many things, but never of being an abuser of children. I did what any woman would do in New York at that time. I helped her get out. In fact, she was not the first young woman I assisted.
Great. Can they kill us on anything else?
Well...

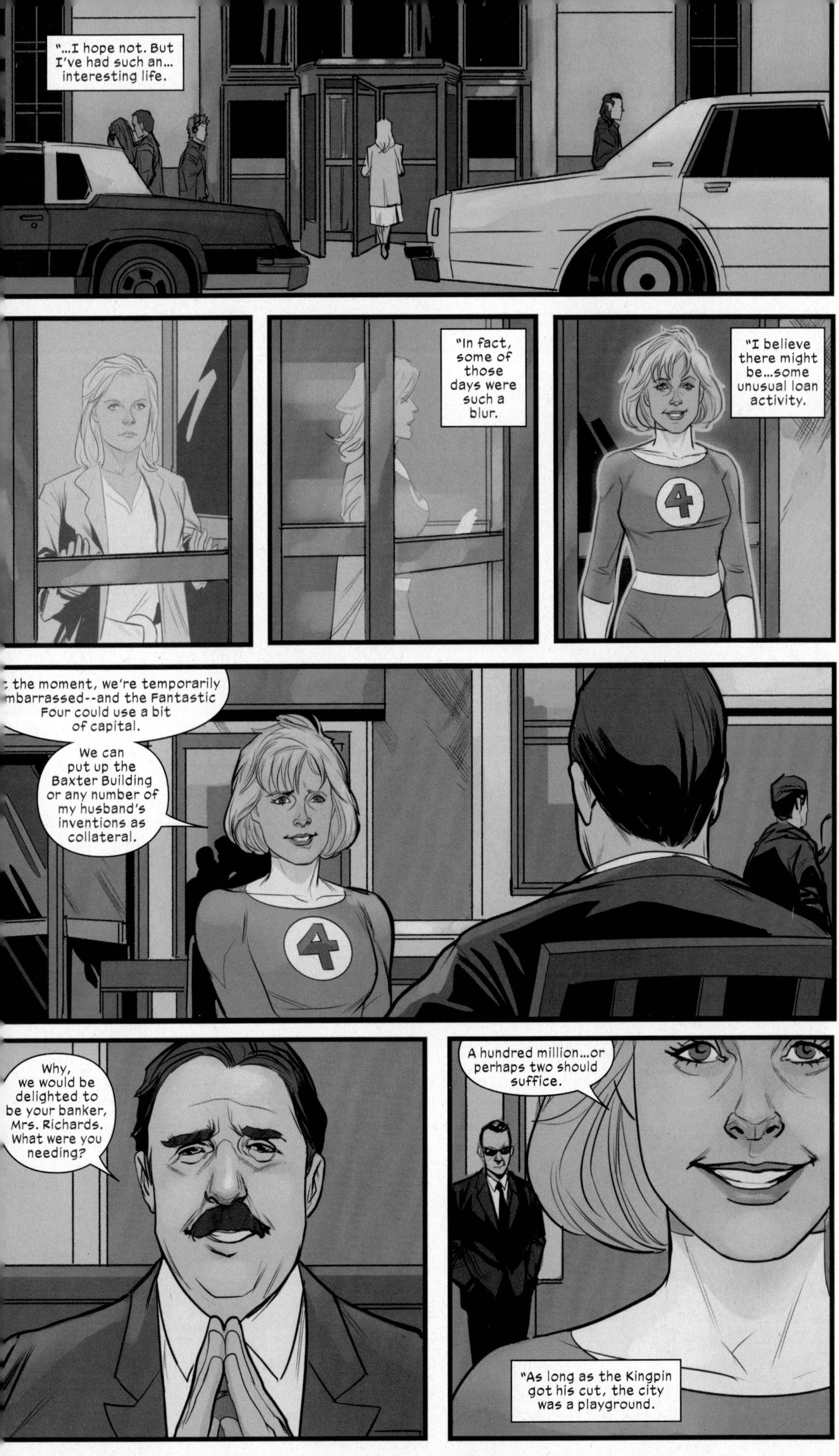
"...I hope not. But I've had such an... interesting life.
"In fact, some of those days were such a blur.
"I believe there might be...some unusual loan activity.
the moment, we're temporarily mbarrassed--and the Fantastic Four could use a bit of capital.
We can put up the Baxter Building or any number of my husband's inventions as collateral.
Why, we would be delighted to be your banker, Mrs. Richards. What were you needing?
A hundred million...or perhaps two should suffice.
"As long as the Kingpin got his cut, the city was a playground.

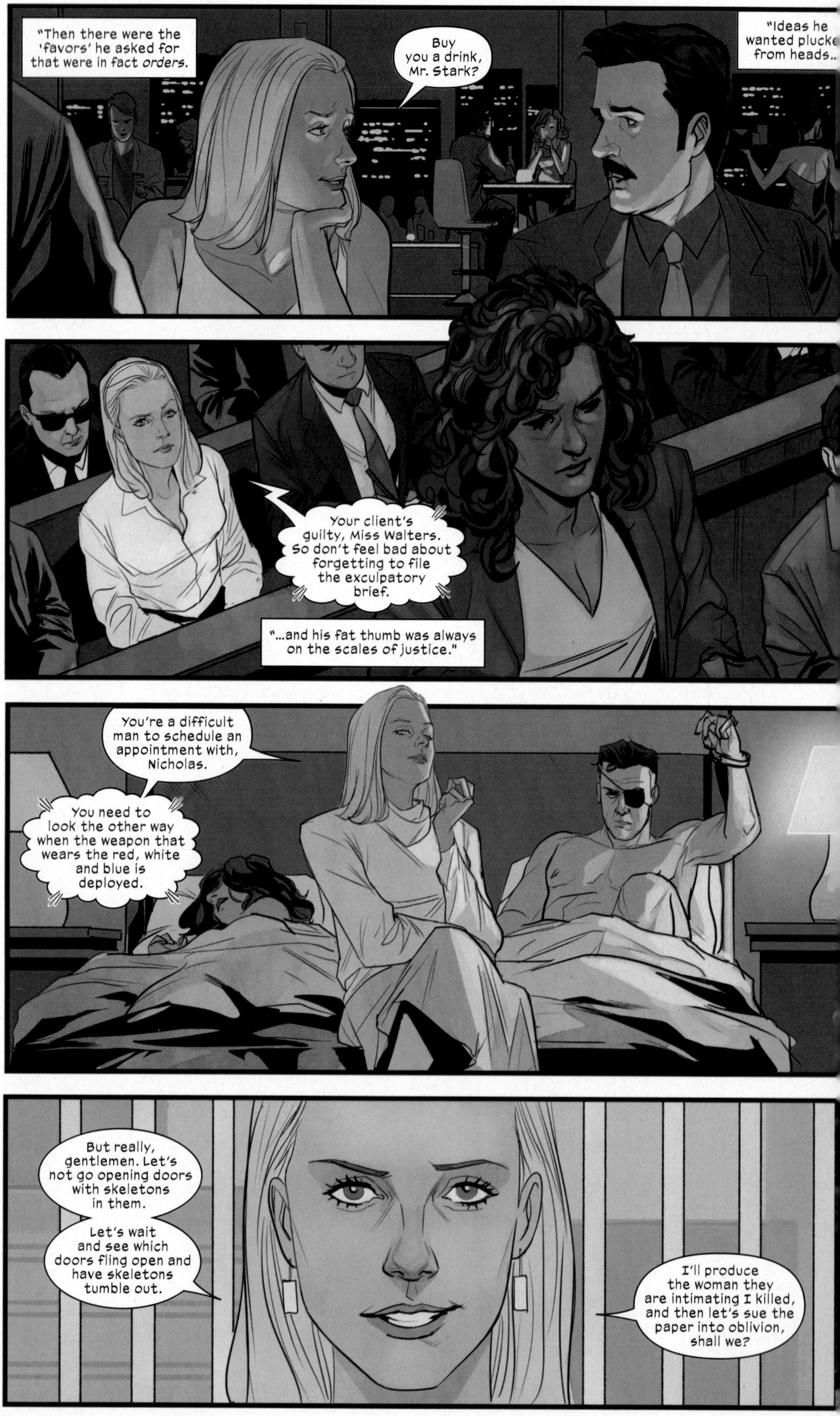
"Then there were the 'favors' he asked for that were in fact *orders*.
Buy you a drink, Mr. Stark?
"Ideas he wanted plucke from heads..
Your client's guilty, Miss Walters. So don't feel bad about forgetting to file the exculpatory brief.
"...and his fat thumb was always on the scales of justice."
You're a difficult man to schedule an appointment with, Nicholas.
You need to look the other way when the weapon that wears the red, white and blue is deployed.
But really, gentlemen. Let's not go opening doors with skeletons in them.
Let's wait and see which doors fling open and have skeletons tumble out.
I'll produce the woman they are intimating I killed, and then let's sue the paper into oblivion, shall we?

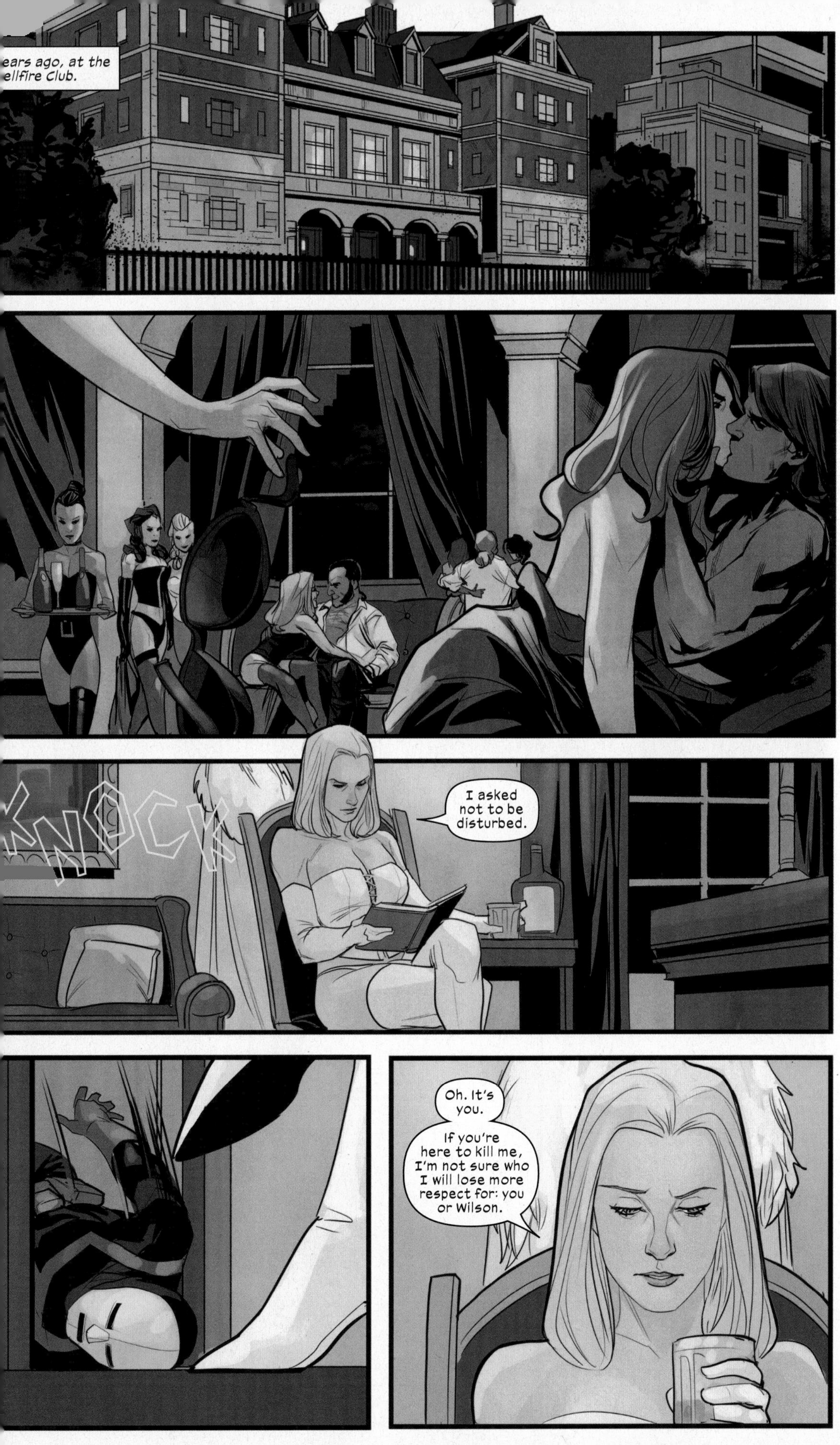
ears ago, at the
ellfire Club.
KNOCK
I asked not to be disturbed.
Oh. It's you.
If you're here to kill me, I'm not sure who I will lose more respect for: you or Wilson.

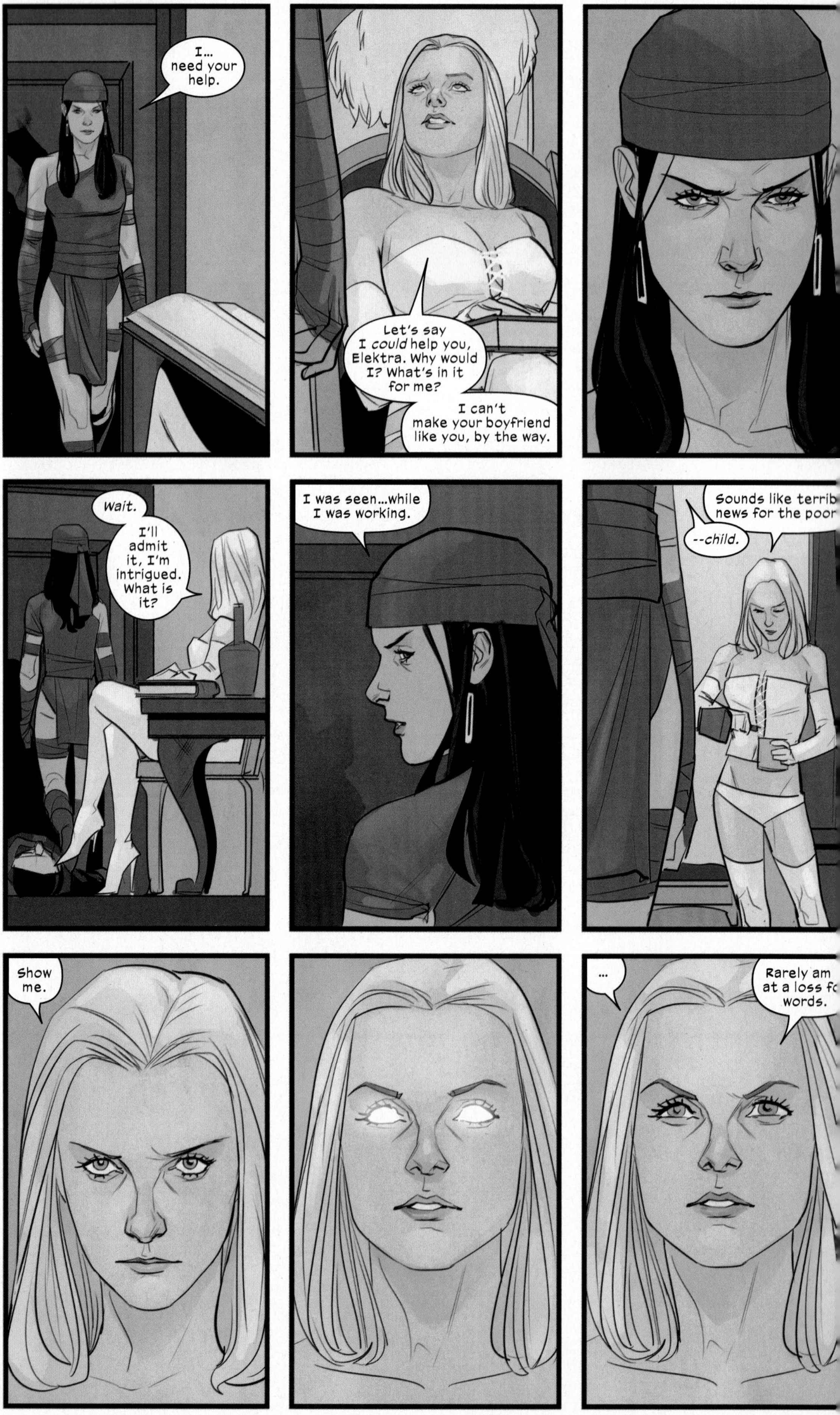

I... need your help.
Let's say I *could* help you, Elektra. Why would I? What's in it for me?
I can't make your boyfriend like you, by the way.
Wait.
I'll admit it, I'm intrigued. What is it?
I was seen...while I was working.
Sounds like terrib news for the poor
--*child.*
Show me.
...
Rarely am at a loss fo words.

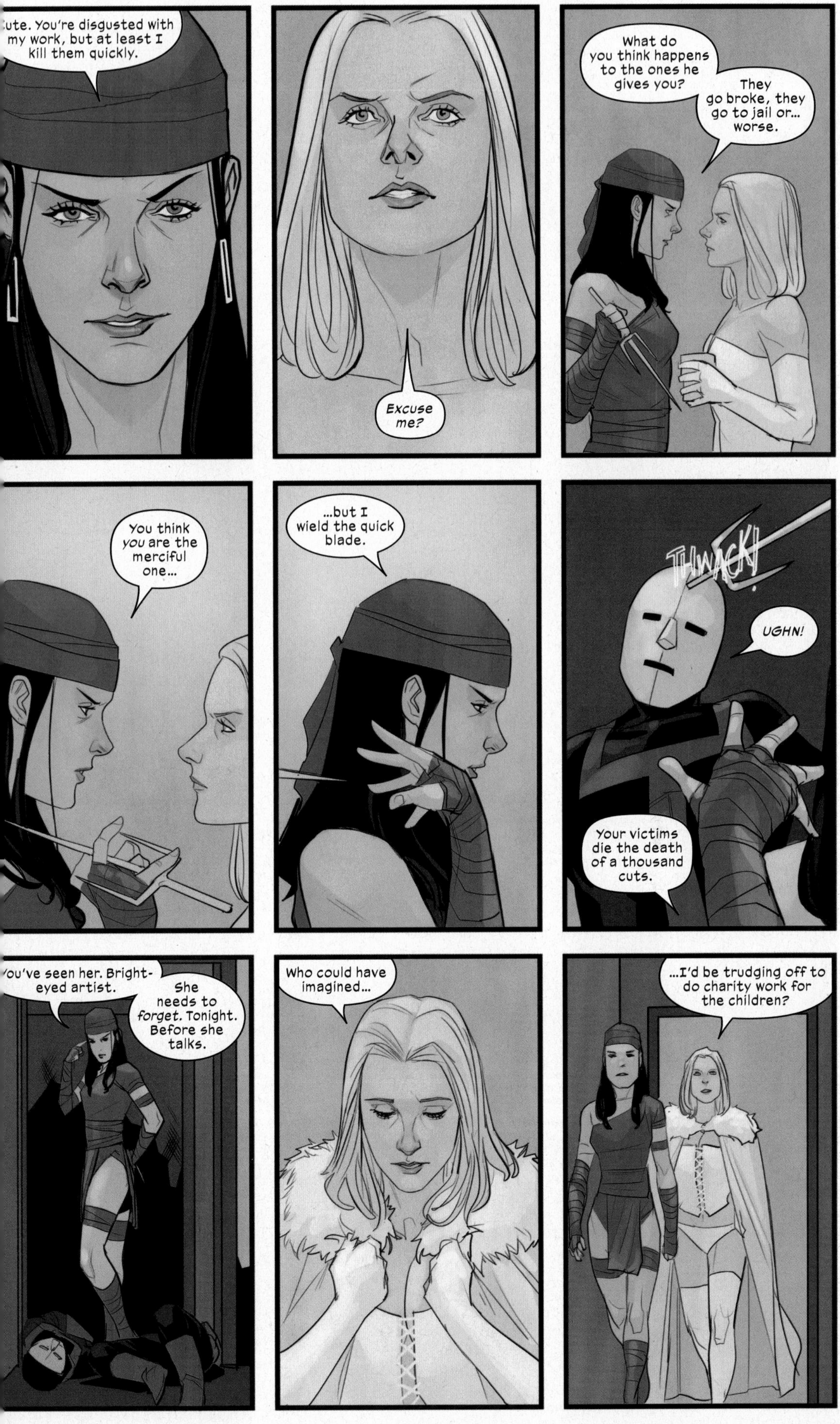
Cute. You're disgusted with my work, but at least I kill them quickly.
Excuse me?
What do you think happens to the ones he gives you?
They go broke, they go to jail or... worse.
You think *you* are the merciful one...
...but I wield the quick blade.
THWACK!
UGHN!
Your victims die the death of a thousand cuts.
You've seen her. Bright-eyed artist.
She needs to *forget*. Tonight. Before she talks.
Who could have imagined...
...I'd be trudging off to do charity work for the children?

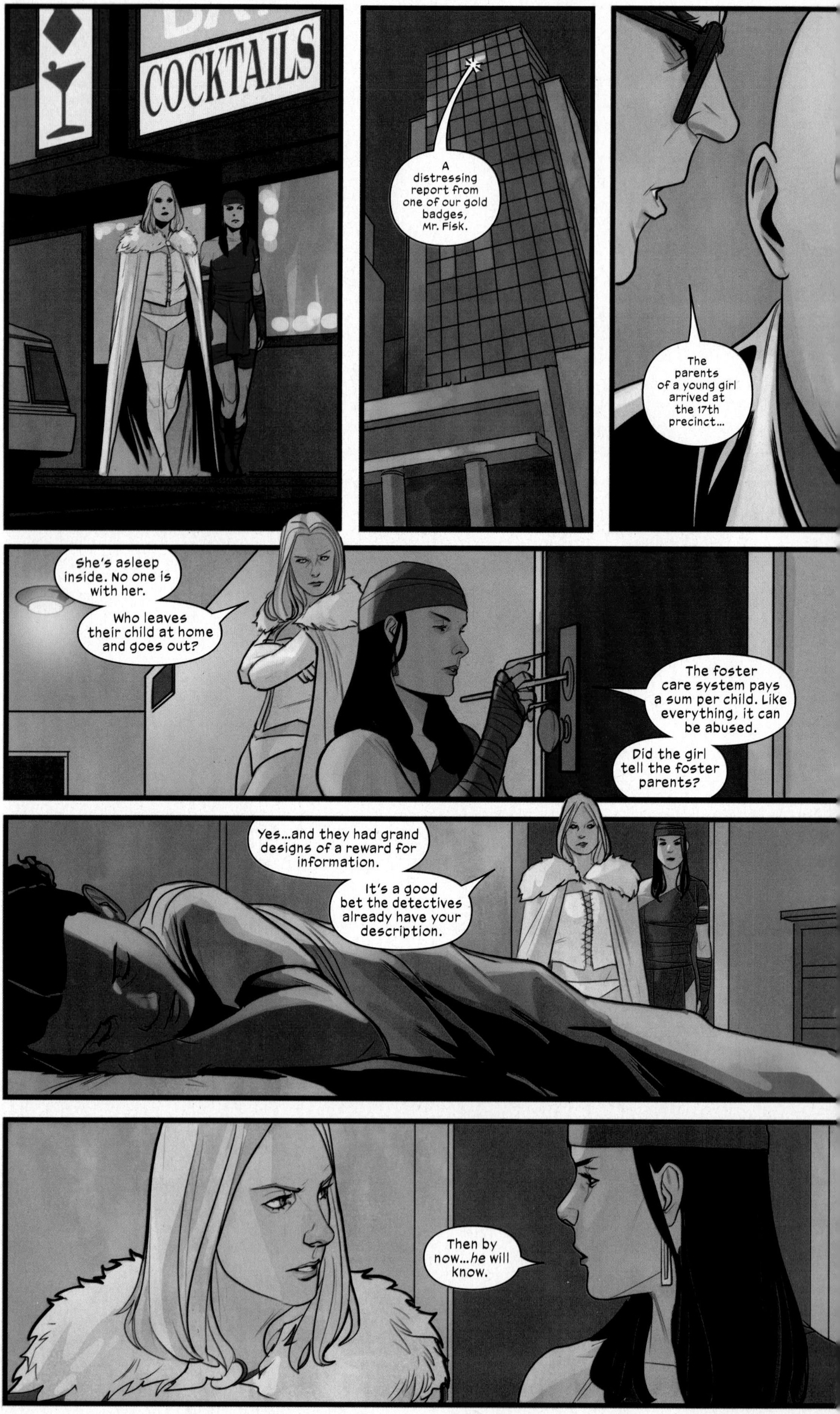
COCKTAILS
A distressing report from one of our gold badges, Mr. Fisk.
The parents of a young girl arrived at the 17th precinct...
She's asleep inside. No one is with her.
Who leaves their child at home and goes out?
The foster care system pays a sum per child. Like everything, it can be abused.
Did the girl tell the foster parents?
Yes...and they had grand designs of a reward for information.
It's a good bet the detectives already have your description.
Then by now...*he* will know.

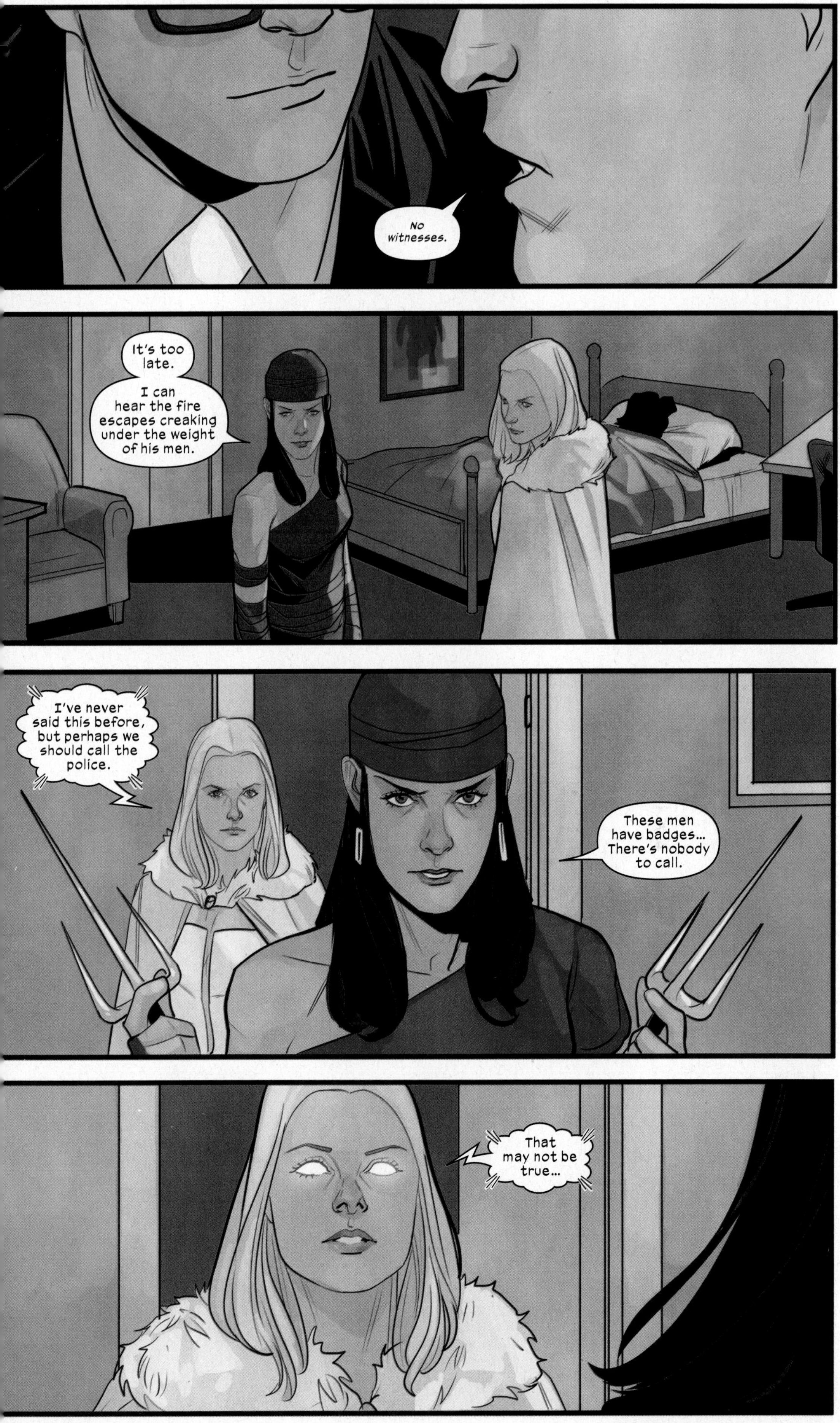
No witnesses.
It's too late.
I can hear the fire escapes creaking under the weight of his men.
I've never said this before, but perhaps we should call the police.
These men have badges... There's nobody to call.
That may not be true...

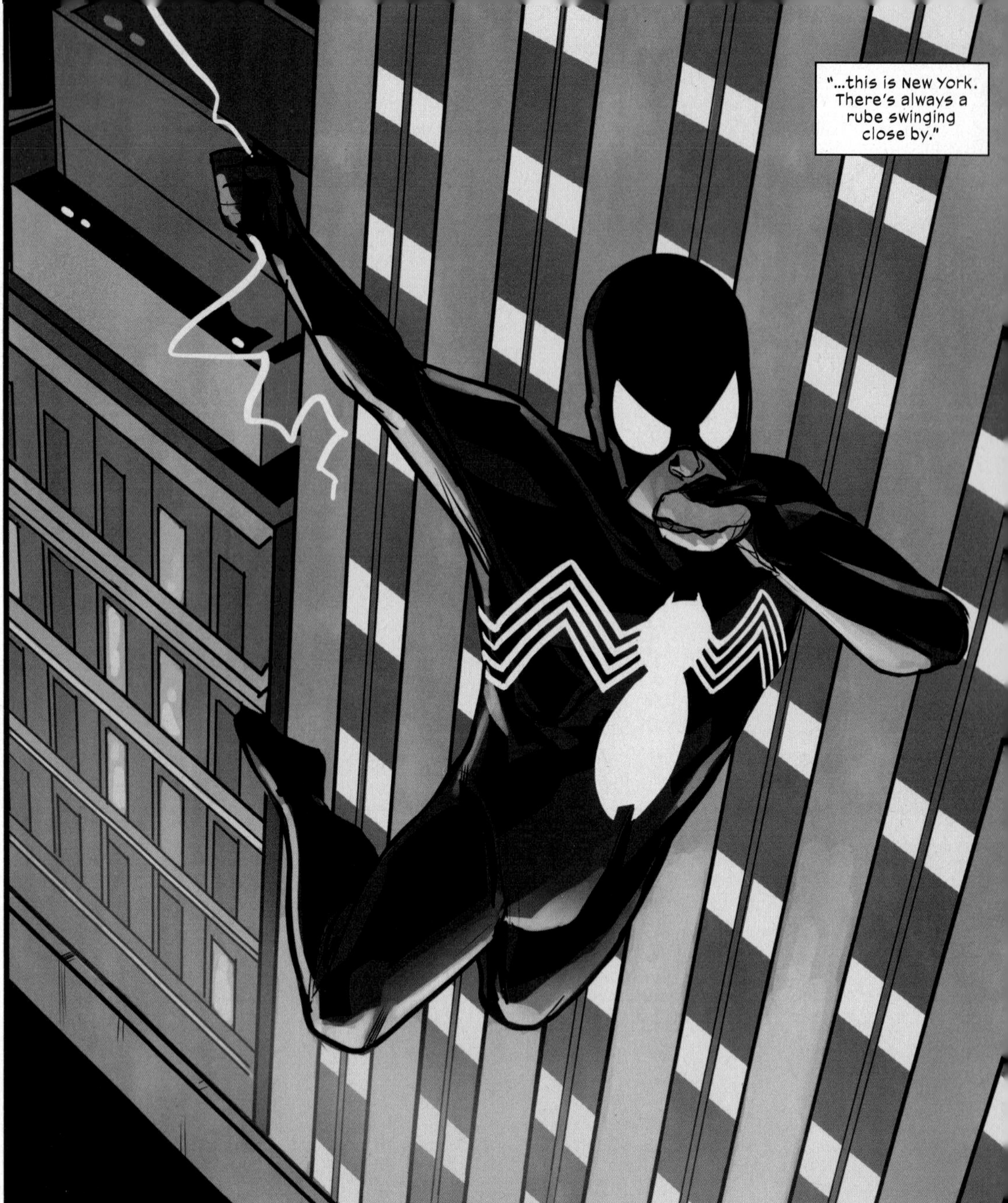
"...this is New York. There's always a rube swinging close by."

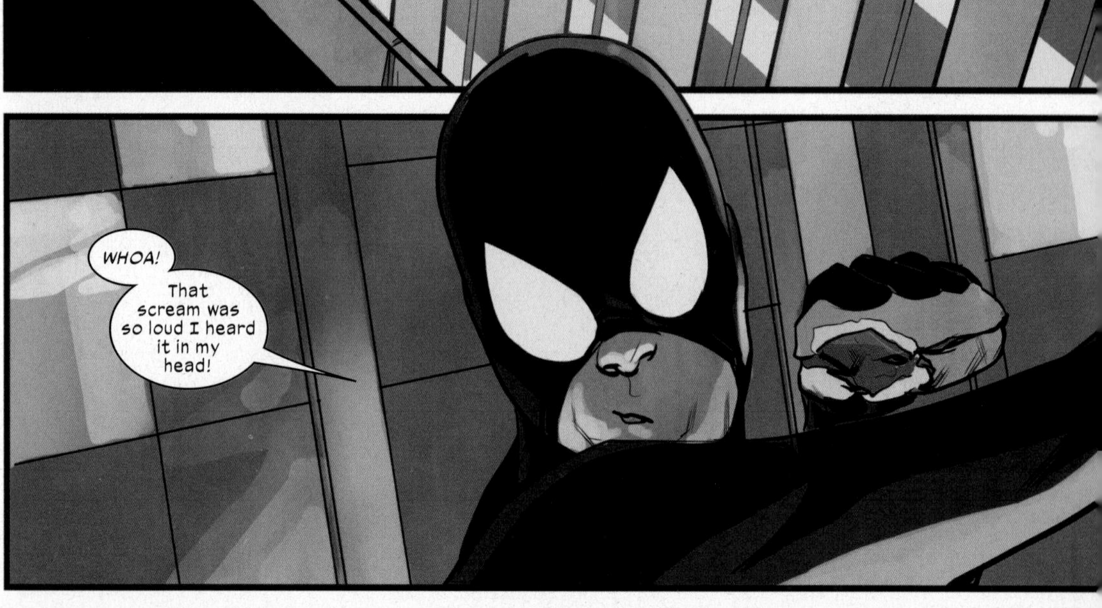
WHOA!
That scream was so loud I heard it in my head!

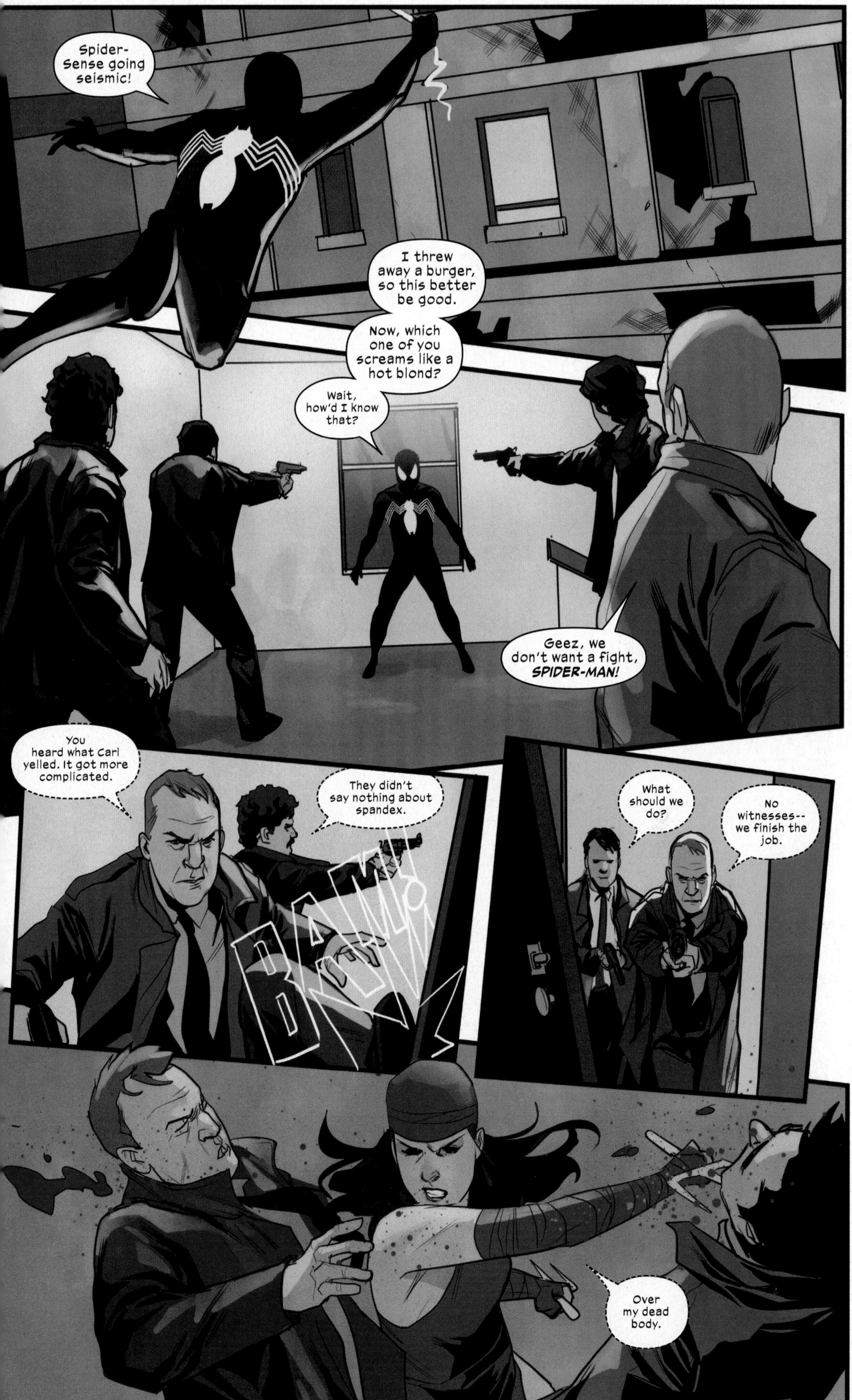
Spider-Sense going seismic!
I threw away a burger, so this better be good.
Now, which one of you screams like a hot blond?
Wait, how'd I know that?
Geez, we don't want a fight, SPIDER-MAN!
You heard what Carl yelled. It got more complicated.
They didn't say nothing about spandex.
BAM!
What should we do?
No witnesses--we finish the job.
Over my dead body.

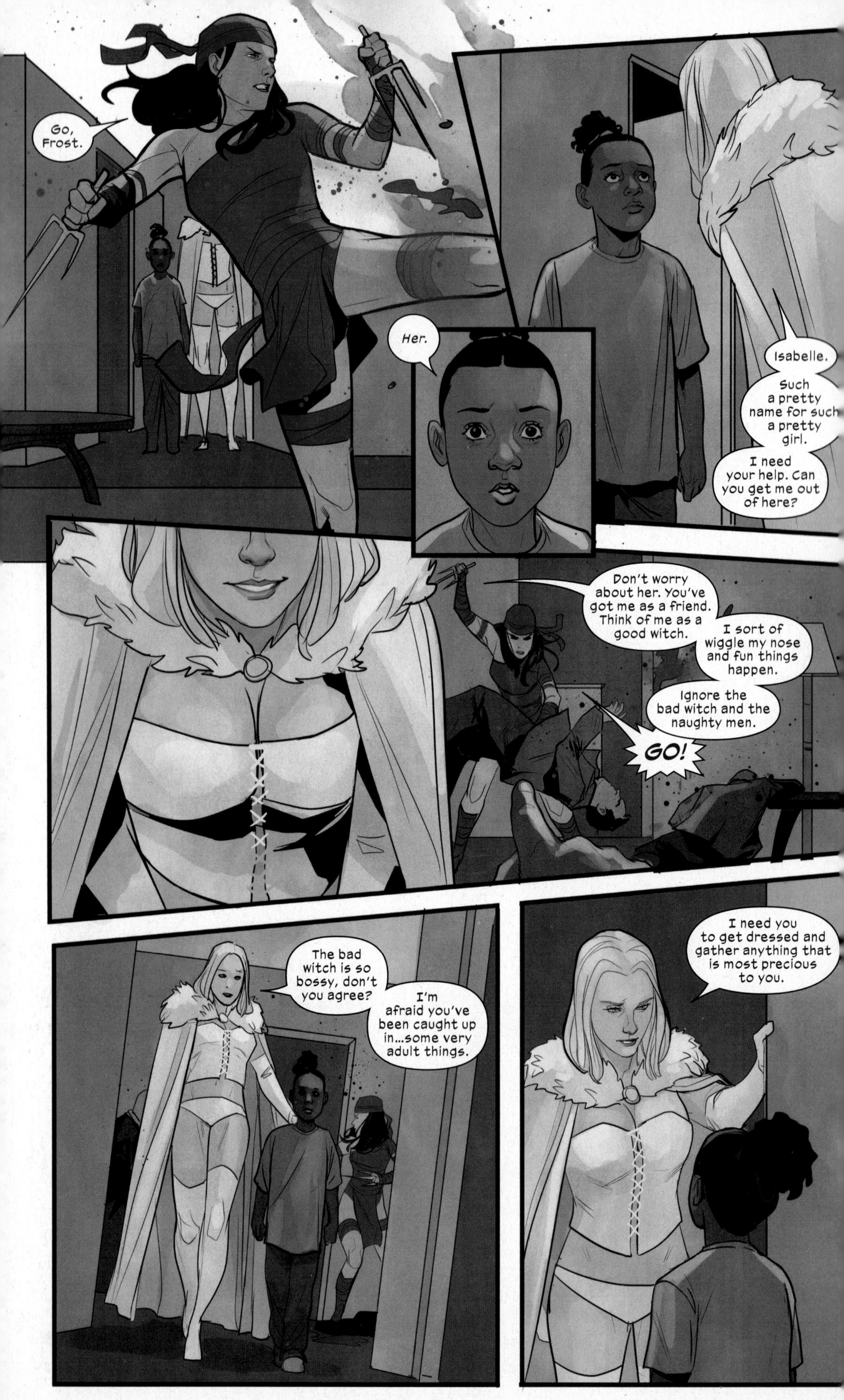
Go, Frost.
Her.
Isabelle.
Such a pretty name for such a pretty girl.
I need your help. Can you get me out of here?
Don't worry about her. You've got me as a friend. Think of me as a good witch.
I sort of wiggle my nose and fun things happen.
Ignore the bad witch and the naughty men.
GO!
The bad witch is so bossy, don't you agree?
I'm afraid you've been caught up in...some very adult things.
I need you to get dressed and gather anything that is most precious to you.

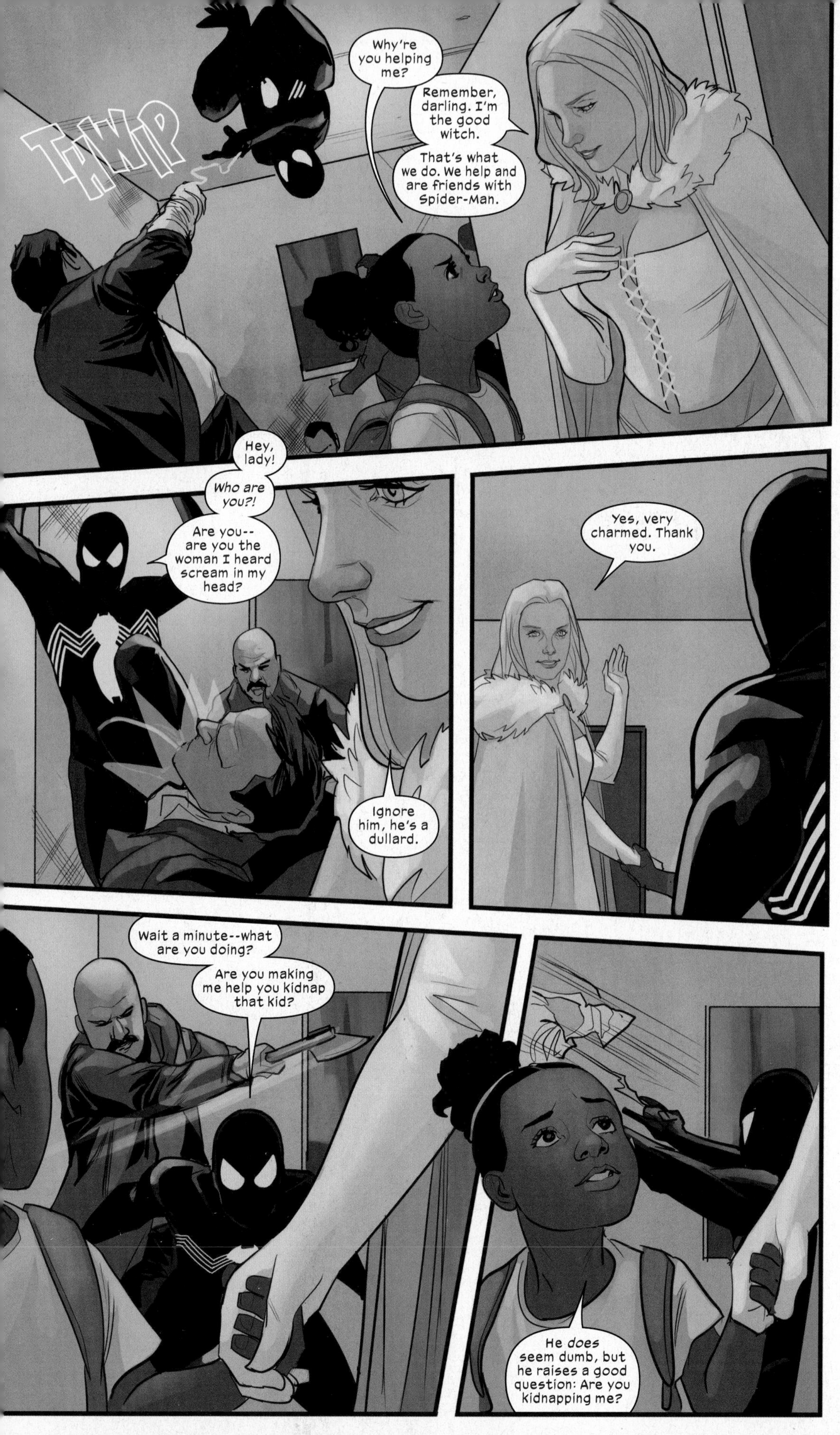
THWIP
Why're you helping me?
Remember, darling. I'm the good witch.
That's what we do. We help and are friends with Spider-Man.
Hey, lady!
Who are you?!
Are you--are you the woman I heard scream in my head?
Ignore him, he's a dullard.
Yes, very charmed. Thank you.
Wait a minute--what are you doing?
Are you making me help you kidnap that kid?
He *does* seem dumb, but he raises a good question: Are you kidnapping me?

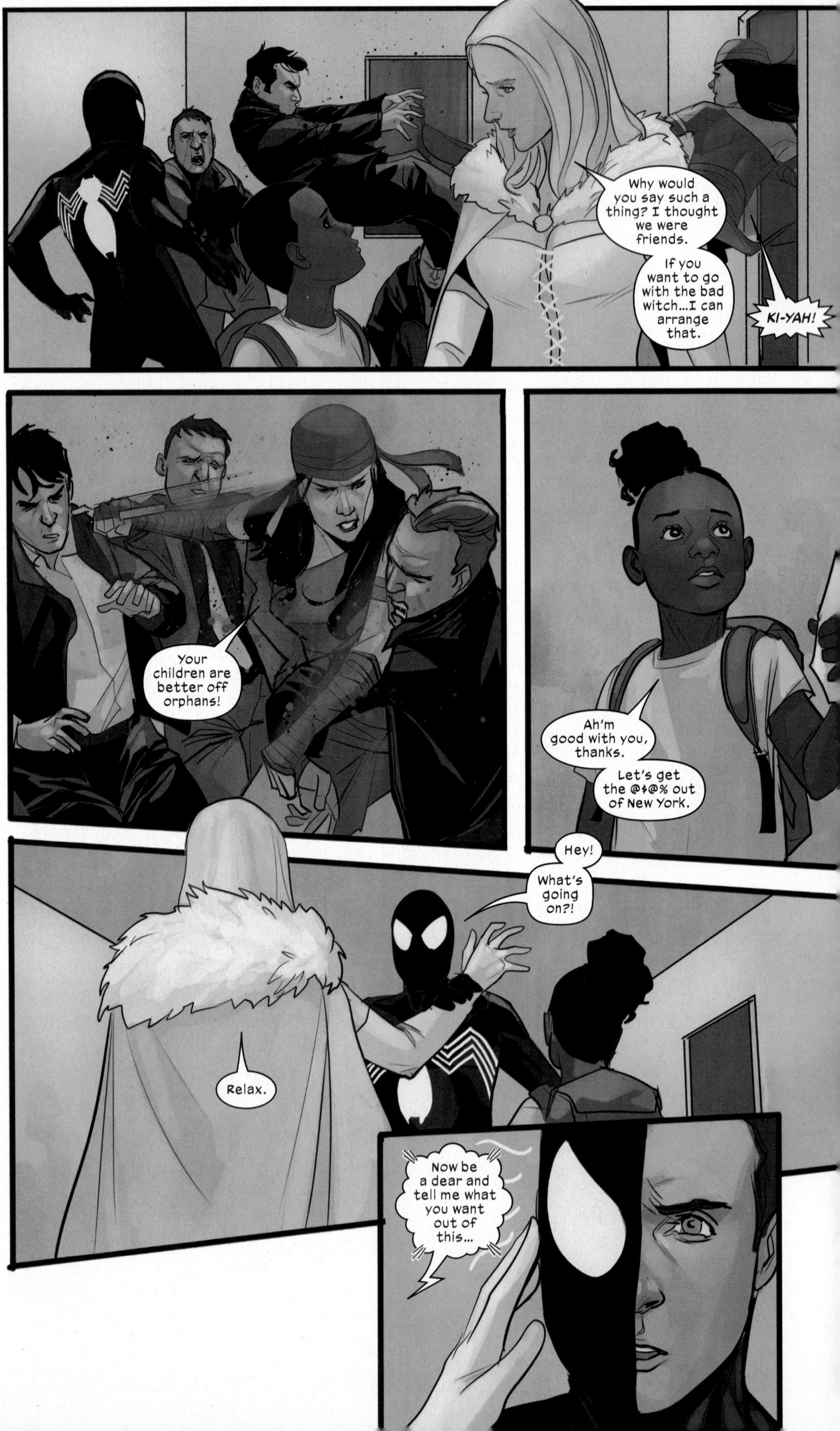

Why would you say such a thing? I thought we were friends.
If you want to go with the bad witch...I can arrange that.
KI-YAH!
Your children are better off orphans!
Ah'm good with you, thanks.
Let's get the @$@% out of New York.
Hey!
What's going on?!
Relax.
Now be a dear and tell me what you want out of this...

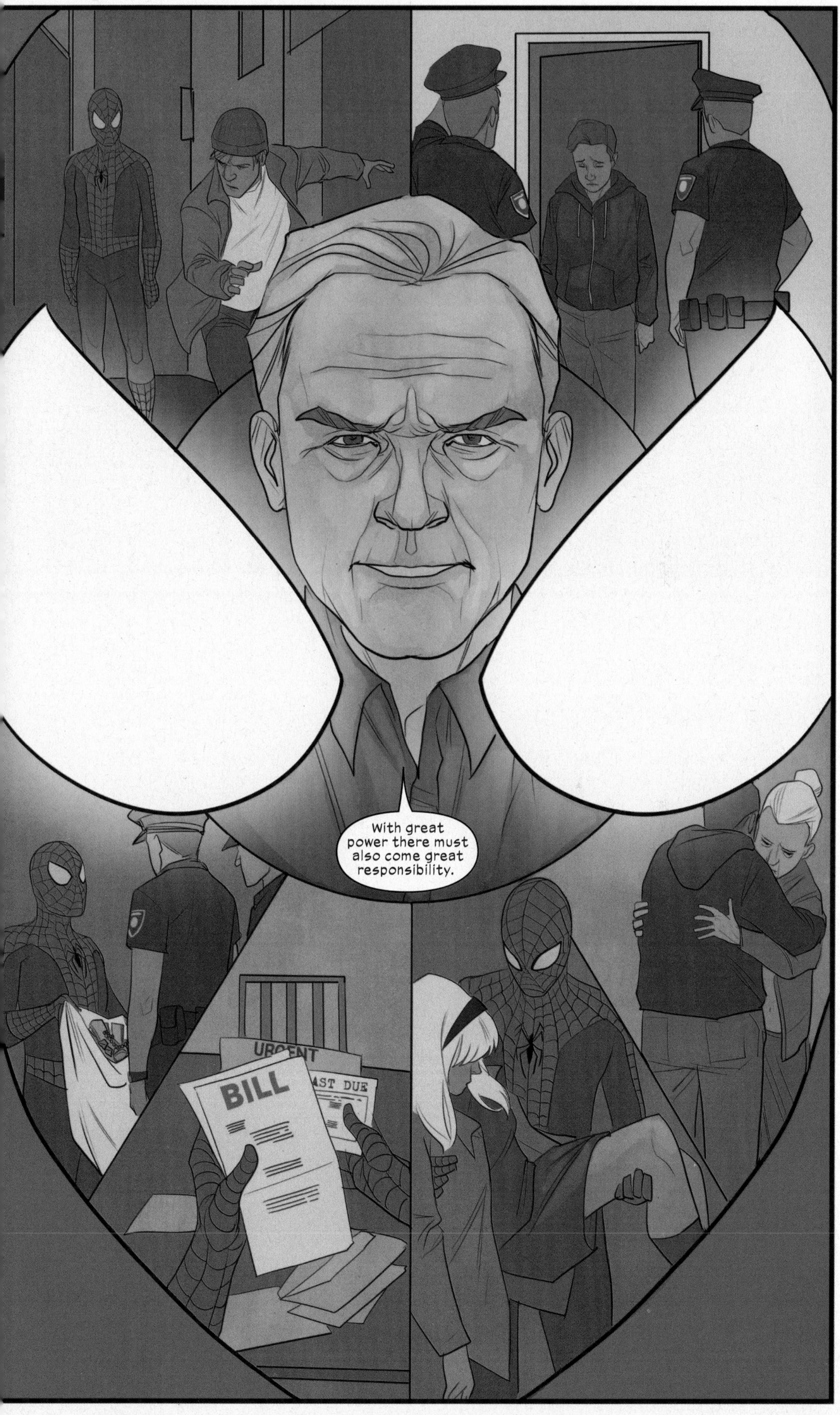
With great power there must also come great responsibility.
URGENT
BILL
PAST DUE

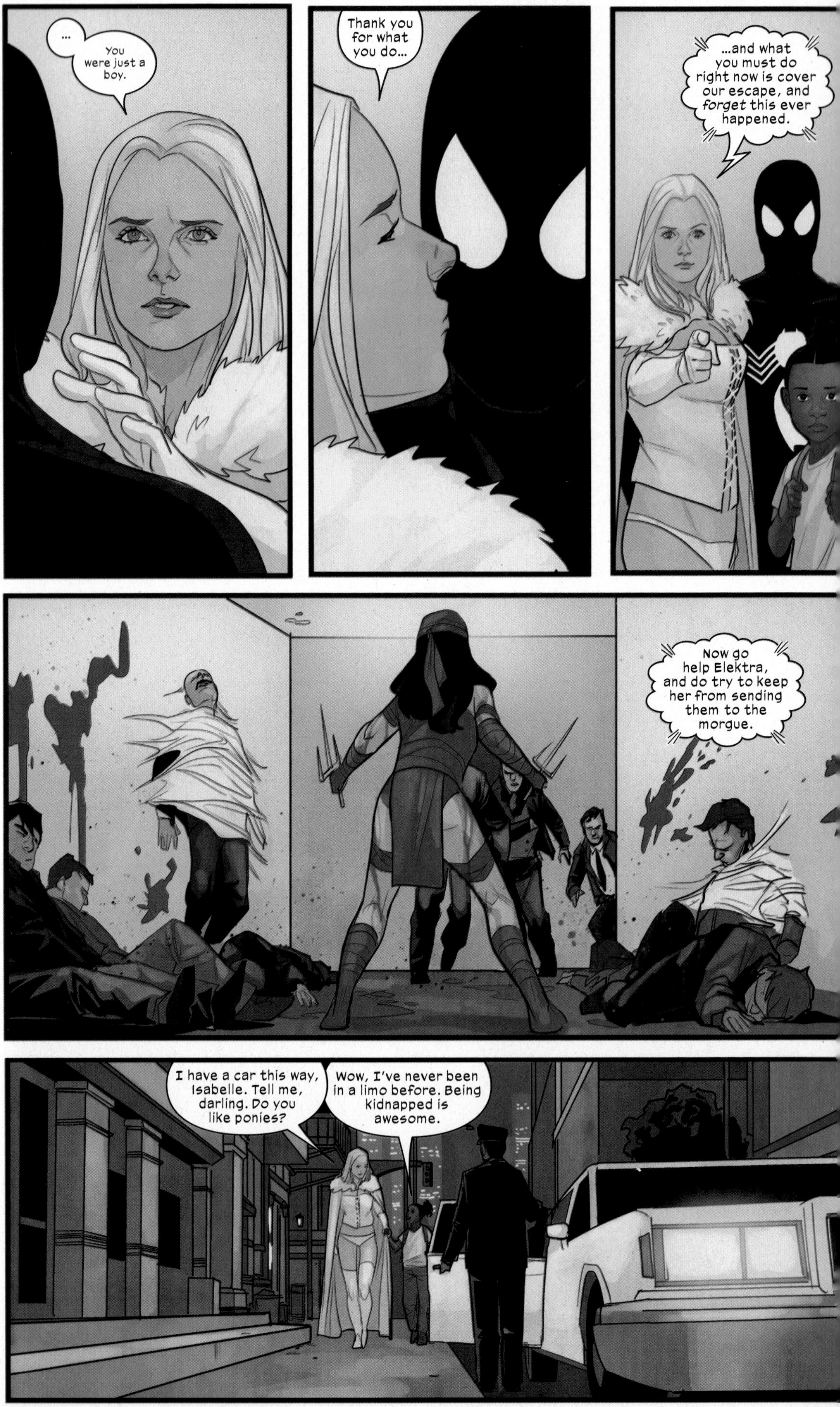

... You were just a boy.
Thank you for what you do...
...and what you must do right now is cover our escape, and *forget* this ever happened.
Now go help Elektra, and do try to keep her from sending them to the morgue.
I have a car this way, Isabelle. Tell me, darling. Do you like ponies?
Wow, I've never been in a limo before. Being kidnapped is awesome.

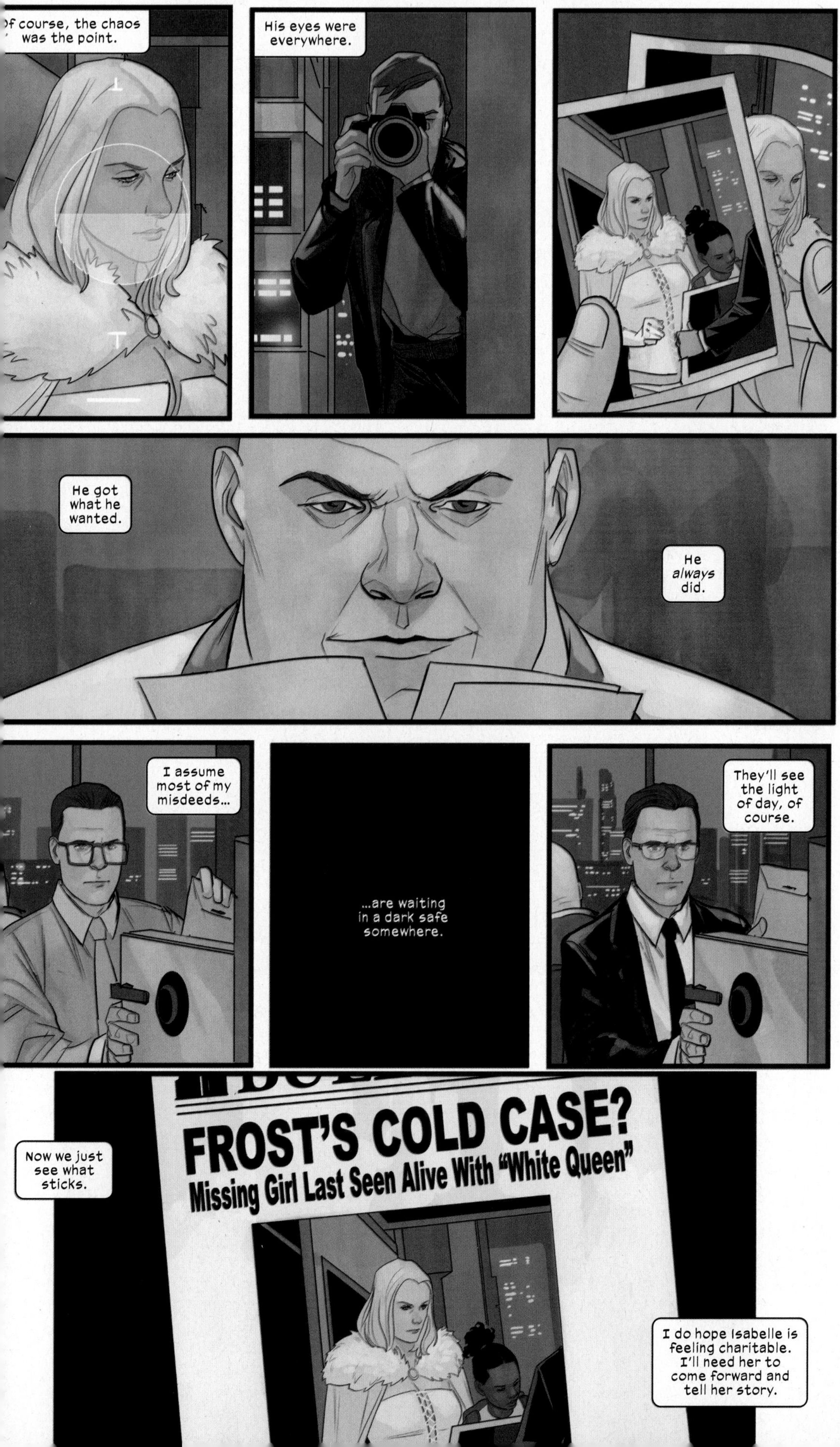
Of course, the chaos was the point.
His eyes were everywhere.
He got what he wanted.
He *always* did.
I assume most of my misdeeds...
...are waiting in a dark safe somewhere.
They'll see the light of day, of course.
FROST'S COLD CASE?
Missing Girl Last Seen Alive With "White Queen"
Now we just see what sticks.
I do hope Isabelle is feeling charitable. I'll need her to come forward and tell her story.

[ENCRYPTED]

FAO: **JAMES WESLEY**

CONTENTS OF THIS FILE ARE SUBJECT TO ATTORNEY-CLIENT PRIVILEGE WITH **FISK HOLDING, LLC**

PERSONAL FILE OF **EMMA GRACE FROST**

ATTACHED ARE THE PHOTOGRAPHS AND DETAILS OF SUBJECT'S WORK AND EXTRACURRICULARS. WHEN OUR SHOOTER WAS MADE BY THE SUBJECT, IT IS NOTED. SAFEST DISTANCE TO FLY UNDER HER RADAR IN CROWDS WAS ONE HUNDRED METERS. -- FISK HOLDING, LLC HR DEPARTMENT

CONTENTS

1-11 - BIOGRAPHICAL, FAMILY HISTORY AND KNOWN ASSOCIATES

12 - EMPLOYMENT HISTORY [DUAL ENCRYPTED]

13 - EXTRACURRICULARS

14-20 - BANK FRAUD, INSIDER TRADING, WITNESS TAMPERING, SPORTS-FIXING, PONZI SCHEMES

15 - SUBJECT OBSERVED KILLING A PONY WITH HER MIND?

16 - CHILD ENDANGERMENT?

17 - TENURE WITH SUPER HEROES

18 - SURVEILLANCE TERMINATED

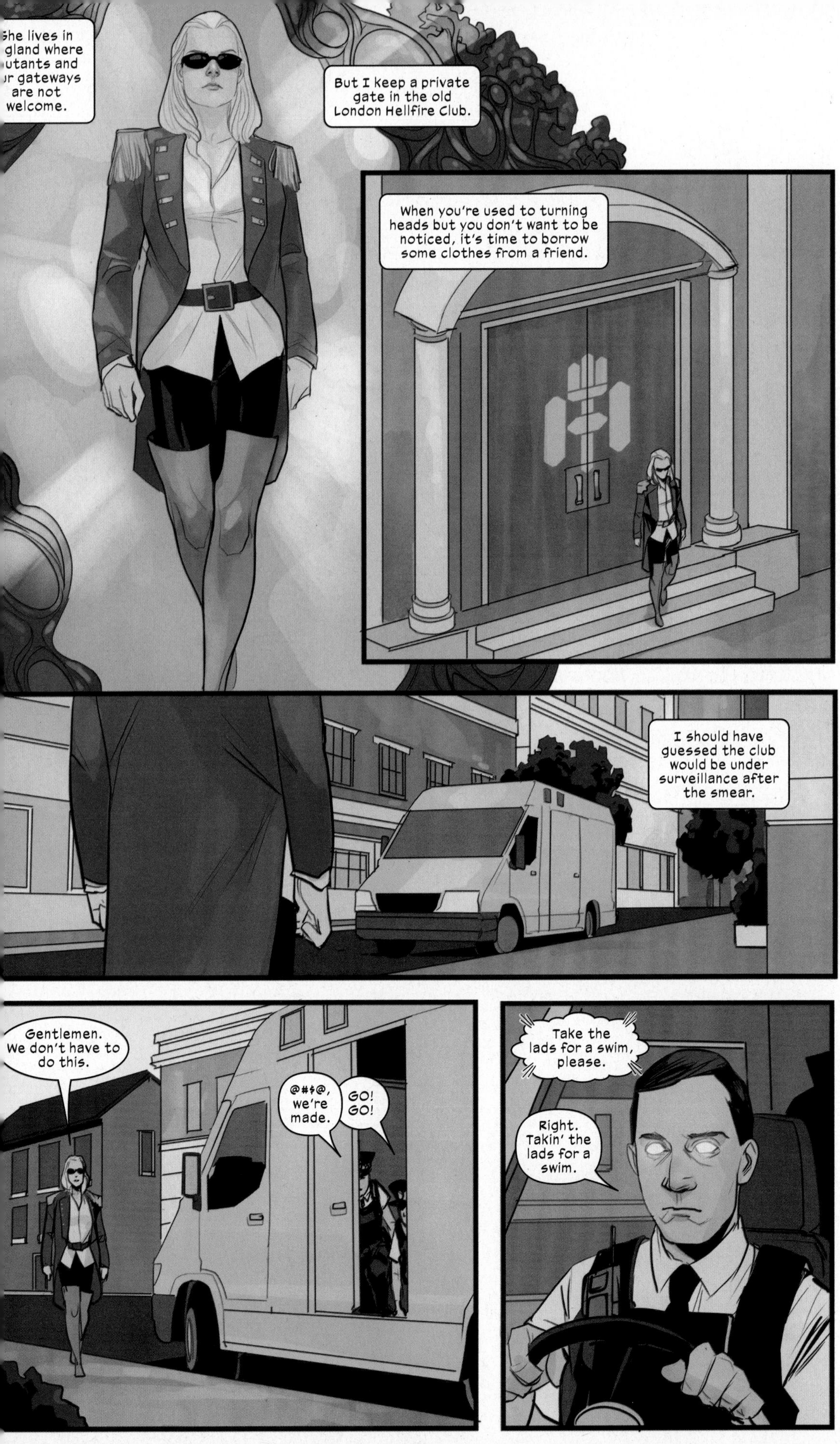

she lives in gland where utants and r gateways are not welcome.
But I keep a private gate in the old London Hellfire Club.
When you're used to turning heads but you don't want to be noticed, it's time to borrow some clothes from a friend.
I should have guessed the club would be under surveillance after the smear.
Gentlemen. We don't have to do this.
@#$@, we're made.
GO! GO!
Take the lads for a swim, please.
Right. Takin' the lads for a swim.

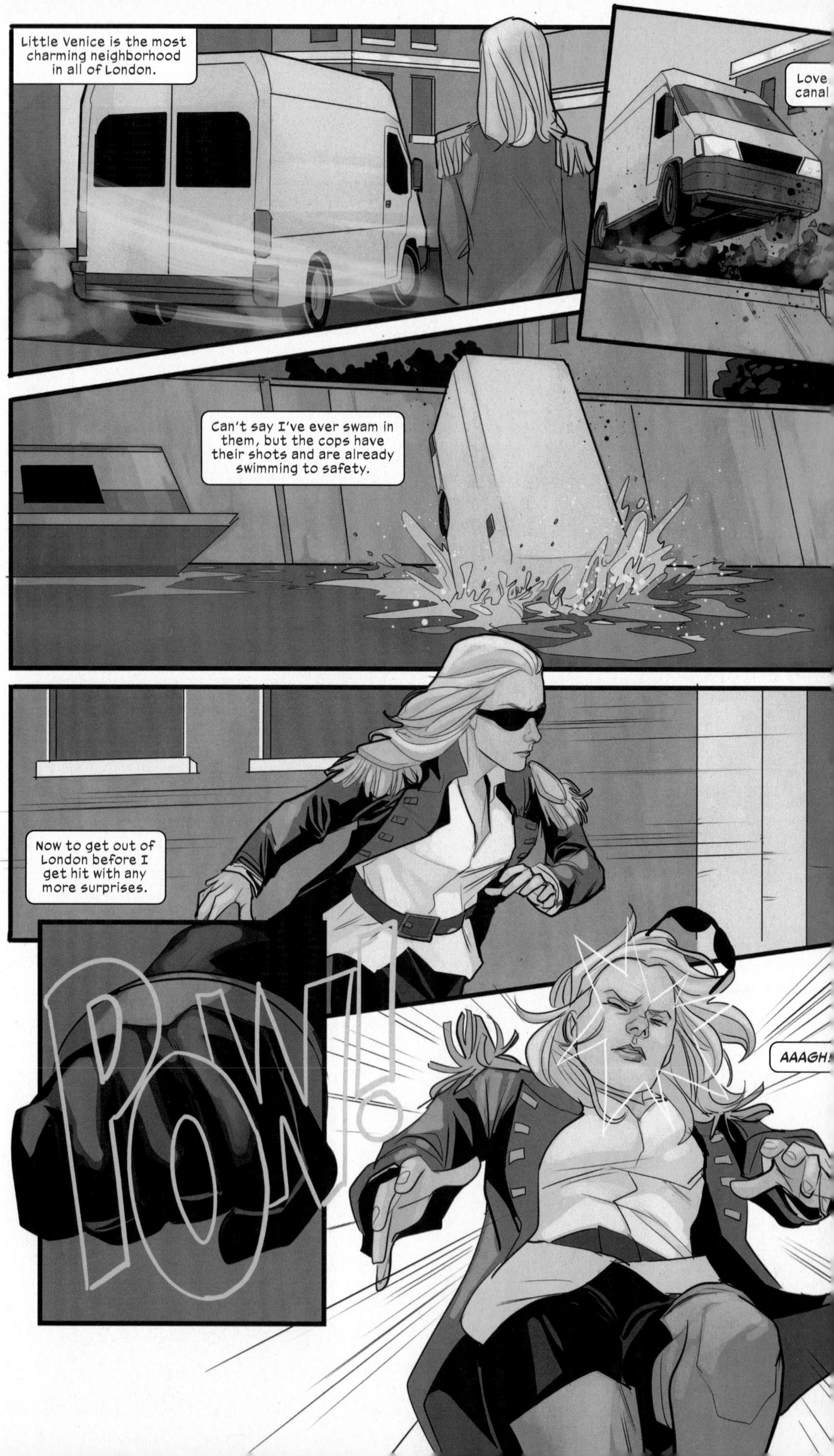
Little Venice is the most charming neighborhood in all of London.
Love canal
Can't say I've ever swam in them, but the cops have their shots and are already swimming to safety.
Now to get out of London before I get hit with any more surprises.
POW!
AAAGH!

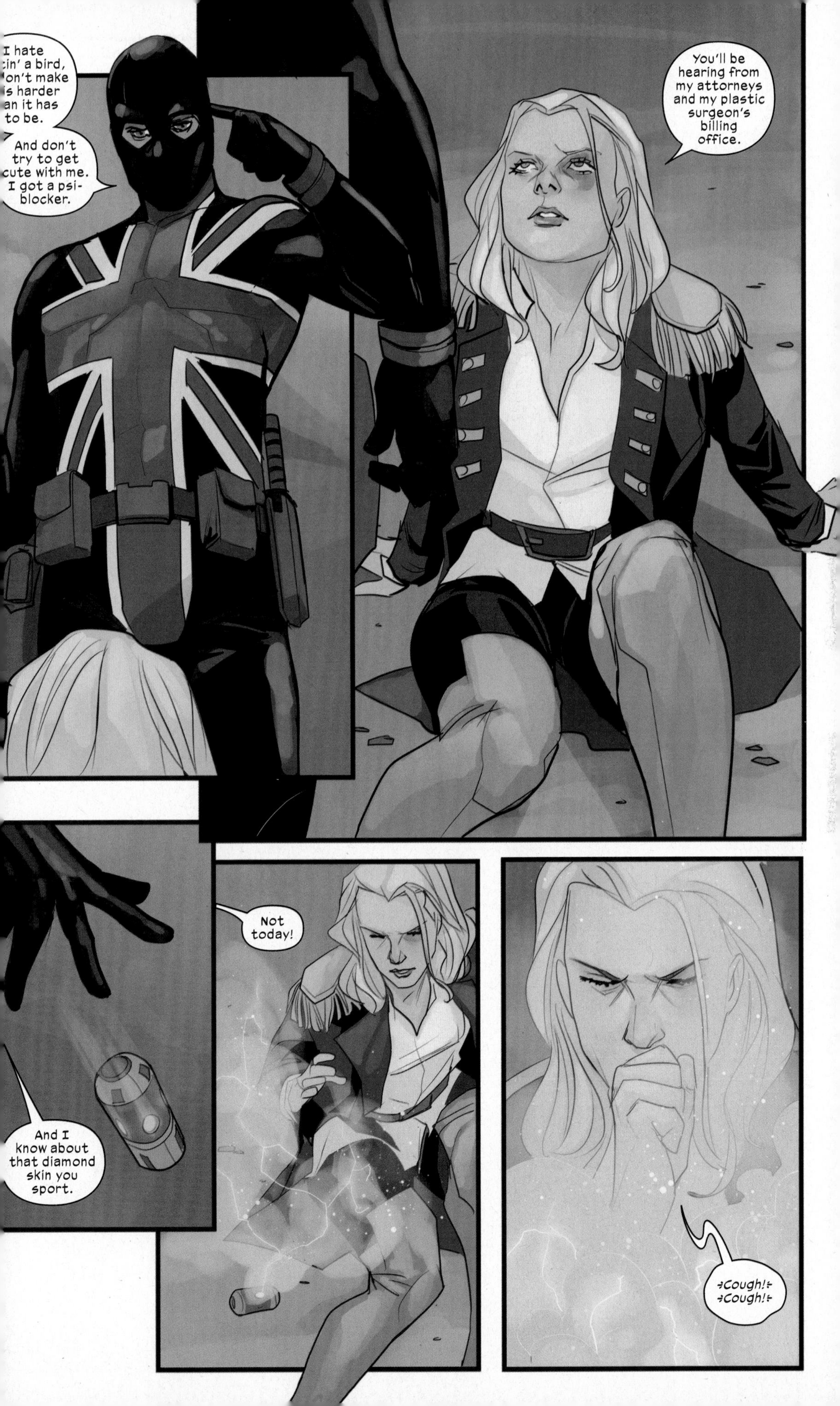

I hate
:in' a bird,
'on't make
is harder
an it has
to be.
And don't
try to get
cute with me.
I got a psi-
blocker.
You'll be hearing from my attorneys and my plastic surgeon's billing office.
And I know about that diamond skin you sport.
Not today!
Cough! Cough!

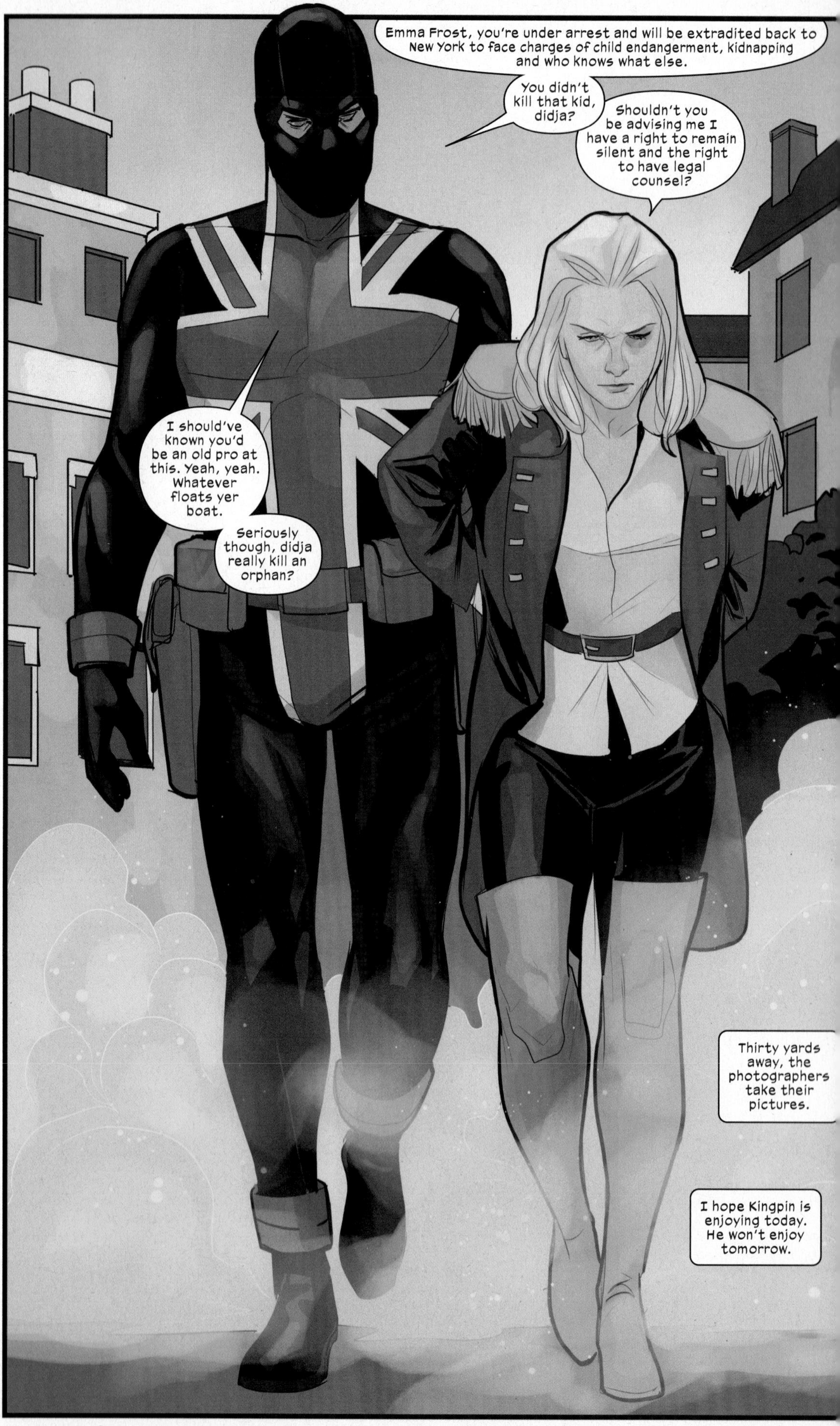
Emma Frost, you're under arrest and will be extradited back to New York to face charges of child endangerment, kidnapping and who knows what else.
You didn't kill that kid, didja?
Shouldn't you be advising me I have a right to remain silent and the right to have legal counsel?
I should've known you'd be an old pro at this. Yeah, yeah. Whatever floats yer boat.
Seriously though, didja really kill an orphan?
Thirty yards away, the photographers take their pictures.
I hope Kingpin is enjoying today. He won't enjoy tomorrow.

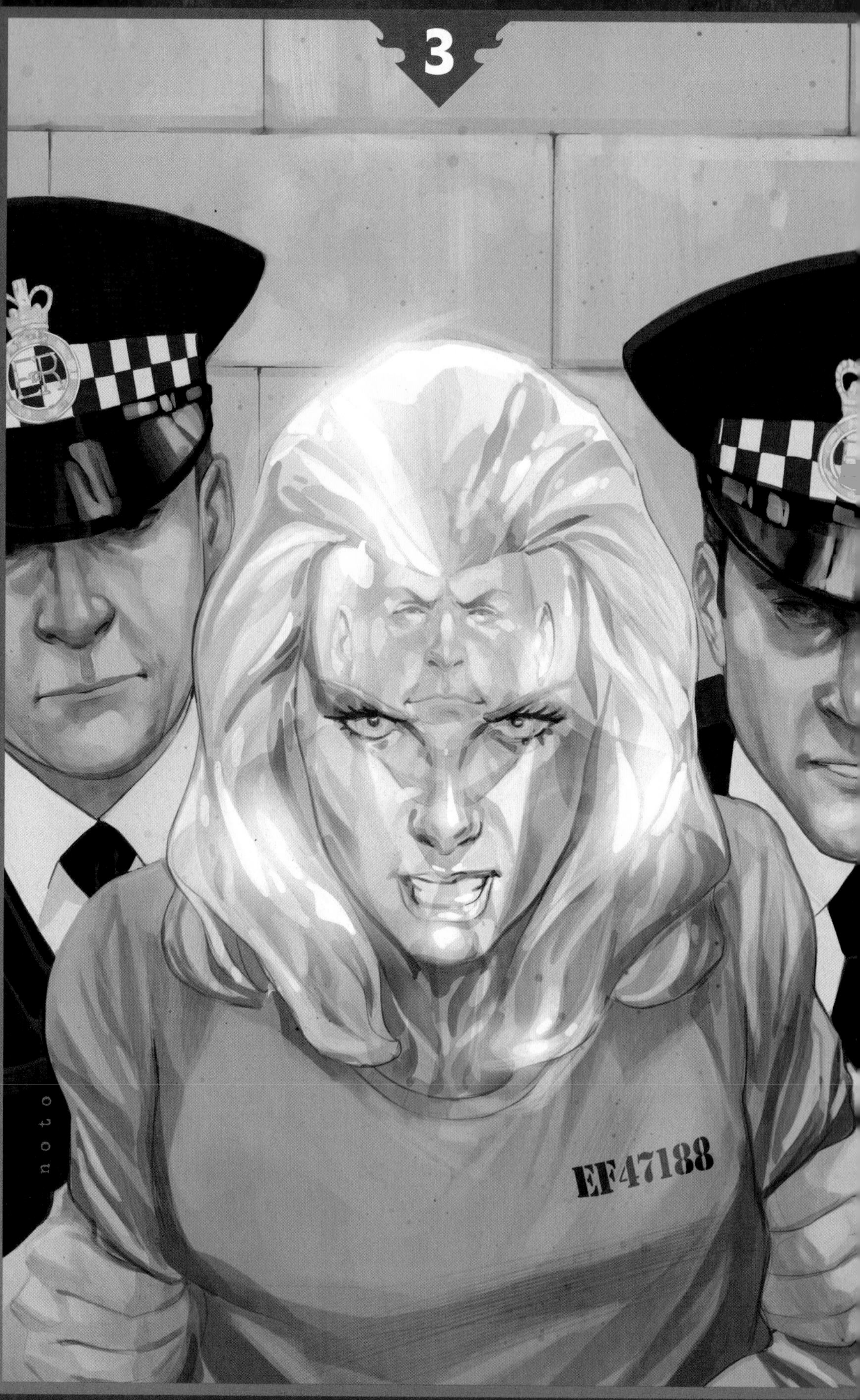
3
EF47188
noto

[devilsre....[0.1]
[ignxmen.....[0.3]

"Frost scared me more than the Kingpin did back in the day. I know she got off on that too. Best to give that woman a wide berth. I never want to be on her $@#% list."

-- TURK BARRETT

[devilsre....[0.1]
[ignxmen.....[0.3]

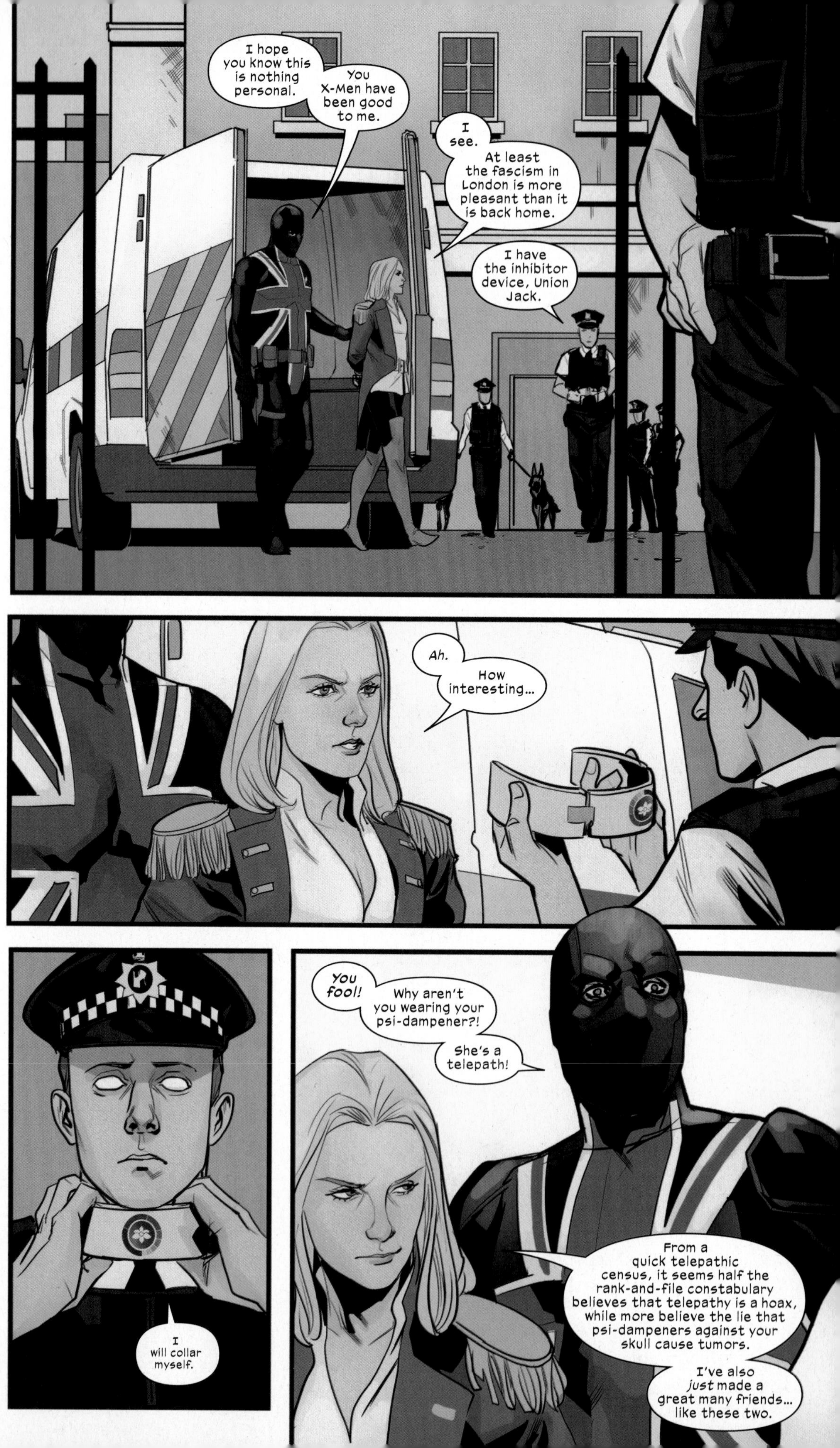

I hope you know this is nothing personal.
You X-Men have been good to me.
I see.
At least the fascism in London is more pleasant than it is back home.
I have the inhibitor device, Union Jack.
Ah.
How interesting...
I will collar myself.
You fool!
Why aren't you wearing your psi-dampener?!
She's a telepath!
From a quick telepathic census, it seems half the rank-and-file constabulary believes that telepathy is a hoax, while more believe the lie that psi-dampeners against your skull cause tumors.
I've also *just* made a great many friends... like these two.

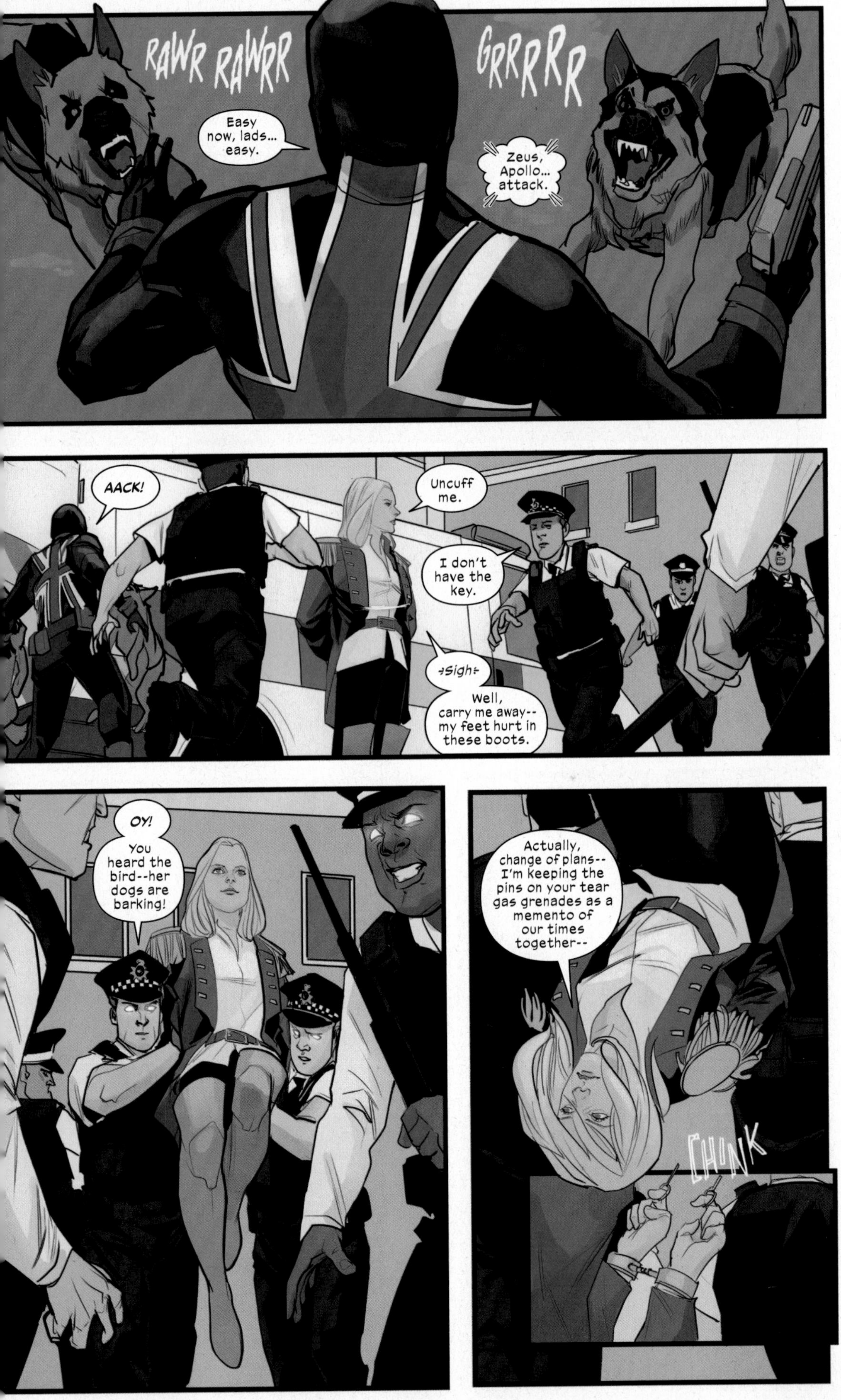
RAWR RAWRR
GRRRRR
Easy now, lads... easy.
Zeus, Apollo... attack.
AACK!
Uncuff me.
I don't have the key.
+Sigh+
Well, carry me away-- my feet hurt in these boots.
OY!
You heard the bird--her dogs are barking!
Actually, change of plans-- I'm keeping the pins on your tear gas grenades as a memento of our times together--
CHINK

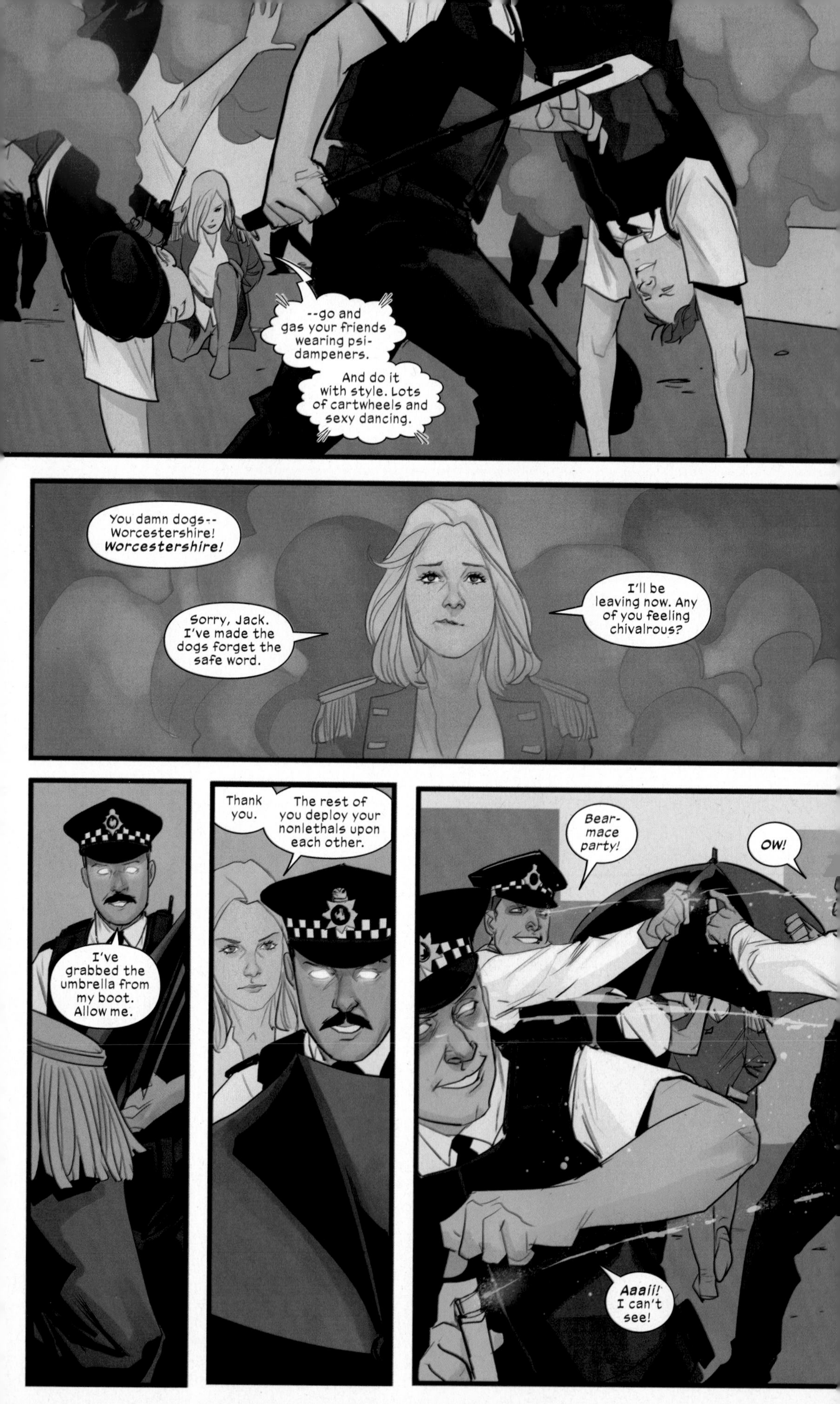
--go and gas your friends wearing psi-dampeners.
And do it with style. Lots of cartwheels and sexy dancing.
You damn dogs--Worcestershire! **Worcestershire!**
Sorry, Jack. I've made the dogs forget the safe word.
I'll be leaving now. Any of you feeling chivalrous?
I've grabbed the umbrella from my boot. Allow me.
Thank you.
The rest of you deploy your nonlethals upon each other.
Bear-mace party!
OW!
Aaaii! I can't see!

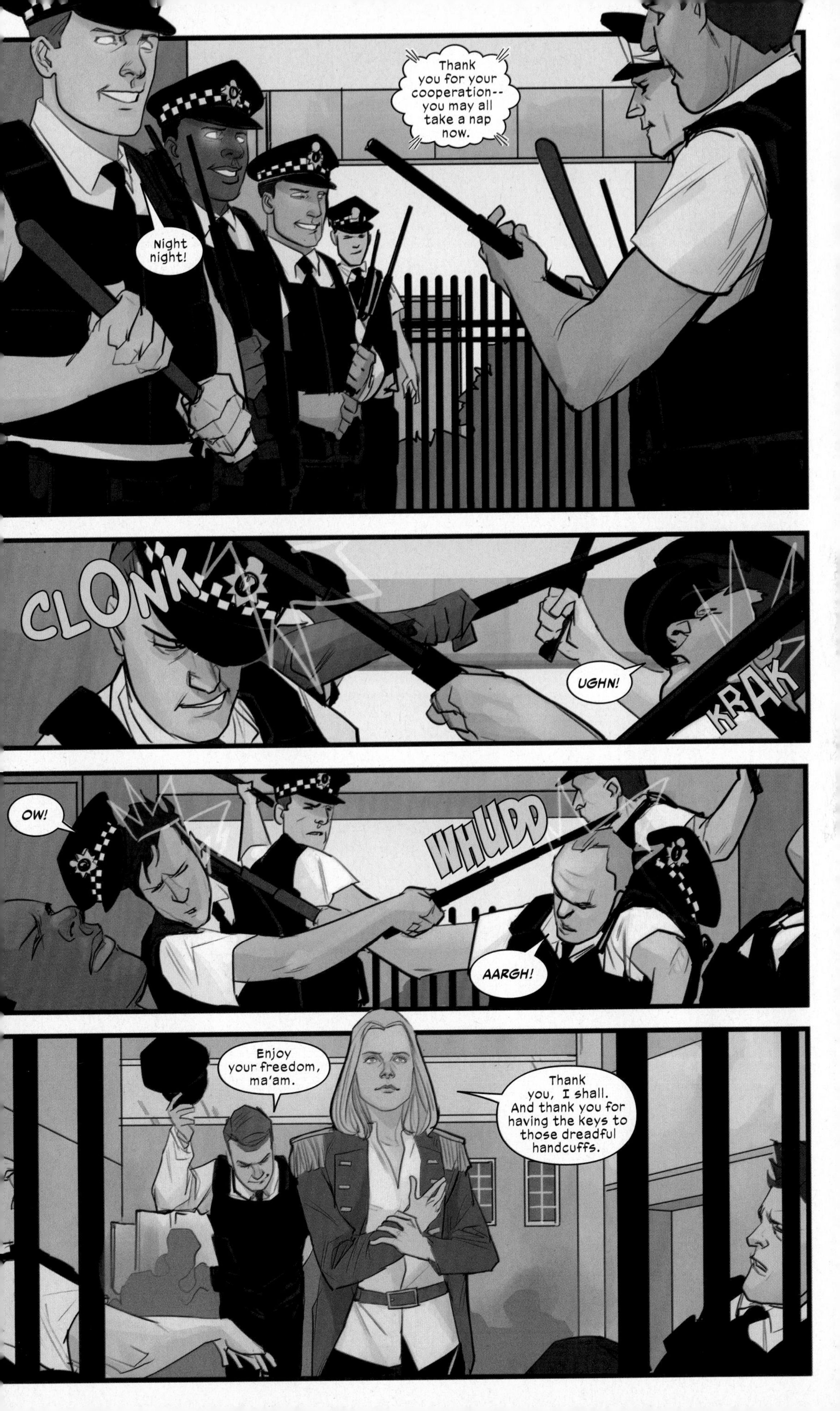
Thank you for your cooperation--you may all take a nap now.
Night night!
CLONK
UGHN!
KRAK
OW!
WHUDD
AARGH!
Enjoy your freedom, ma'am.
Thank you, I shall. And thank you for having the keys to those dreadful handcuffs.

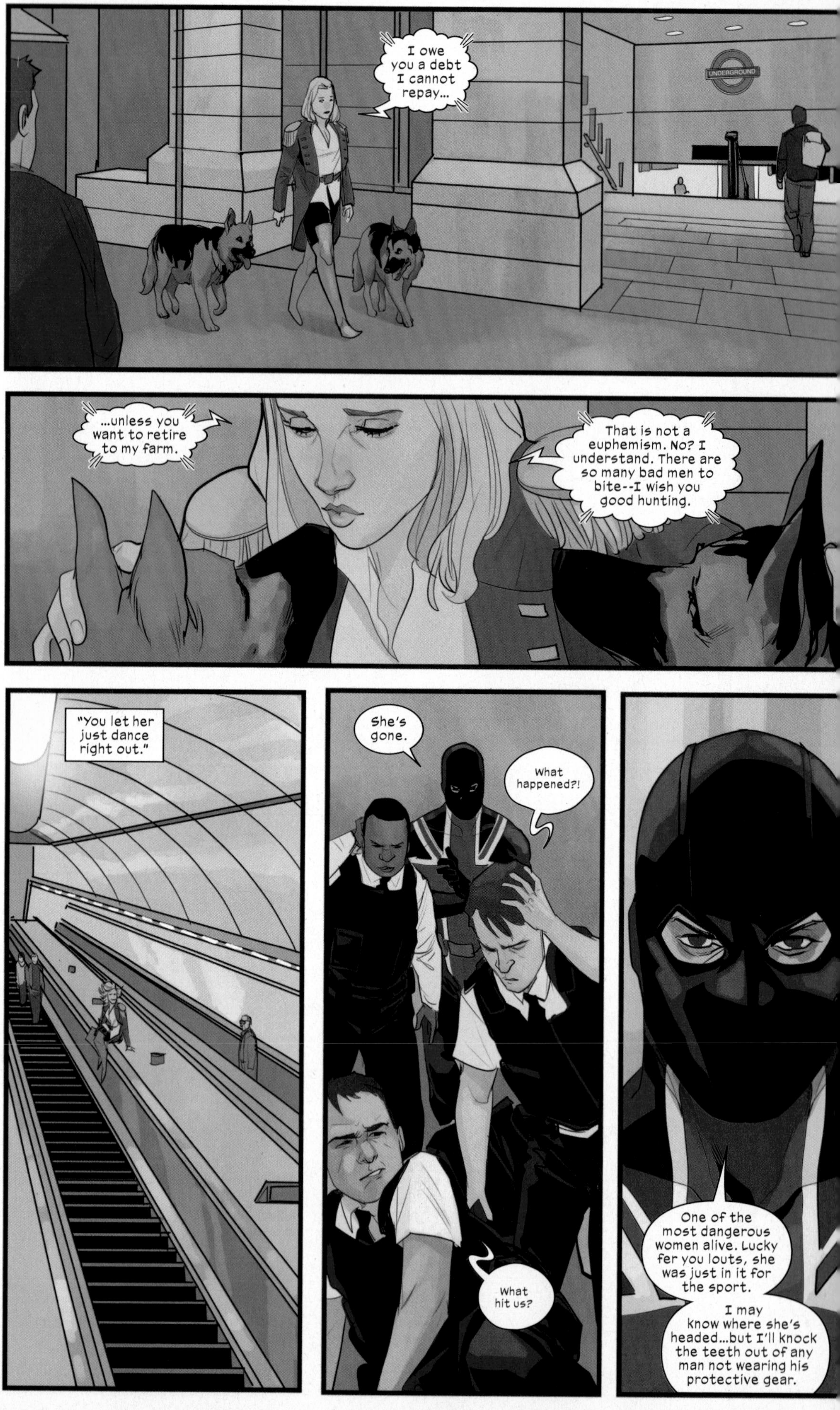
I owe you a debt I cannot repay...
UNDERGROUND
...unless you want to retire to my farm.
That is not a euphemism. No? I understand. There are so many bad men to bite--I wish you good hunting.
"You let her just dance right out."
She's gone.
What happened?!
What hit us?
One of the most dangerous women alive. Lucky fer you louts, she was just in it for the sport.
I may know where she's headed...but I'll knock the teeth out of any man not wearing his protective gear.

Dear Isabelle,

When you wake up, I will be gone. I'm on a night flight back to New York City. I do not wish to endanger you any further than I have.

I know the last few days have been traumatizing, but the family I have placed you with have been vetted thoroughly and I trust them implicitly. They are plain, old English farmers, and you should draw no unwanted attention while in their care. I understand from them that you're resisting visiting the therapist I've arranged for you, and I'd ask you to reconsider. Go sit and be quiet, and see what happens. The mood may overtake you.

I've arranged for a new name and identity for you, keeping your first name and giving you my mother's maiden name of Donovan. My mother, Hazel, was a complicated woman, but she fought valiantly against her demons. The name is not permanent if you do not wish it to be so.

Keep up with your art -- you're very talented -- study hard and do not lose that sense of humor. An old friend once told me, "it's chaos, be kind", and that is how you find yourself out of questionable foster care and into a home of privilege with a stable out back. I'm trying to be kind -- you will be the final adjudicator on whether or not I succeeded. If I have added to your troubles, I ask you to forgive me. I have no experience with children. When you get older, you may understand that adults have to pick the lesser of evils. We girls have to look out for each other.

You know how to reach me when you need me.

-- EF

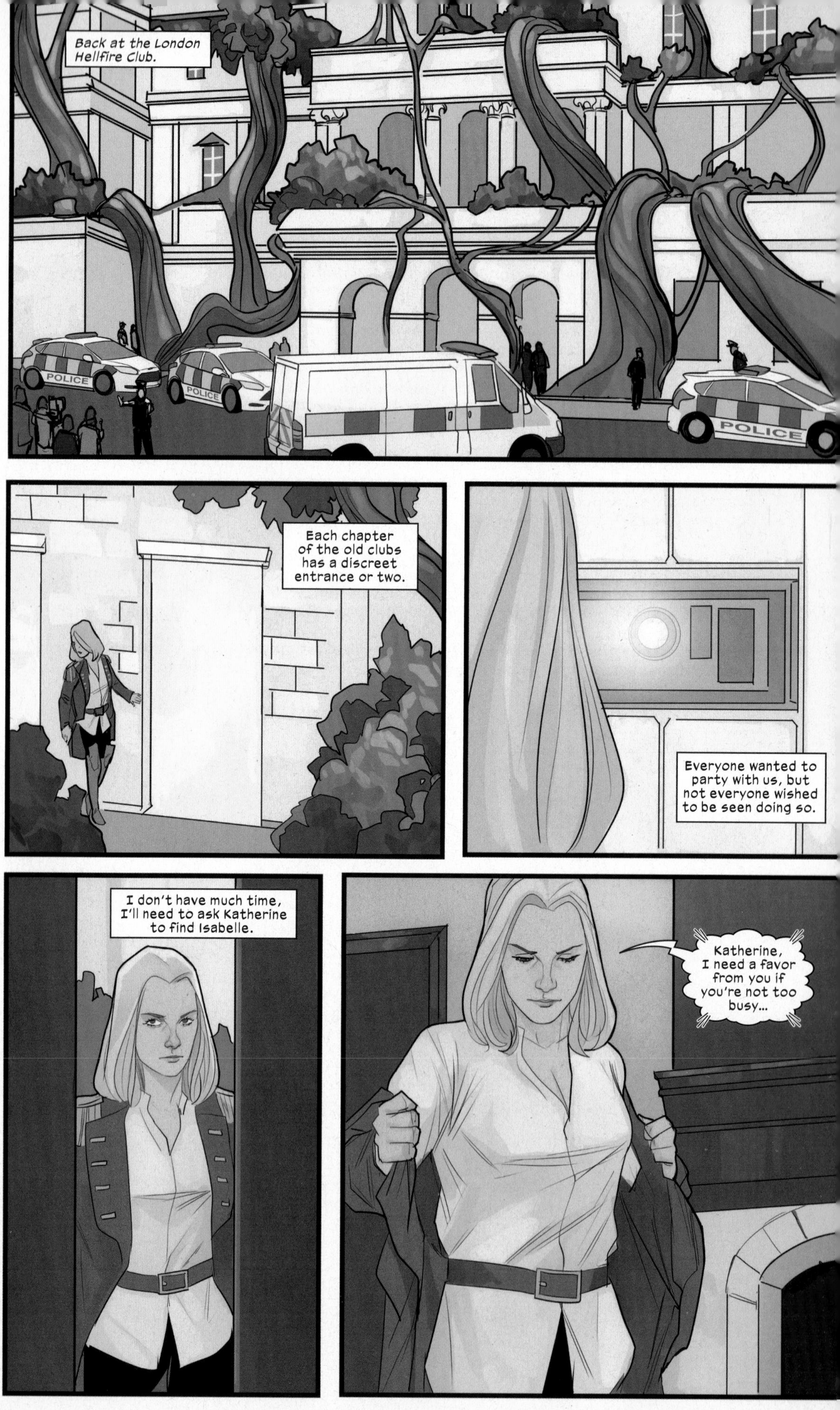

Back at the London Hellfire Club.
POLICE
POLICE
POLICE
Each chapter of the old clubs has a discreet entrance or two.
Everyone wanted to party with us, but not everyone wished to be seen doing so.
I don't have much time, I'll need to ask Katherine to find Isabelle.
Katherine, I need a favor from you if you're not too busy...

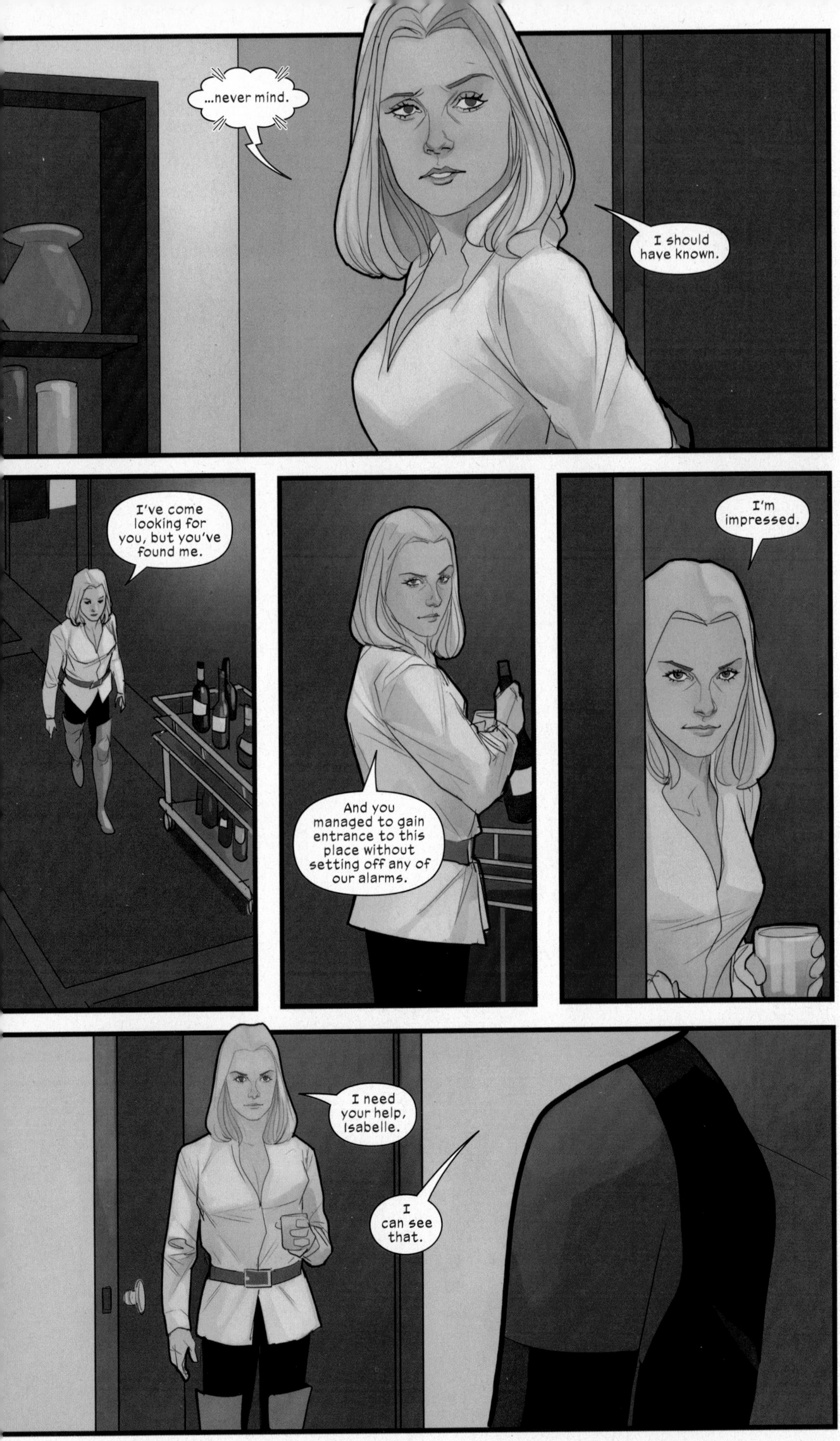
...never mind.
I should have known.
I've come looking for you, but you've found me.
And you managed to gain entrance to this place without setting off any of our alarms.
I'm impressed.
I need your help, Isabelle.
I can see that.

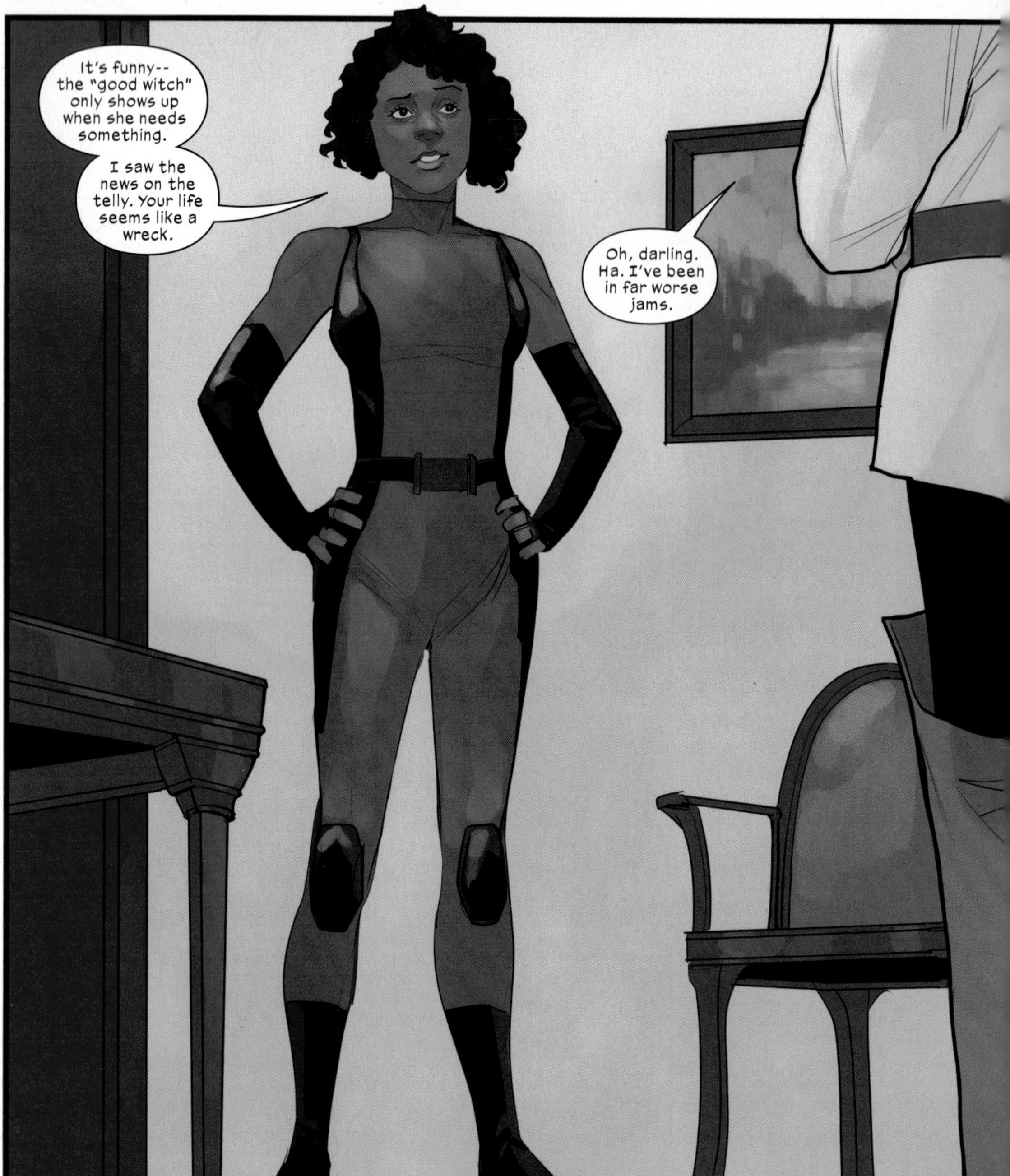
It's funny-- the "good witch" only shows up when she needs something.
I saw the news on the telly. Your life seems like a wreck.
Oh, darling. Ha. I've been in far worse jams.

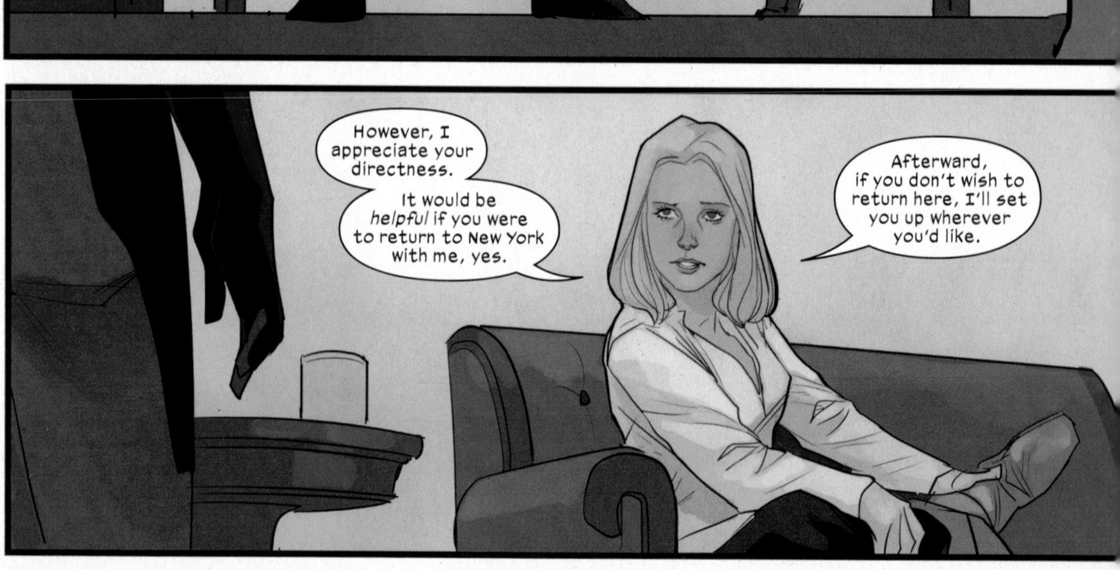
However, I appreciate your directness.
It would be *helpful* if you were to return to New York with me, yes.
Afterward, if you don't wish to return here, I'll set you up wherever you'd like.

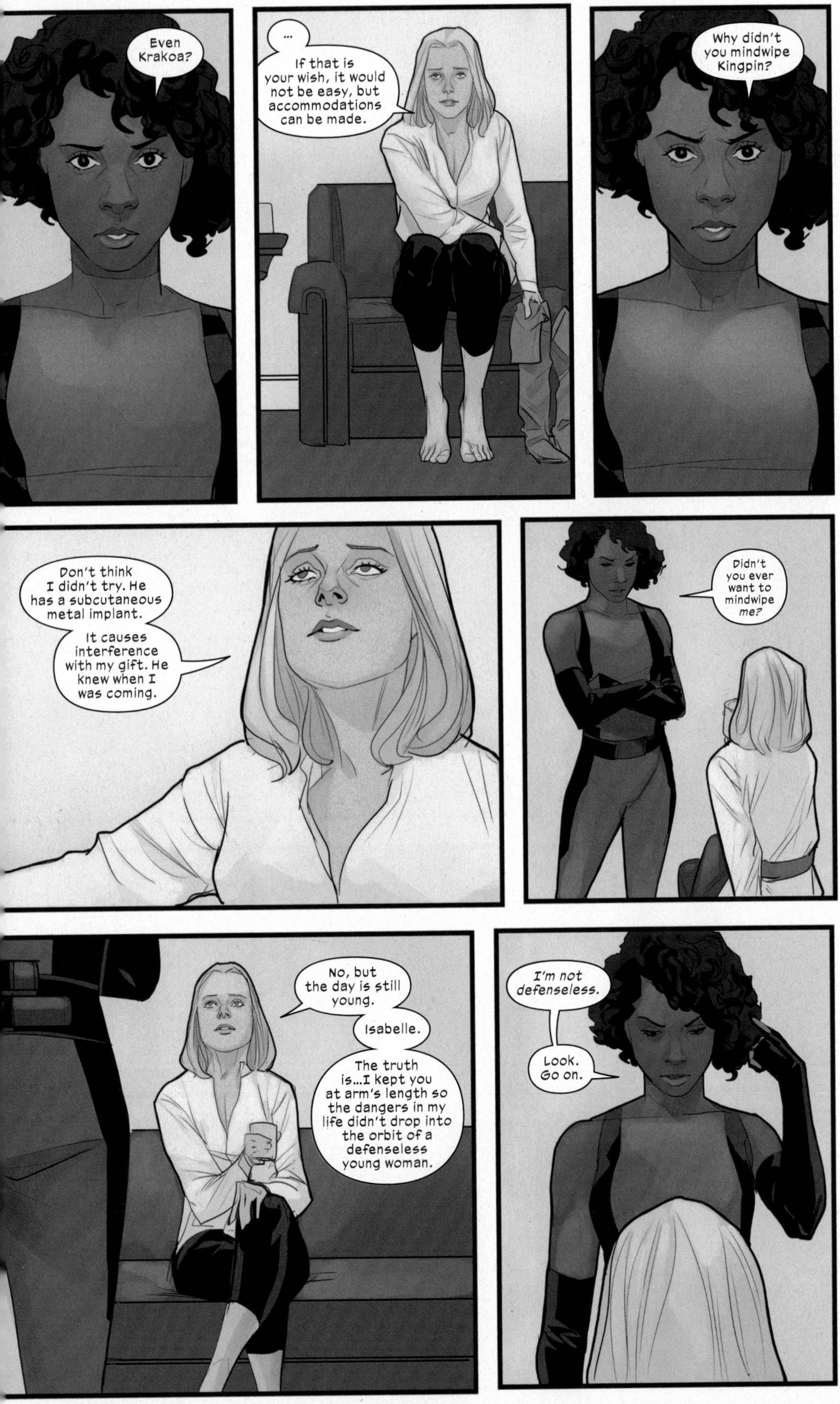
Even Krakoa?
...
If that is your wish, it would not be easy, but accommodations can be made.
Why didn't you mindwipe Kingpin?
Don't think I didn't try. He has a subcutaneous metal implant.
It causes interference with my gift. He knew when I was coming.
Didn't you ever want to mindwipe *me*?
No, but the day is still young.
Isabelle.
The truth is...I kept you at arm's length so the dangers in my life didn't drop into the orbit of a defenseless young woman.
I'm not defenseless.
Look. Go on.

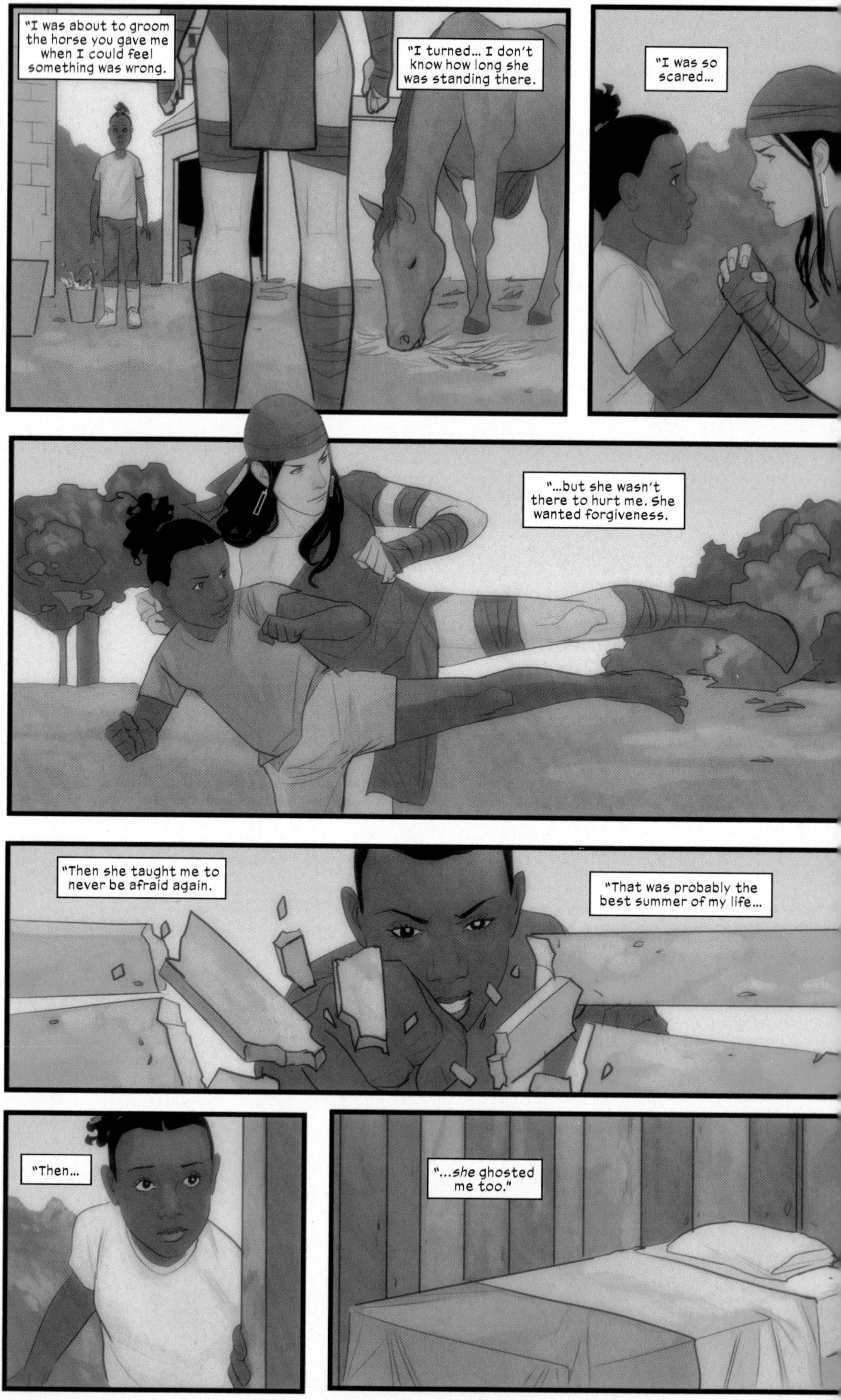
"I was about to groom the horse you gave me when I could feel something was wrong.
"I turned... I don't know how long she was standing there.
"I was so scared...
"...but she wasn't there to hurt me. She wanted forgiveness.
"Then she taught me to never be afraid again.
"That was probably the best summer of my life...
"Then...
"...*she* ghosted me too."

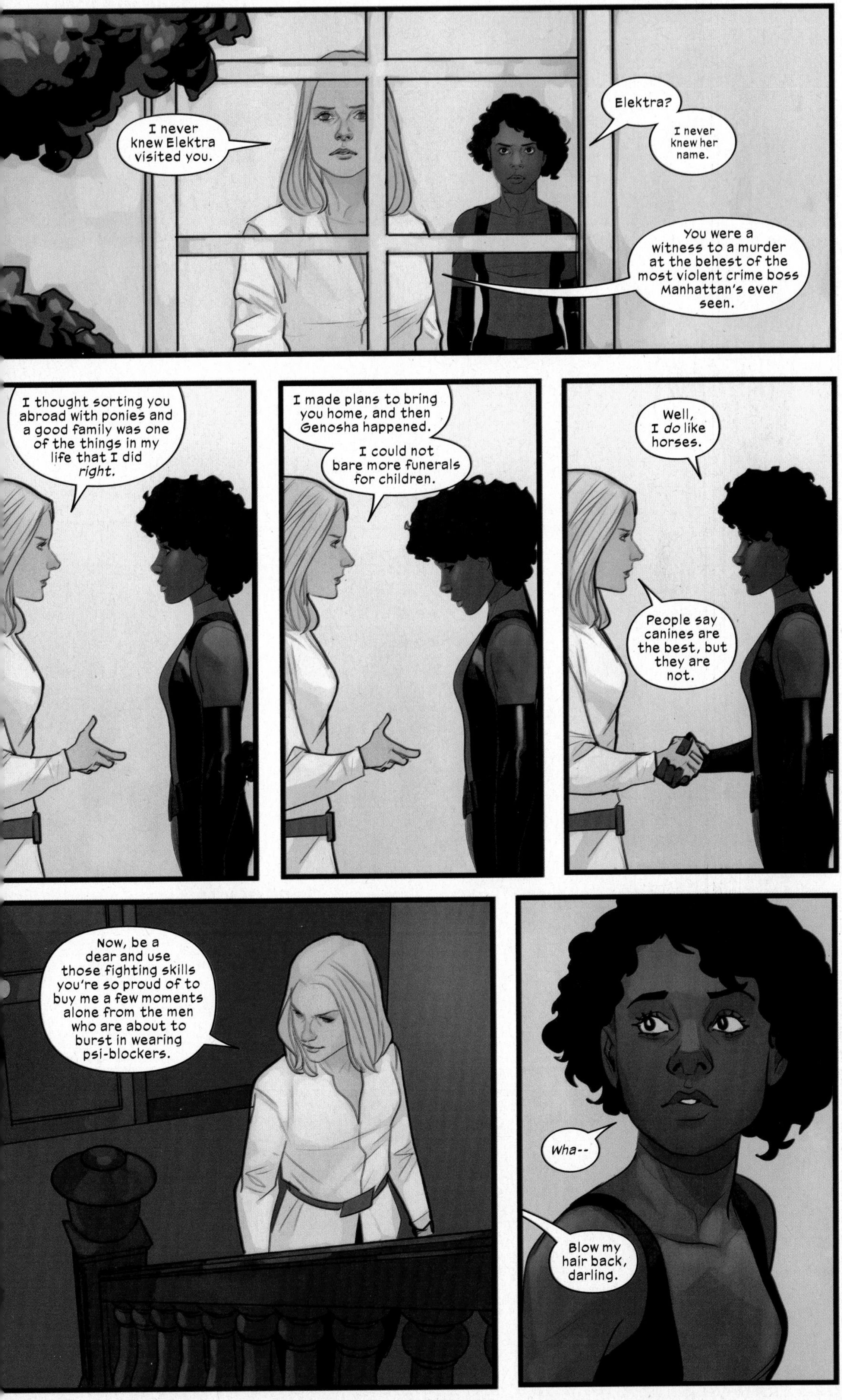
I never knew Elektra visited you.
Elektra?
I never knew her name.
You were a witness to a murder at the behest of the most violent crime boss Manhattan's ever seen.
I thought sorting you abroad with ponies and a good family was one of the things in my life that I did *right*.
I made plans to bring you home, and then Genosha happened.
I could not bare more funerals for children.
Well, I *do* like horses.
People say canines are the best, but they are not.
Now, be a dear and use those fighting skills you're so proud of to buy me a few moments alone from the men who are about to burst in wearing psi-blockers.
Wha--
Blow my hair back, darling.

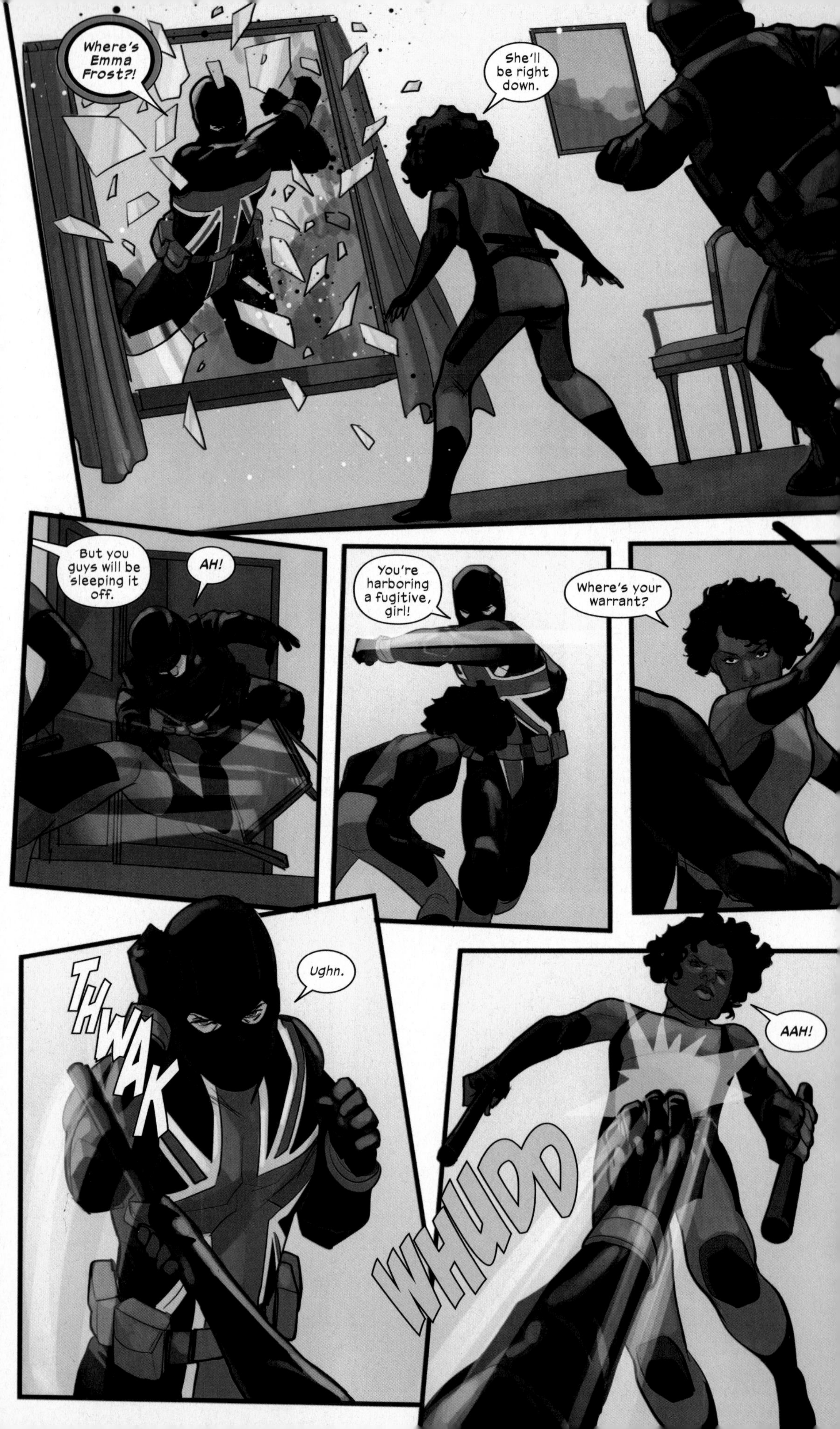

Where's Emma Frost?!
She'll be right down.
But you guys will be sleeping it off.
AH!
You're harboring a fugitive, girl!
Where's your warrant?
THWAK
Ughn.
AAH!
WHUDD

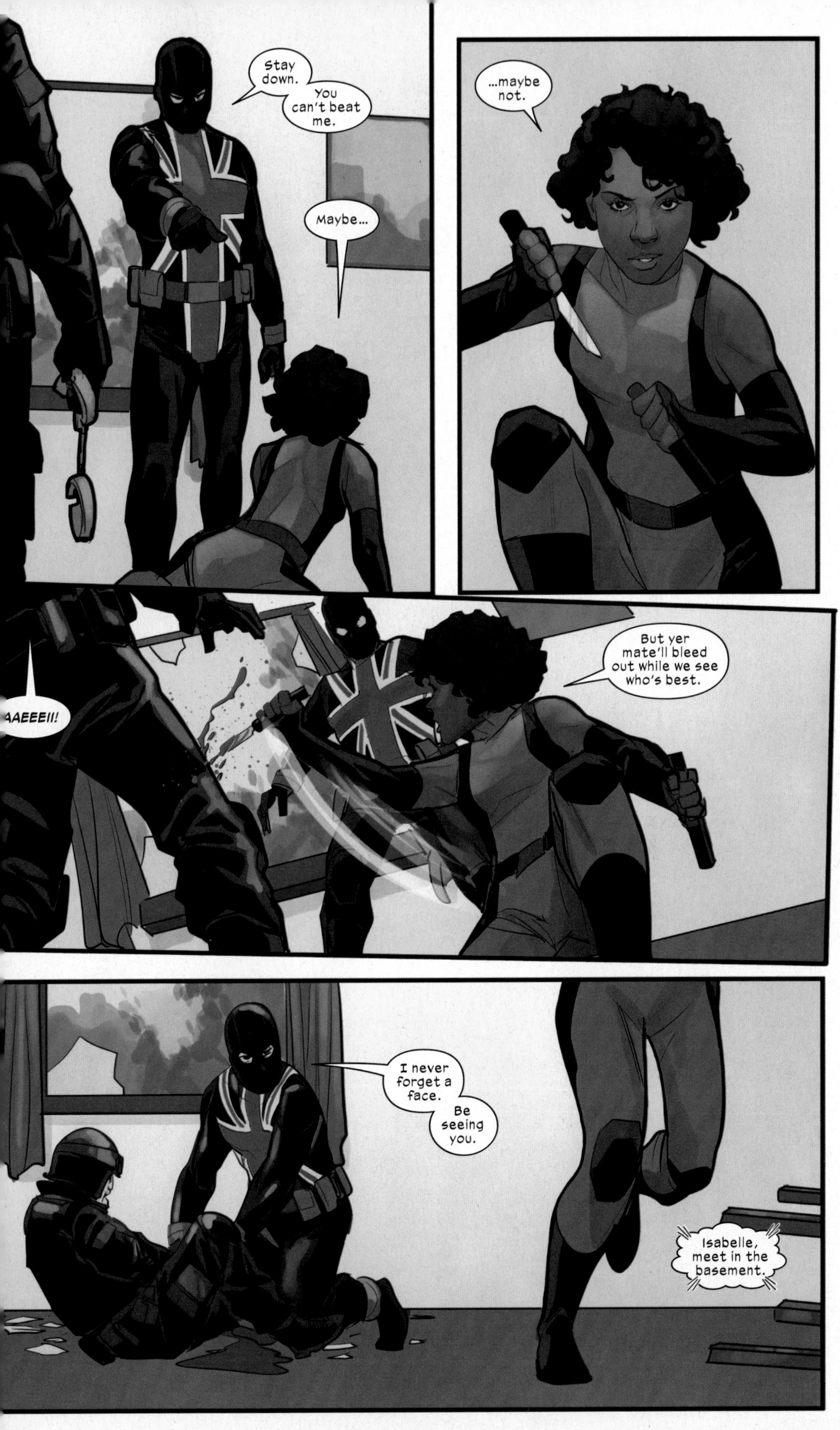
Stay down.
You can't beat me.
Maybe...
...maybe not.
AAEEEII!
But yer mate'll bleed out while we see who's best.
I never forget a face.
Be seeing you.
Isabelle, meet in the basement.

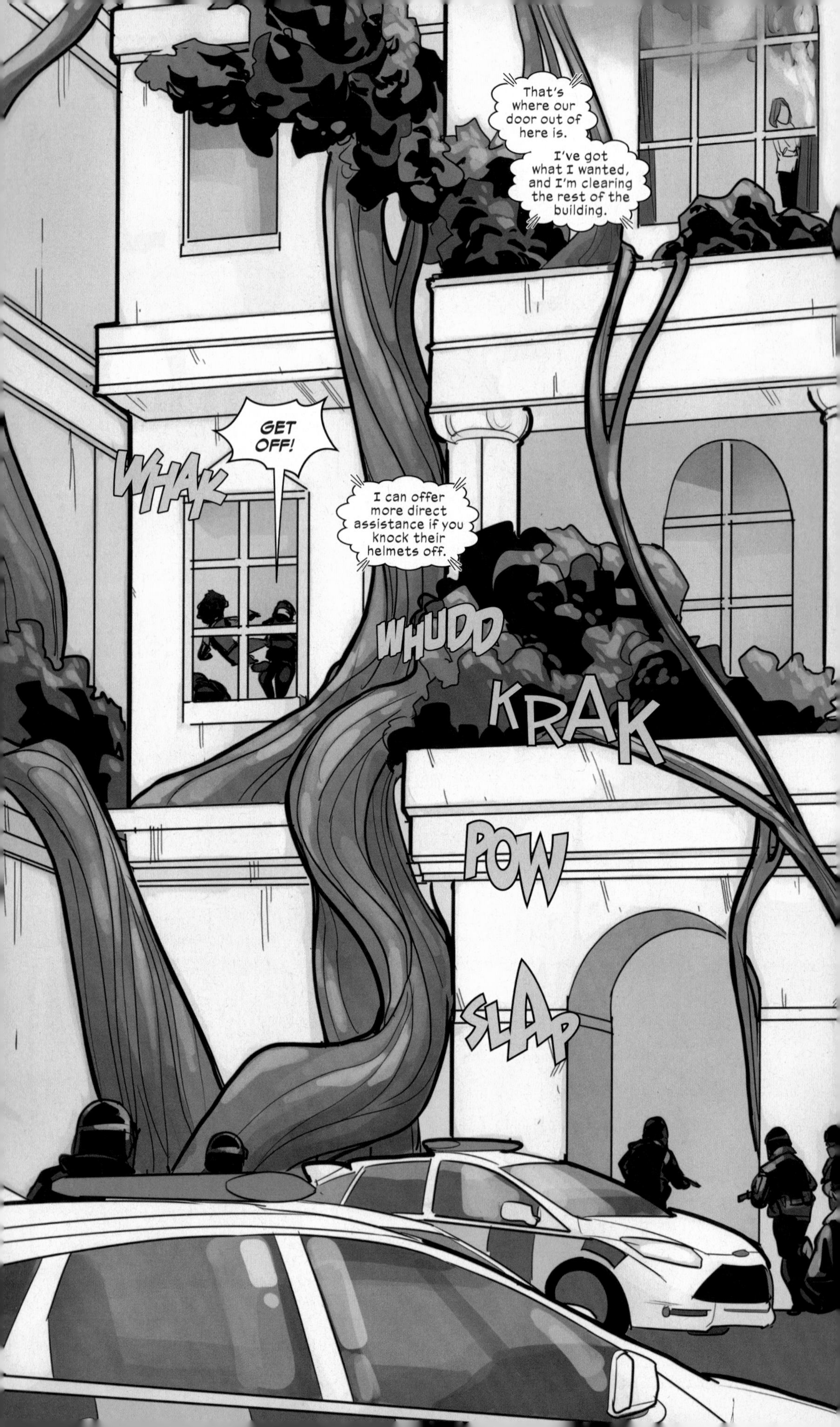
That's where our door out of here is.
I've got what I wanted, and I'm clearing the rest of the building.
GET OFF!
WHAK
I can offer more direct assistance if you knock their helmets off.
WHUDD
KRAK
POW
SLAP

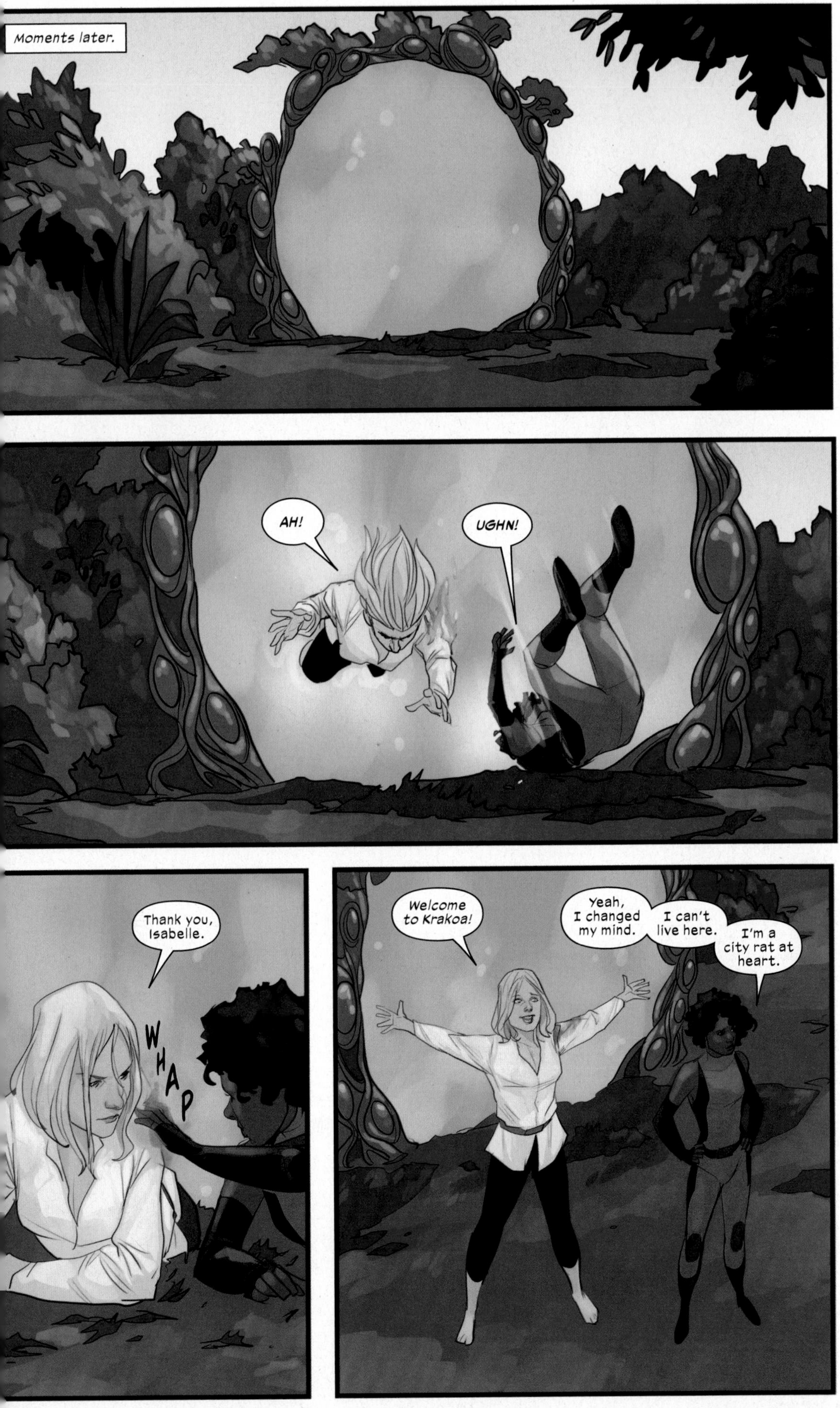
Moments later.
AH!
UGHN!
Thank you, Isabelle.
WHAP
Welcome to Krakoa!
Yeah, I changed my mind.
I can't live here.
I'm a city rat at heart.

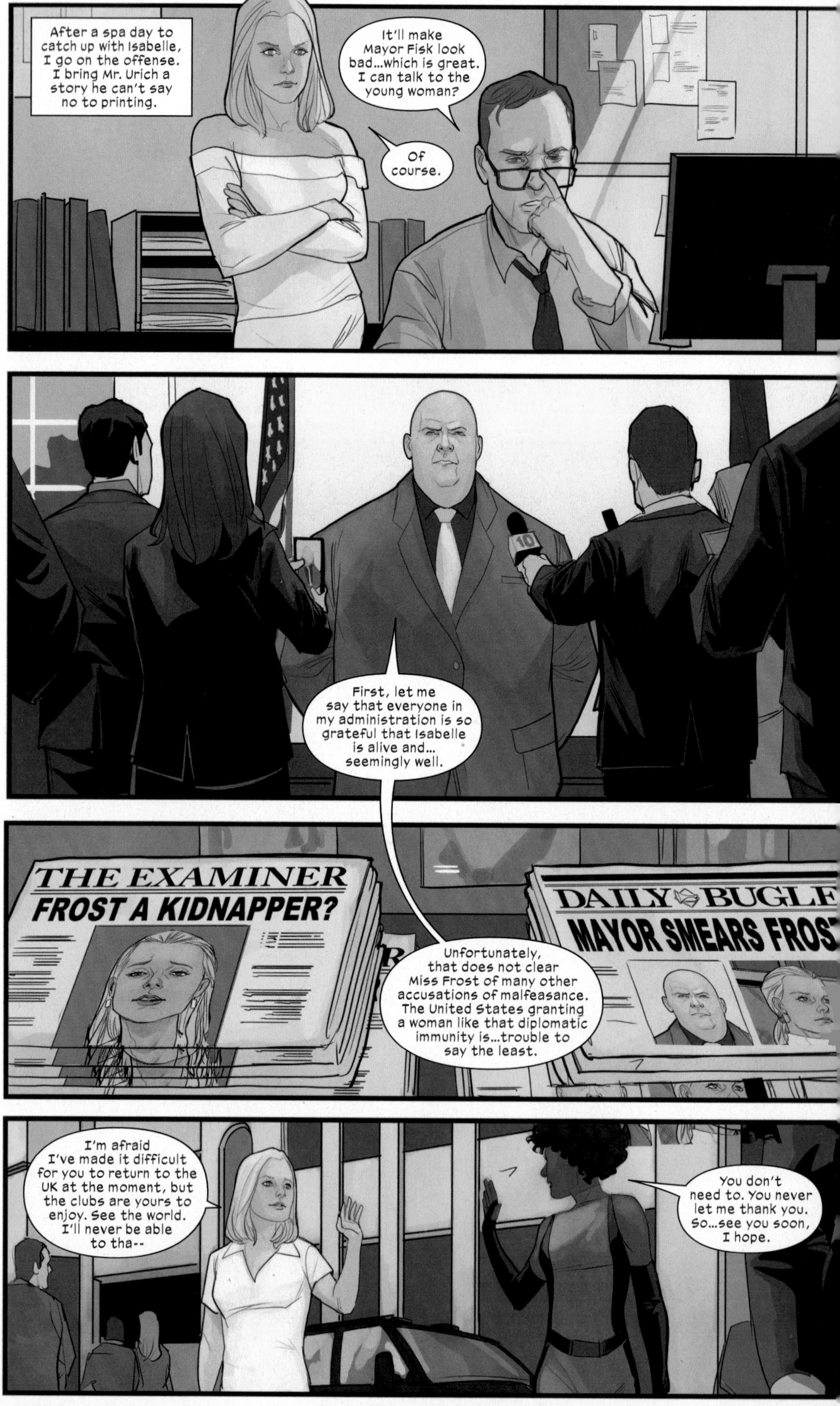
After a spa day to catch up with Isabelle, I go on the offense. I bring Mr. Urich a story he can't say no to printing.
It'll make Mayor Fisk look bad...which is great. I can talk to the young woman?
Of course.
First, let me say that everyone in my administration is so grateful that Isabelle is alive and... seemingly well.
THE EXAMINER
FROST A KIDNAPPER?
DAILY BUGLE
MAYOR SMEARS FROST
Unfortunately, that does not clear Miss Frost of many other accusations of malfeasance. The United States granting a woman like that diplomatic immunity is...trouble to say the least.
I'm afraid I've made it difficult for you to return to the UK at the moment, but the clubs are yours to enjoy. See the world. I'll never be able to tha--
You don't need to. You never let me thank you. So...see you soon, I hope.

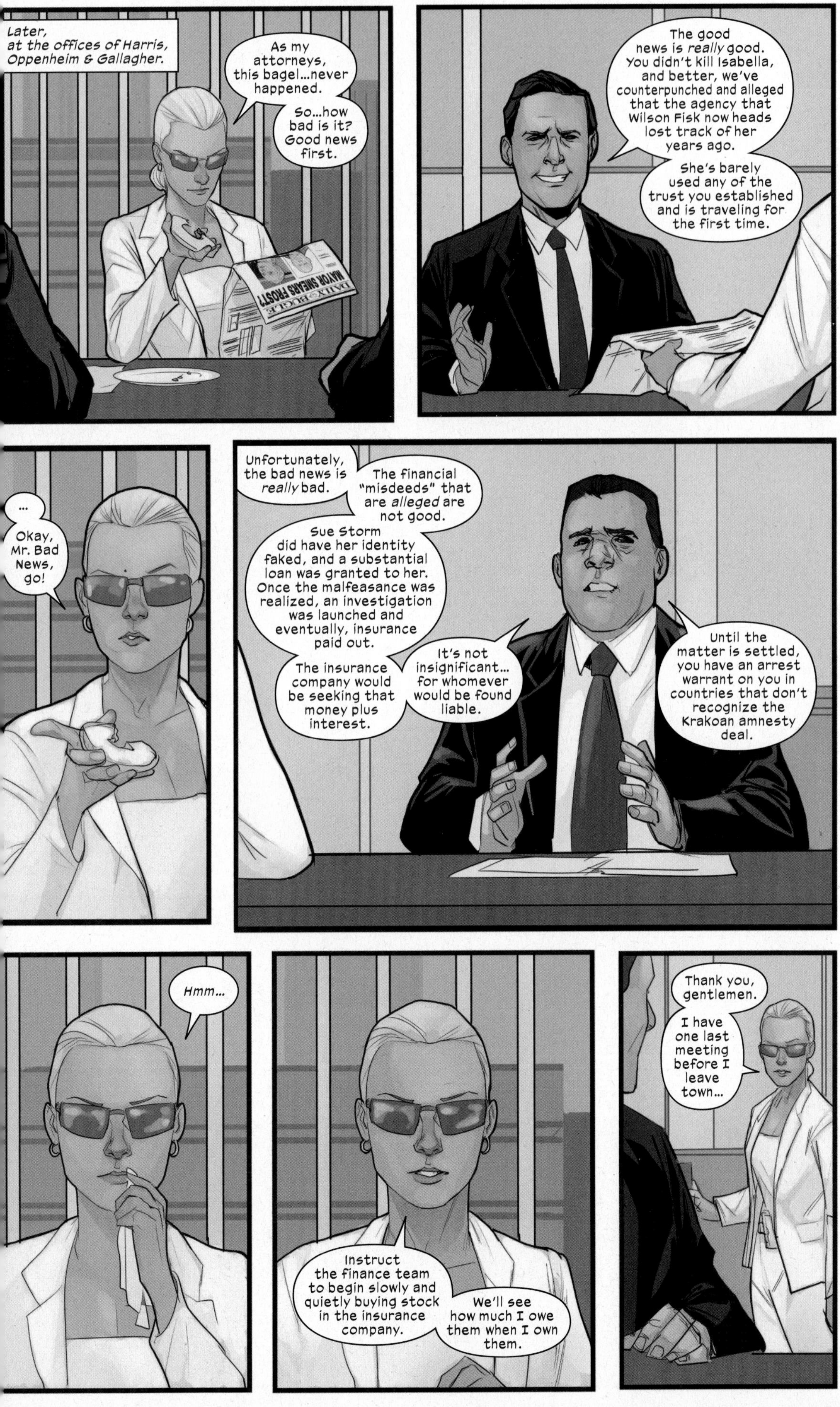
Later, at the offices of Harris, Oppenheim & Gallagher.
As my attorneys, this bagel...never happened.
So...how bad is it? Good news first.
DAILY BUGLE
MAYOR SMEARS FROST?
The good news is *really* good. You didn't kill Isabella, and better, we've counterpunched and alleged that the agency that Wilson Fisk now heads lost track of her years ago.
She's barely used any of the trust you established and is traveling for the first time.
...
Okay, Mr. Bad News, go!
Unfortunately, the bad news is *really* bad.
The financial "misdeeds" that are *alleged* are not good.
Sue Storm did have her identity faked, and a substantial loan was granted to her. Once the malfeasance was realized, an investigation was launched and eventually, insurance paid out.
The insurance company would be seeking that money plus interest.
It's not insignificant... for whomever would be found liable.
Until the matter is settled, you have an arrest warrant on you in countries that don't recognize the Krakoan amnesty deal.
Hmm...
Instruct the finance team to begin slowly and quietly buying stock in the insurance company.
We'll see how much I owe them when I own them.
Thank you, gentlemen.
I have one last meeting before I leave town...

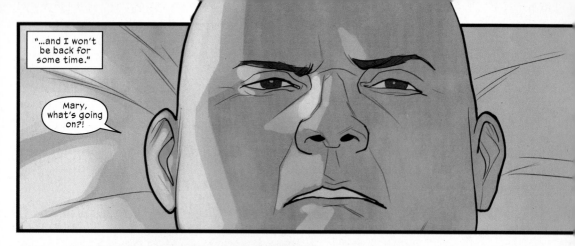

"...and I won't be back for some time."

Mary, what's going on?!

Emma.

How dare you use my wife to put a blade across my neck.

It's okay... I perused her mind...*she's done this before.*

But don't get excited, darling. I'm just passing through.

You must be close by to have dominated Mary so effectively.

Closer than you think, Willie.

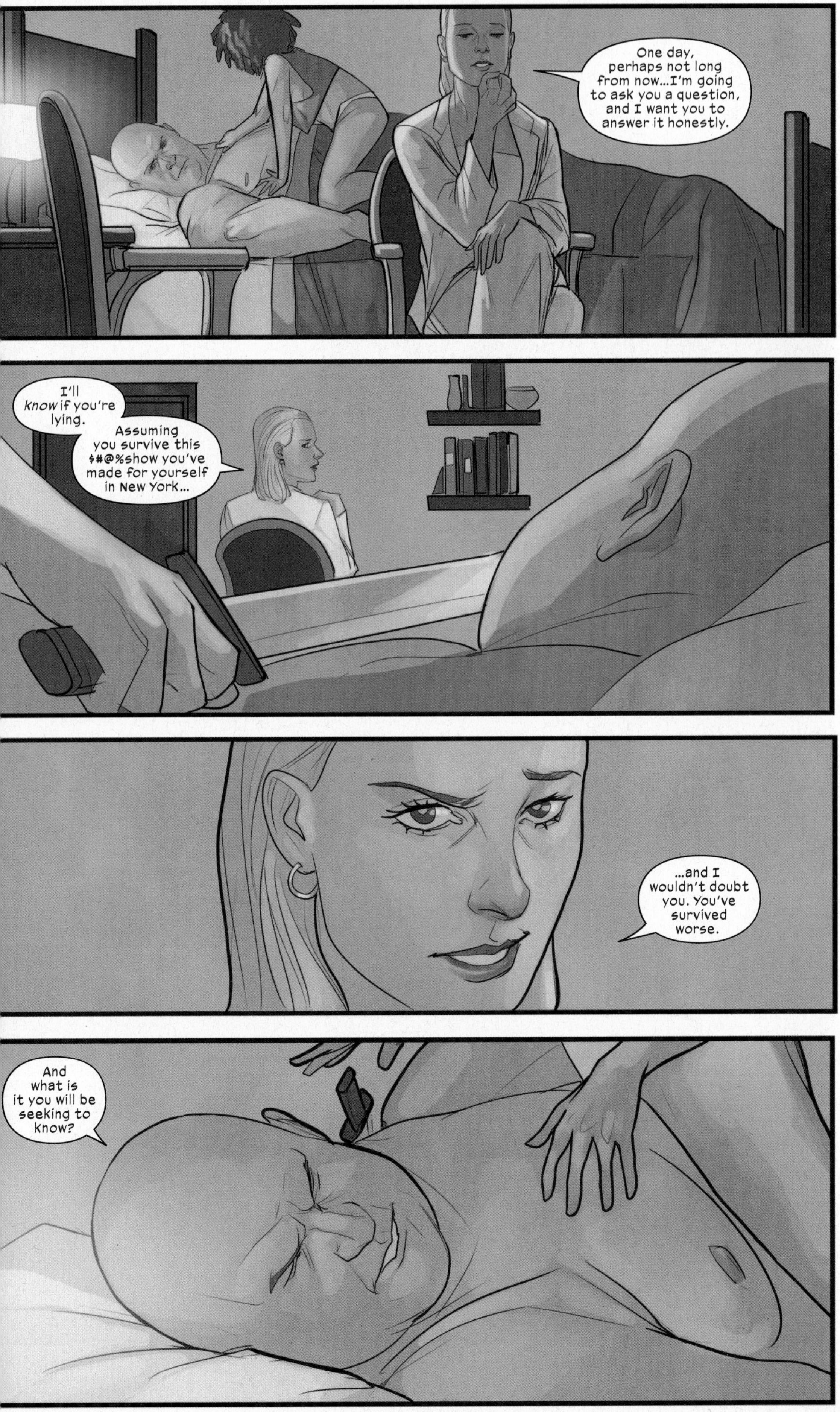
One day, perhaps not long from now...I'm going to ask you a question, and I want you to answer it honestly.
I'll *know* if you're lying.
Assuming you survive this $#@%show you've made for yourself in New York...
...and I wouldn't doubt you. You've survived worse.
And what is it you will be seeking to know?

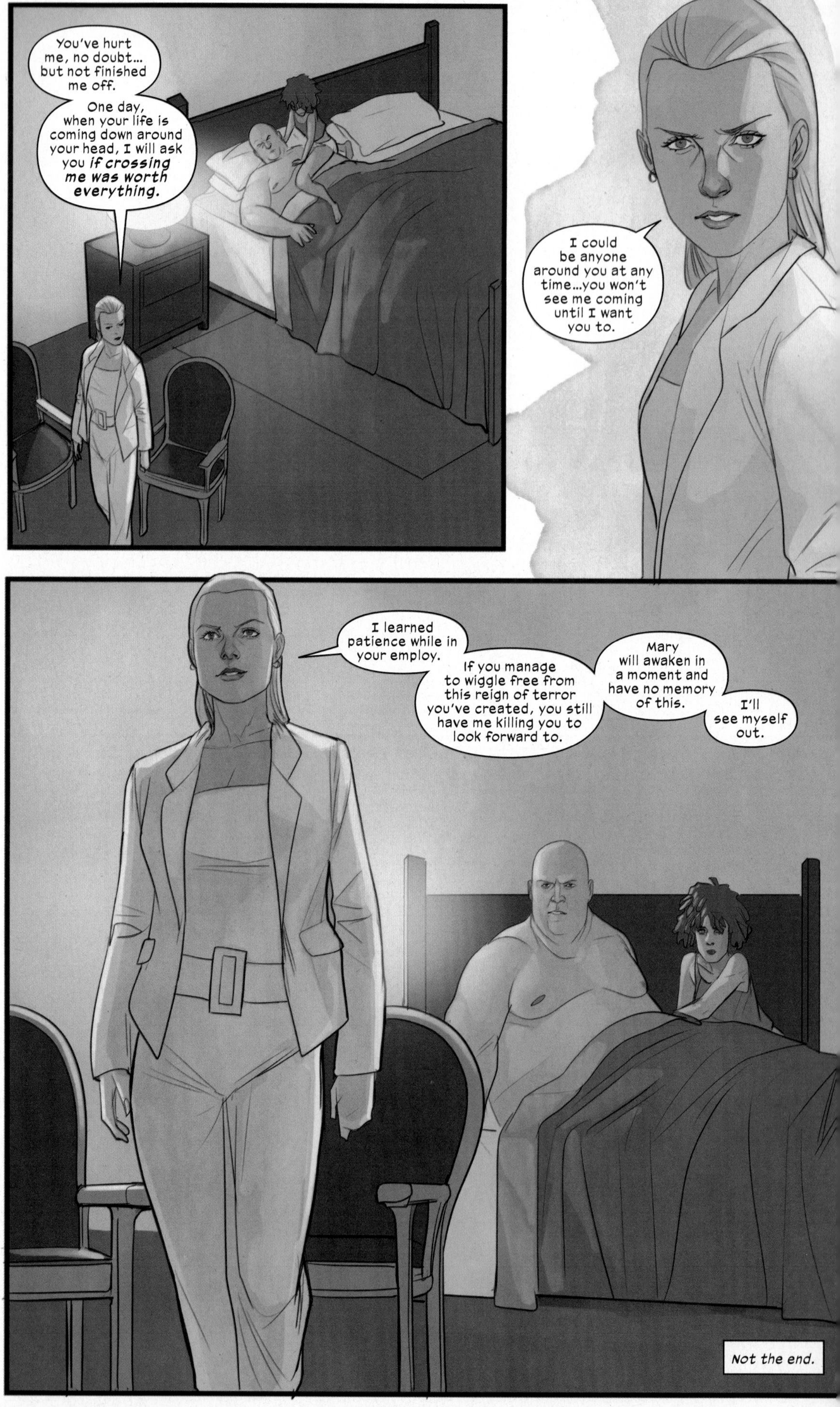
You've hurt me, no doubt... but not finished me off.
One day, when your life is coming down around your head, I will ask you *if crossing me was worth everything.*
I could be anyone around you at any time...you won't see me coming until I want you to.
I learned patience while in your employ.
If you manage to wiggle free from this reign of terror you've created, you still have me killing you to look forward to.
Mary will awaken in a moment and have no memory of this.
I'll see myself out.
Not the end.

WINTER SOLDIER

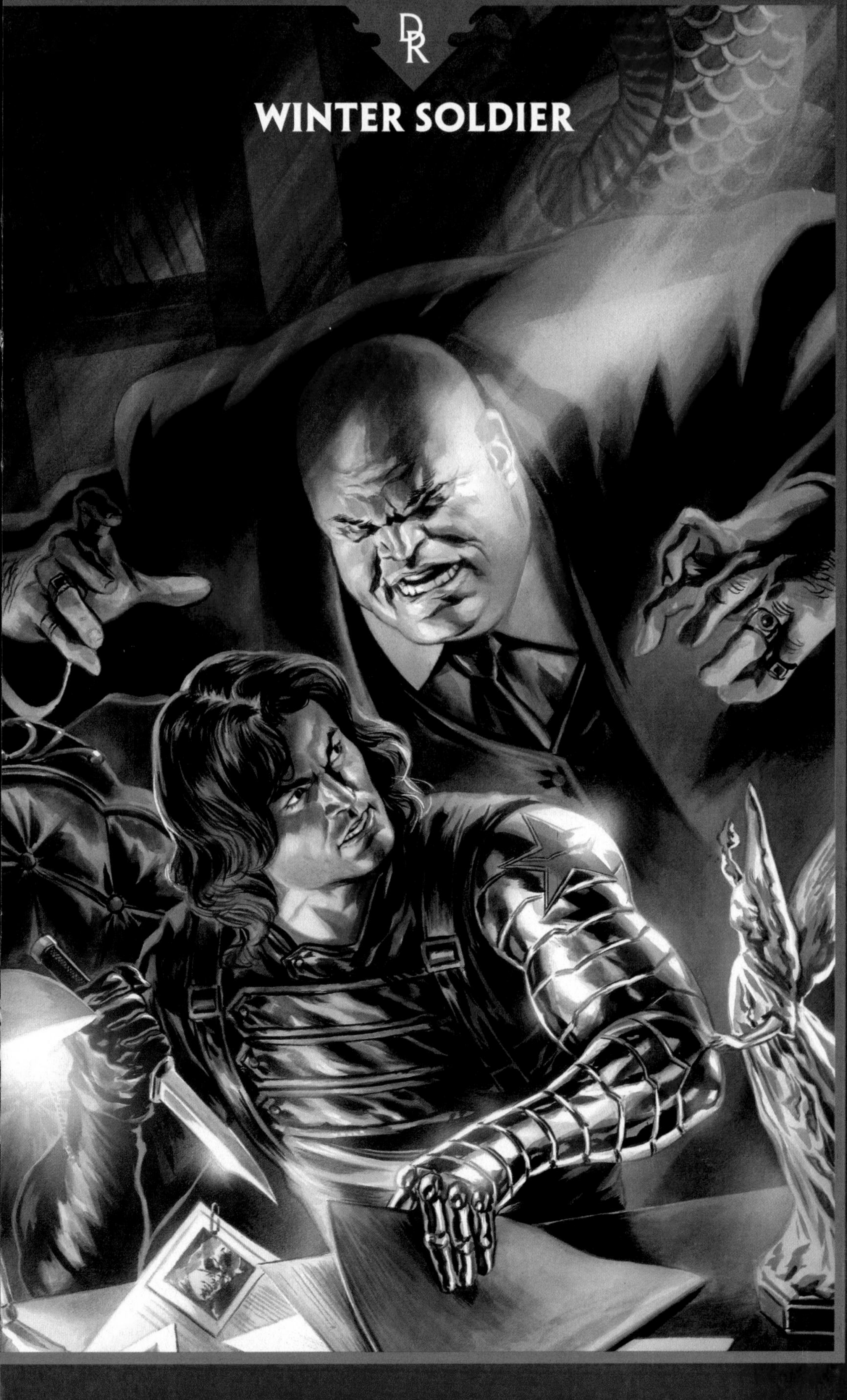

NO OUTLAW HAS EVADED JUSTICE MORE THAN WILSON FISK, FORMERLY THE KINGPIN OF A VAST CRIMINAL EMPIRE THAT TOUCHED EVERY CORNER OF NEW YORK CITY (AND BEYOND). NOW THE DULY ELECTED MAYOR OF NEW YORK, FISK HAS TRIED TO WASH HIS HANDS OF HIS OLD LIFE--AND THE BLOODSHED IT BORE.

BUT THE STEPS THAT DAREDEVIL TOOK TO SUPERNATURALLY CONCEAL HIS TRUE IDENTITY AS MATT MURDOCK HAVE BEEN SLOWLY DRIVING FISK INTO MADNESS, LEADING HIM TO SET HIS IRE UPON THE CITY AND EVERY COSTUMED VIGILANTE IN IT. AS PART OF HIS WAR ON SUPER HEROES, HE'S COMPILED AN IMPRESSIVE STACK OF DOSSIERS ON HIS ENEMIES--AND FOR SOMEONE WHO'S FORGOTTEN AS MUCH OF HIS LIFE AS BUCKY BARNES HAS, THERE'S NOTHING MORE VALUABLE THAN INFORMATION...

DEVIL'S REIGN

WINTER SOLDIER

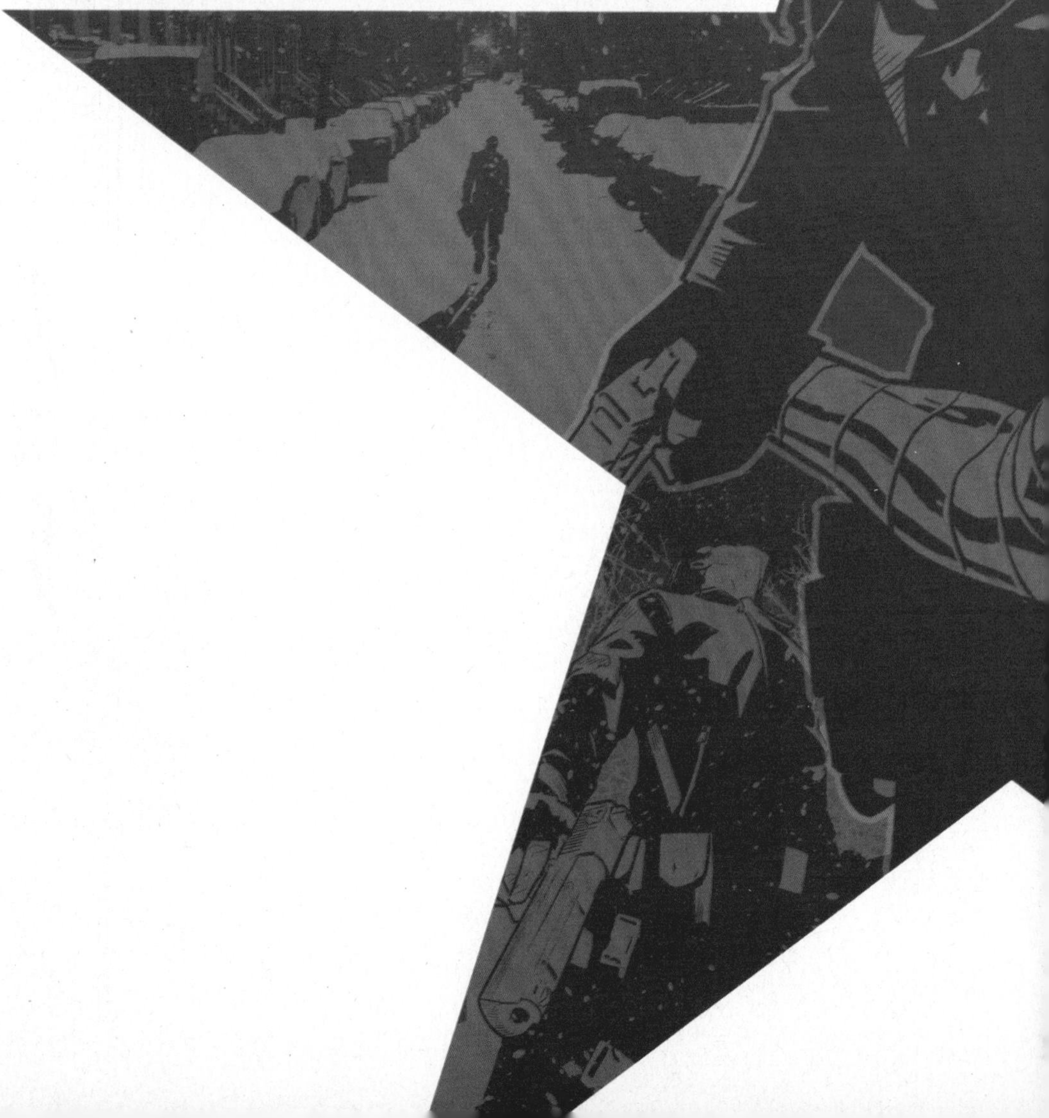

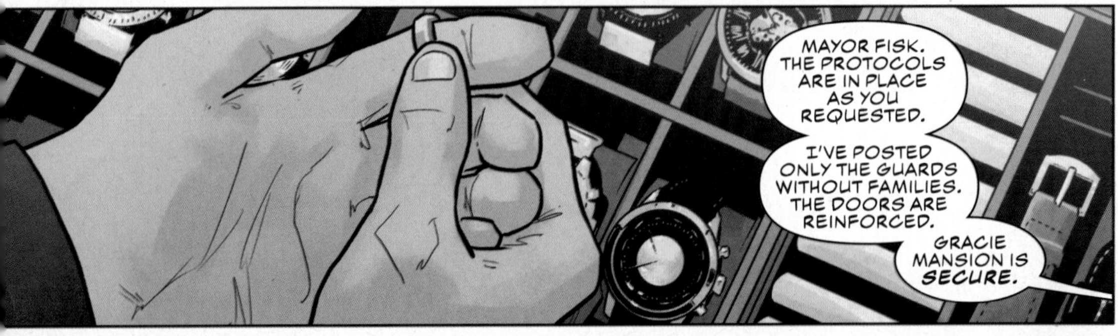
MAYOR FISK. THE PROTOCOLS ARE IN PLACE AS YOU REQUESTED.
I'VE POSTED ONLY THE GUARDS WITHOUT FAMILIES. THE DOORS ARE REINFORCED.
GRACIE MANSION IS **SECURE.**

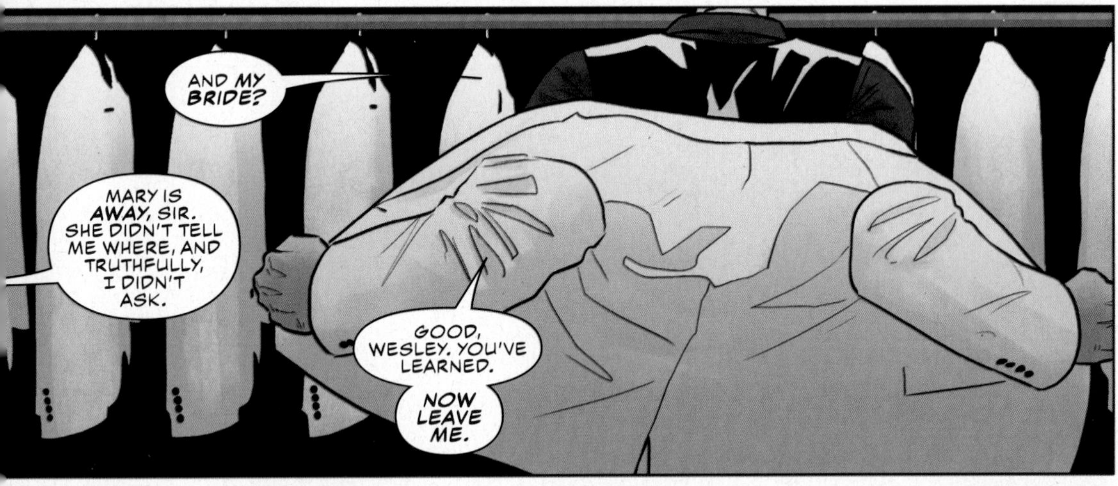
AND MY *BRIDE?*
MARY IS **AWAY,** SIR. SHE DIDN'T TELL ME WHERE, AND TRUTHFULLY, I DIDN'T ASK.
GOOD, WESLEY. YOU'VE LEARNED.
NOW LEAVE ME.

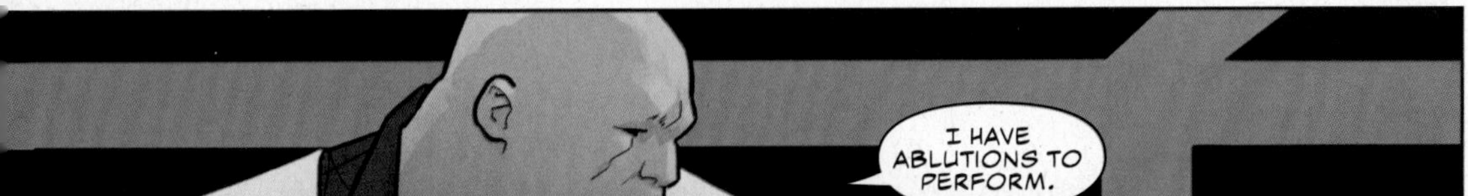
I HAVE ABLUTIONS TO PERFORM.

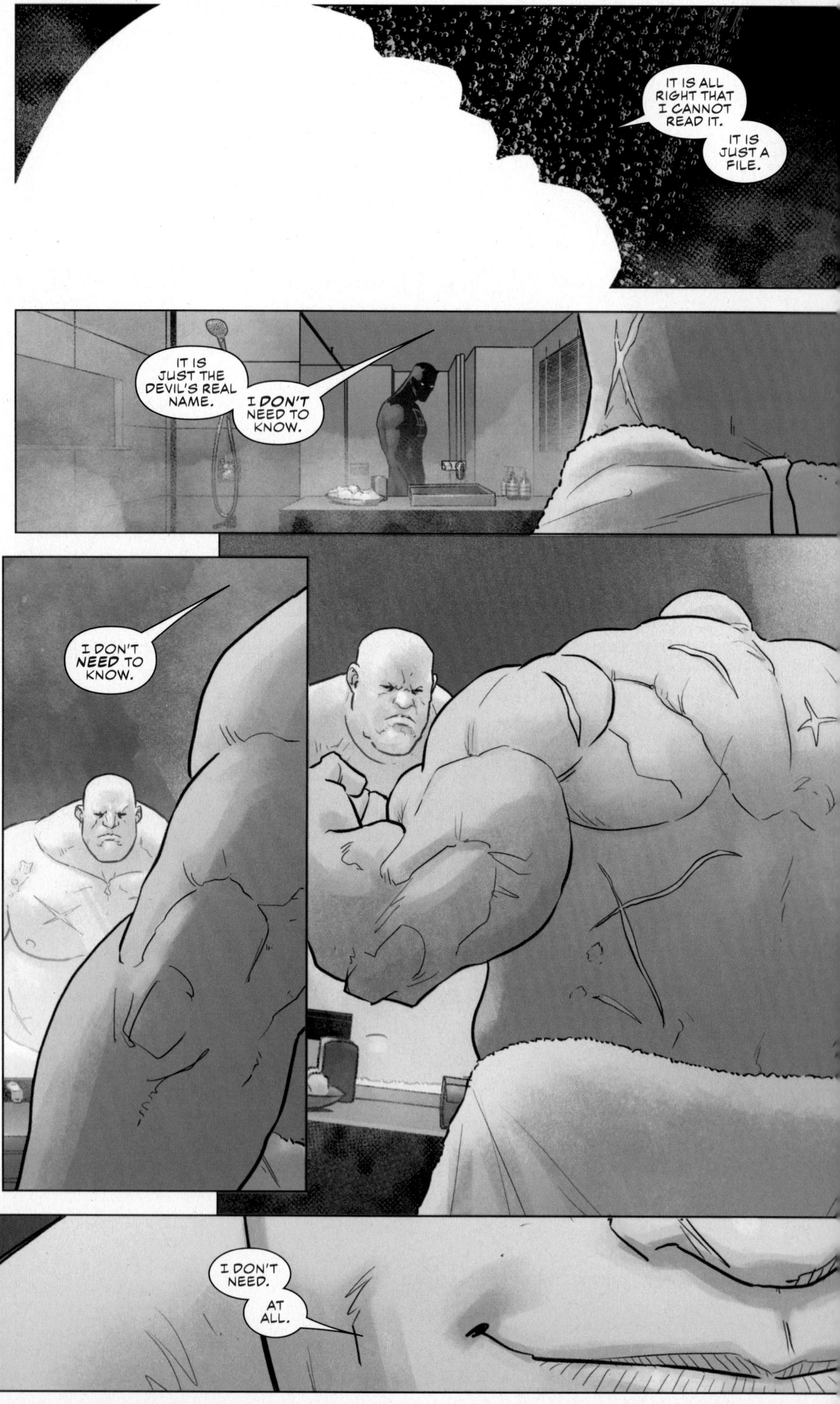
IT IS ALL RIGHT THAT I CANNOT READ IT.
IT IS JUST A FILE.
IT IS JUST THE DEVIL'S REAL NAME.
I DON'T NEED TO KNOW.
I DON'T NEED TO KNOW.
I DON'T NEED.
AT ALL.

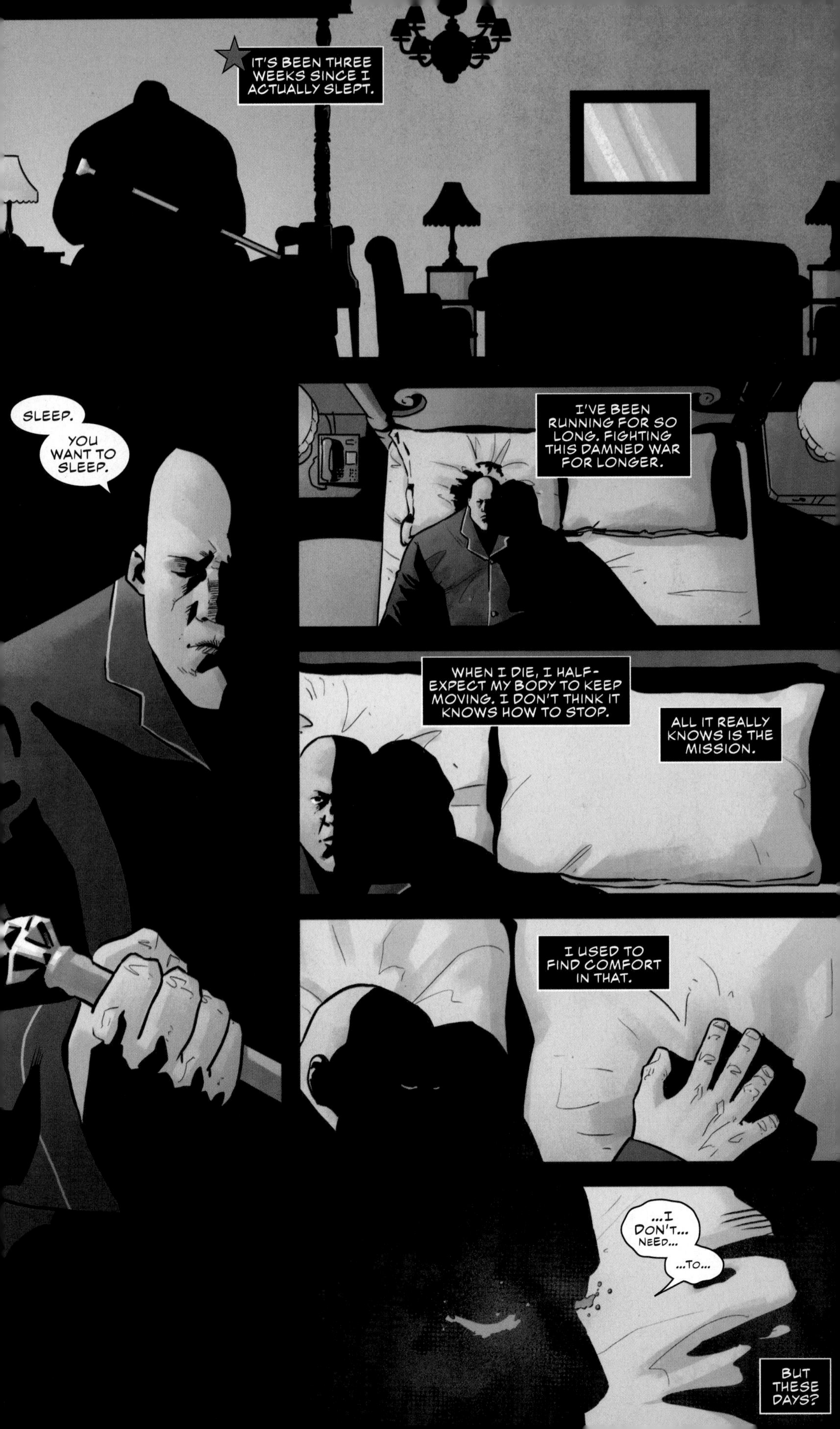
IT'S BEEN THREE WEEKS SINCE I ACTUALLY SLEPT.
SLEEP.
YOU WANT TO SLEEP.
I'VE BEEN RUNNING FOR SO LONG. FIGHTING THIS DAMNED WAR FOR LONGER.
WHEN I DIE, I HALF-EXPECT MY BODY TO KEEP MOVING. I DON'T THINK IT KNOWS HOW TO STOP.
ALL IT REALLY KNOWS IS THE MISSION.
I USED TO FIND COMFORT IN THAT.
...I DON'T... NEED...
...TO...
BUT THESE DAYS?

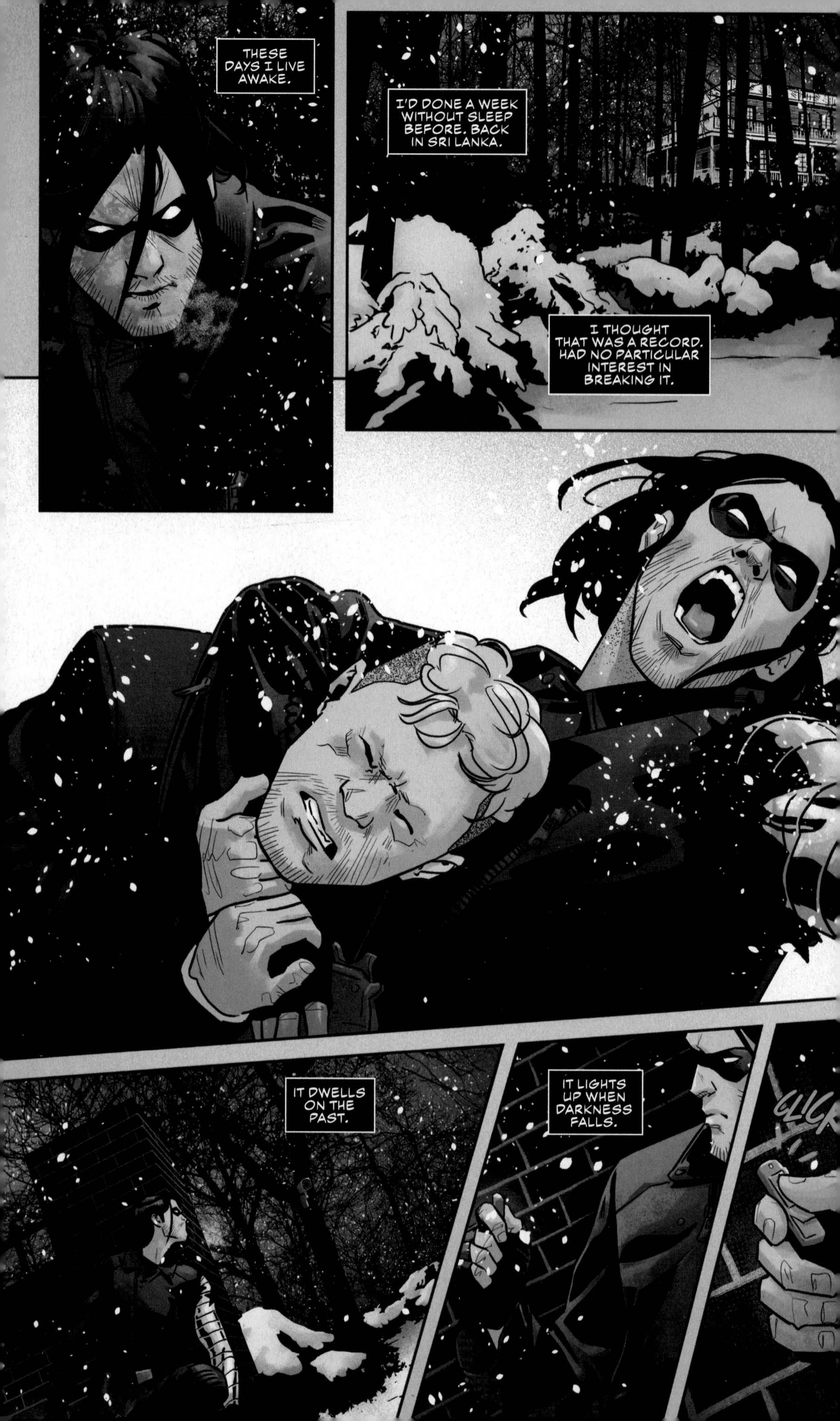
THESE DAYS I LIVE AWAKE.
I'D DONE A WEEK WITHOUT SLEEP BEFORE. BACK IN SRI LANKA.
I THOUGHT THAT WAS A RECORD. HAD NO PARTICULAR INTEREST IN BREAKING IT.
IT DWELLS ON THE PAST.
IT LIGHTS UP WHEN DARKNESS FALLS.
CLICK

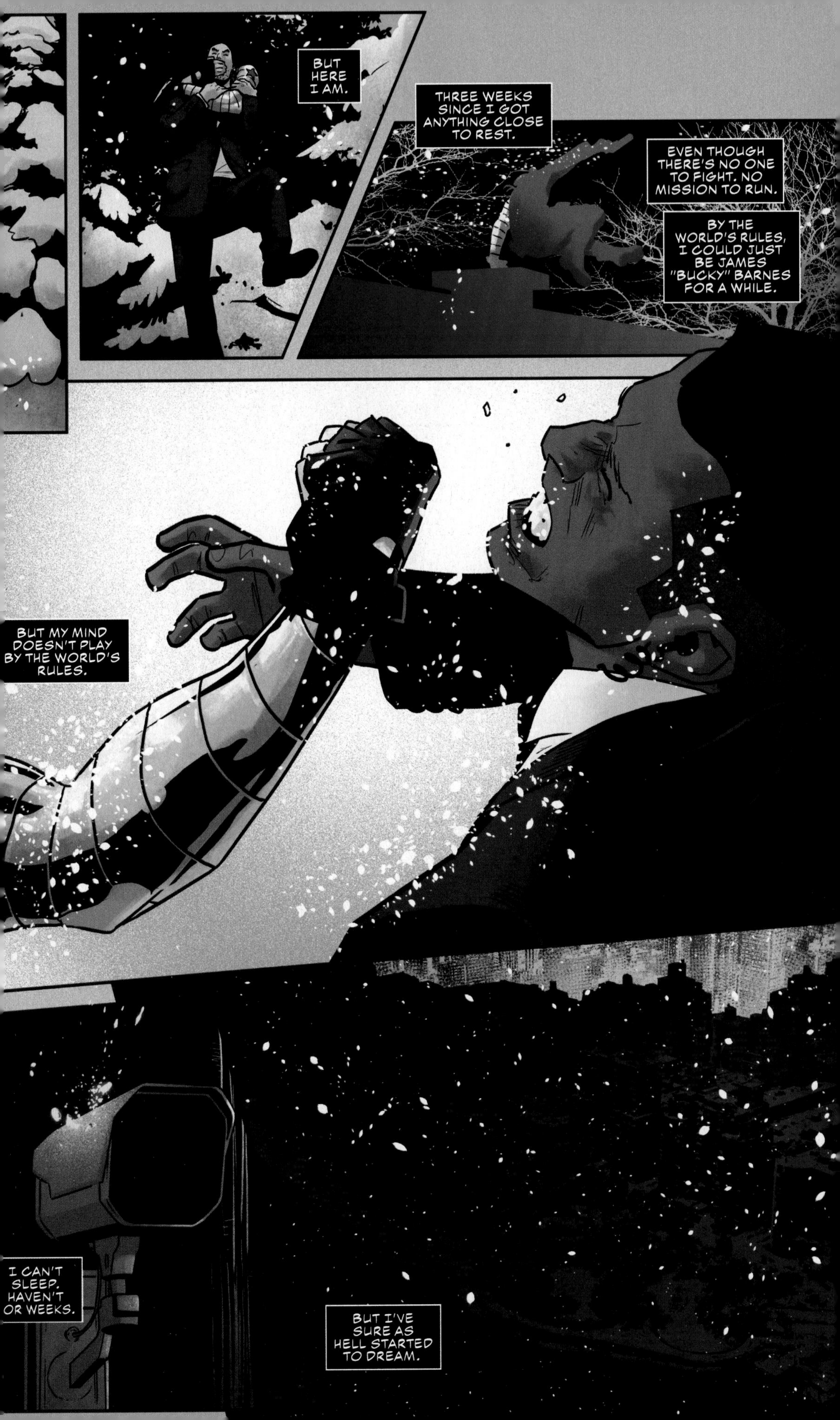
BUT HERE I AM.
THREE WEEKS SINCE I GOT ANYTHING CLOSE TO REST.
EVEN THOUGH THERE'S NO ONE TO FIGHT. NO MISSION TO RUN.
BY THE WORLD'S RULES, I COULD JUST BE JAMES "BUCKY" BARNES FOR A WHILE.
BUT MY MIND DOESN'T PLAY BY THE WORLD'S RULES.
I CAN'T SLEEP. HAVEN'T OR WEEKS.
BUT I'VE SURE AS HELL STARTED TO DREAM.

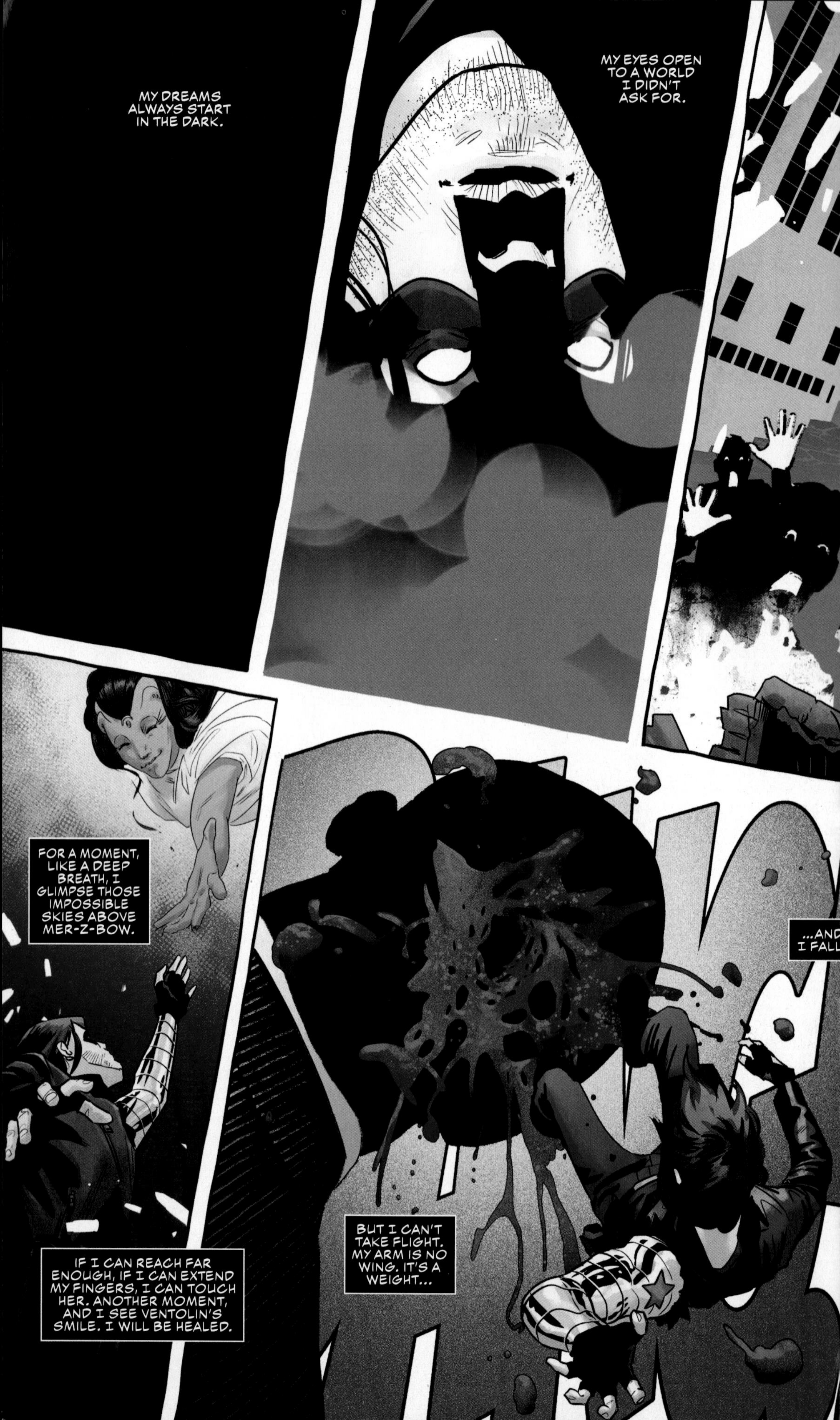
MY DREAMS ALWAYS START IN THE DARK.
MY EYES OPEN TO A WORLD I DIDN'T ASK FOR.
FOR A MOMENT, LIKE A DEEP BREATH, I GLIMPSE THOSE IMPOSSIBLE SKIES ABOVE MER-Z-BOW.
IF I CAN REACH FAR ENOUGH, IF I CAN EXTEND MY FINGERS, I CAN TOUCH HER. ANOTHER MOMENT, AND I SEE VENTOLIN'S SMILE. I WILL BE HEALED.
BUT I CAN'T TAKE FLIGHT. MY ARM IS NO WING. IT'S A WEIGHT...
...AND I FALL

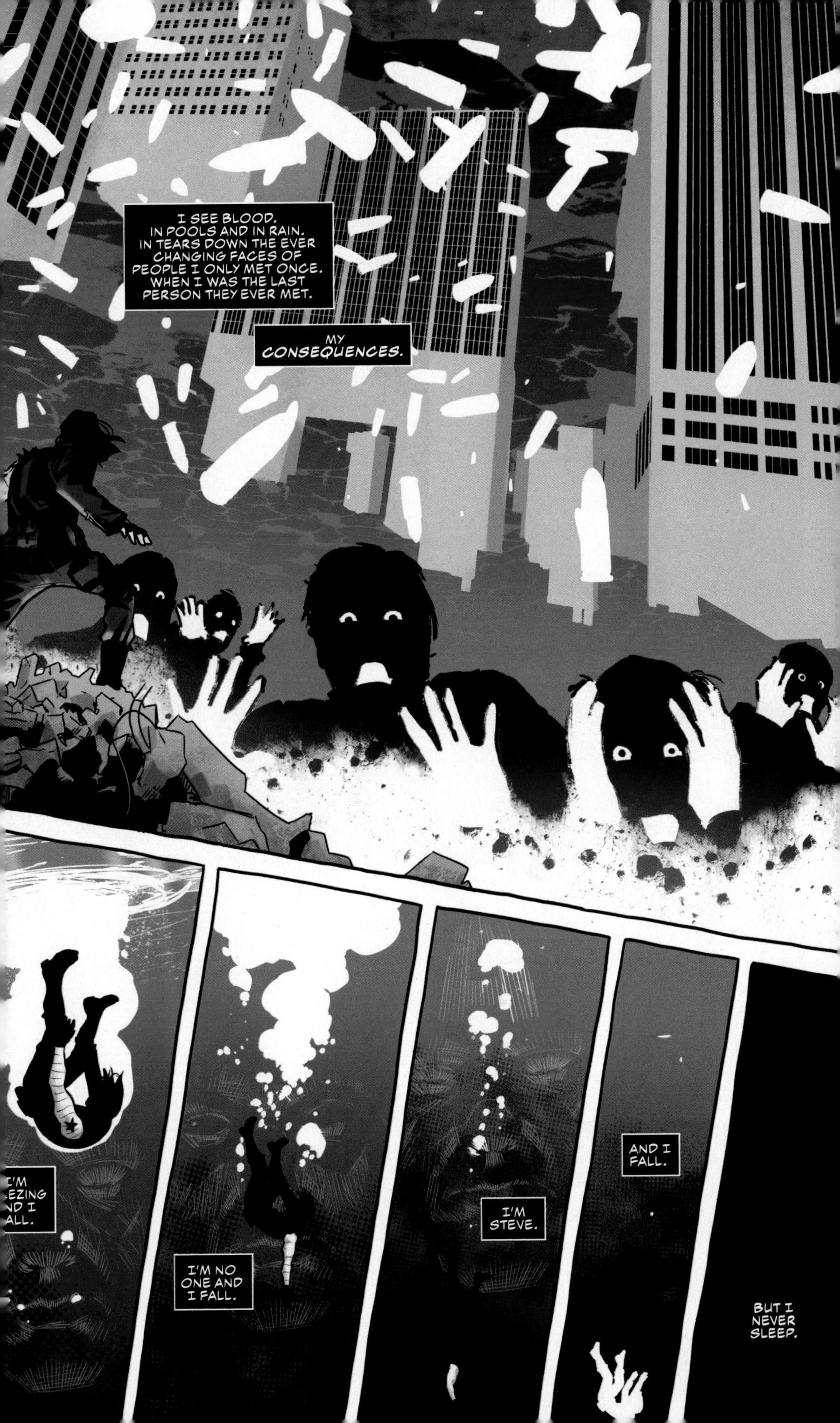
I SEE BLOOD. IN POOLS AND IN RAIN. IN TEARS DOWN THE EVER CHANGING FACES OF PEOPLE I ONLY MET ONCE. WHEN I WAS THE LAST PERSON THEY EVER MET.
MY CONSEQUENCES.
I'M EZING ND I ALL.
I'M NO ONE AND I FALL.
I'M STEVE.
AND I FALL.
BUT I NEVER SLEEP.

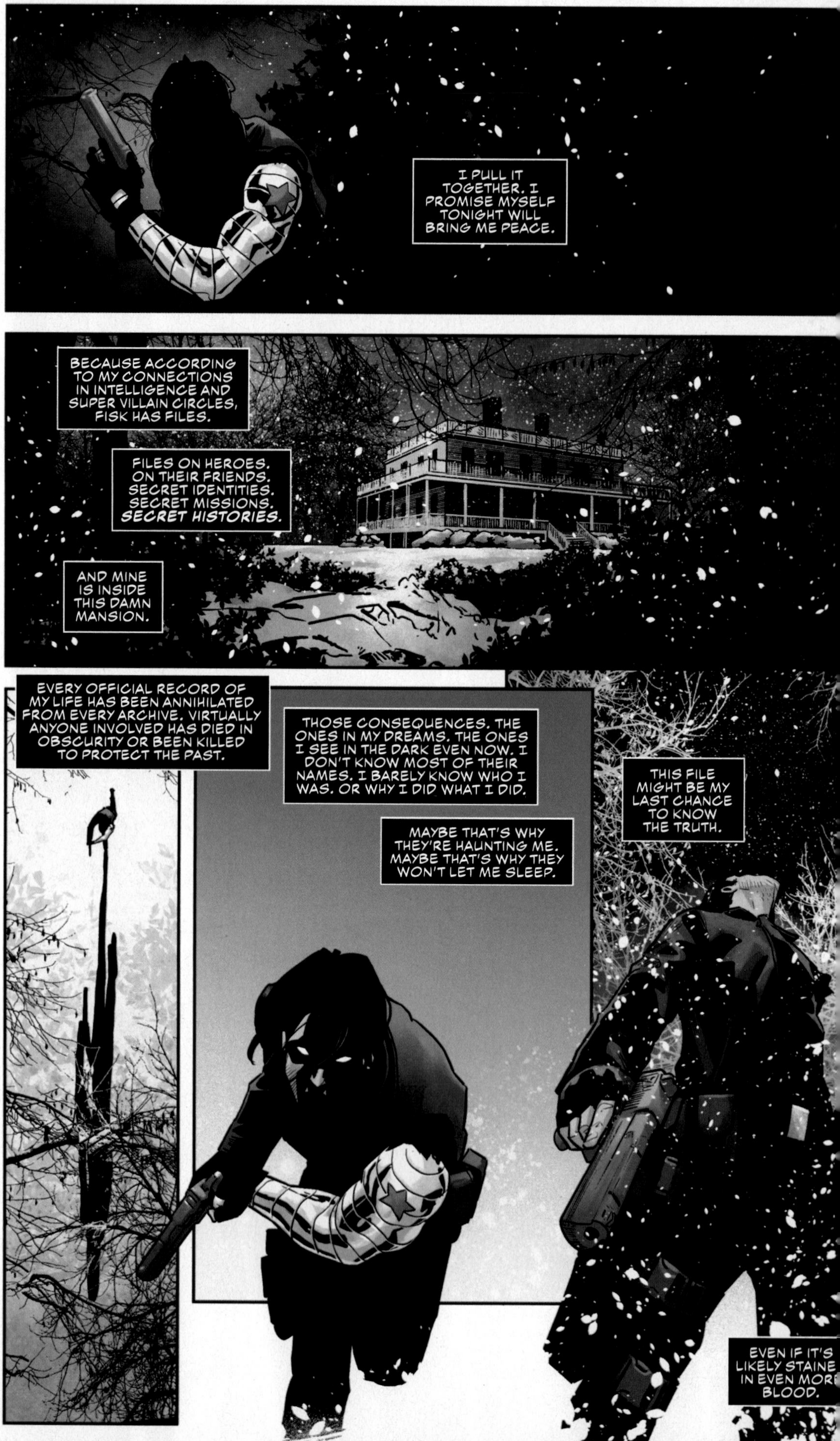

I PULL IT TOGETHER. I PROMISE MYSELF TONIGHT WILL BRING ME PEACE.
BECAUSE ACCORDING TO MY CONNECTIONS IN INTELLIGENCE AND SUPER VILLAIN CIRCLES, FISK HAS FILES.
FILES ON HEROES. ON THEIR FRIENDS. SECRET IDENTITIES. SECRET MISSIONS. *SECRET HISTORIES.*
AND MINE IS INSIDE THIS DAMN MANSION.
EVERY OFFICIAL RECORD OF MY LIFE HAS BEEN ANNIHILATED FROM EVERY ARCHIVE. VIRTUALLY ANYONE INVOLVED HAS DIED IN OBSCURITY OR BEEN KILLED TO PROTECT THE PAST.
THOSE CONSEQUENCES. THE ONES IN MY DREAMS. THE ONES I SEE IN THE DARK EVEN NOW. I DON'T KNOW MOST OF THEIR NAMES. I BARELY KNOW WHO I WAS. OR WHY I DID WHAT I DID.
MAYBE THAT'S WHY THEY'RE HAUNTING ME. MAYBE THAT'S WHY THEY WON'T LET ME SLEEP.
THIS FILE MIGHT BE MY LAST CHANCE TO KNOW THE TRUTH.
EVEN IF IT'S LIKELY STAINE IN EVEN MOR BLOOD.

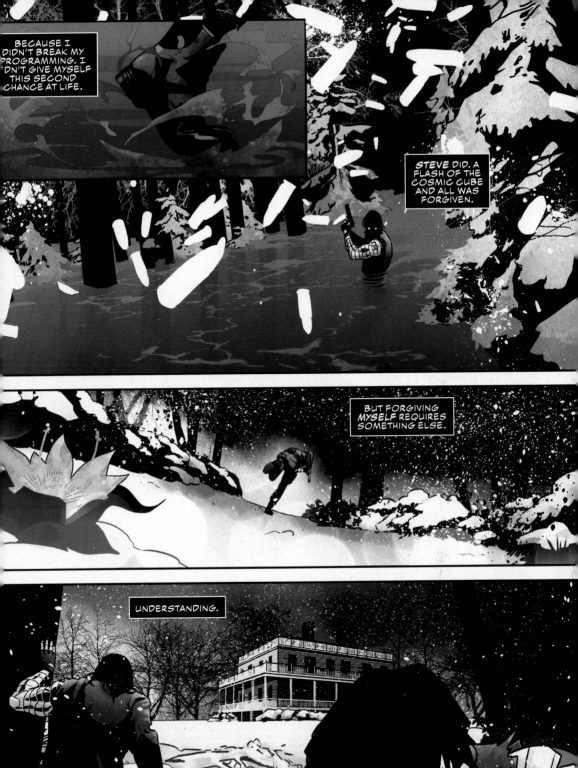

BECAUSE I DIDN'T BREAK MY PROGRAMMING. I DIDN'T GIVE MYSELF THIS SECOND CHANCE AT LIFE.

STEVE DID. A FLASH OF THE COSMIC CUBE AND ALL WAS FORGIVEN.

BUT FORGIVING *MYSELF* REQUIRES SOMETHING ELSE.

UNDERSTANDING.

I NEED TO KNOW WHAT I WAS. ALL OF WHAT I WAS.

I NEED TO FINALLY LOOK THE PAST IN THE EYE.

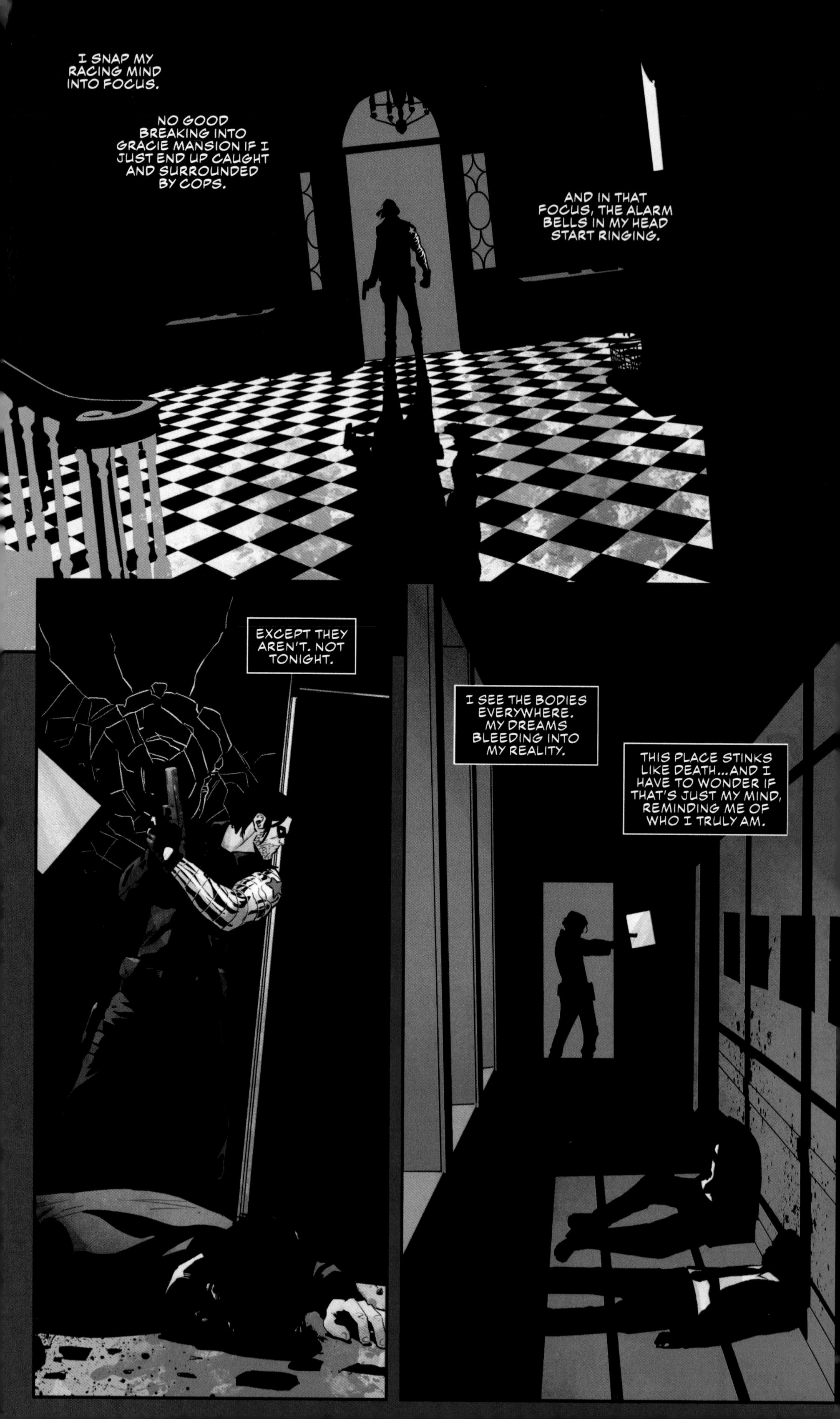
I SNAP MY RACING MIND INTO FOCUS.
NO GOOD BREAKING INTO GRACIE MANSION IF I JUST END UP CAUGHT AND SURROUNDED BY COPS.
AND IN THAT FOCUS, THE ALARM BELLS IN MY HEAD START RINGING.
EXCEPT THEY AREN'T. NOT TONIGHT.
I SEE THE BODIES EVERYWHERE. MY DREAMS BLEEDING INTO MY REALITY.
THIS PLACE STINKS LIKE DEATH...AND I HAVE TO WONDER IF THAT'S JUST MY MIND, REMINDING ME OF WHO I TRULY AM.

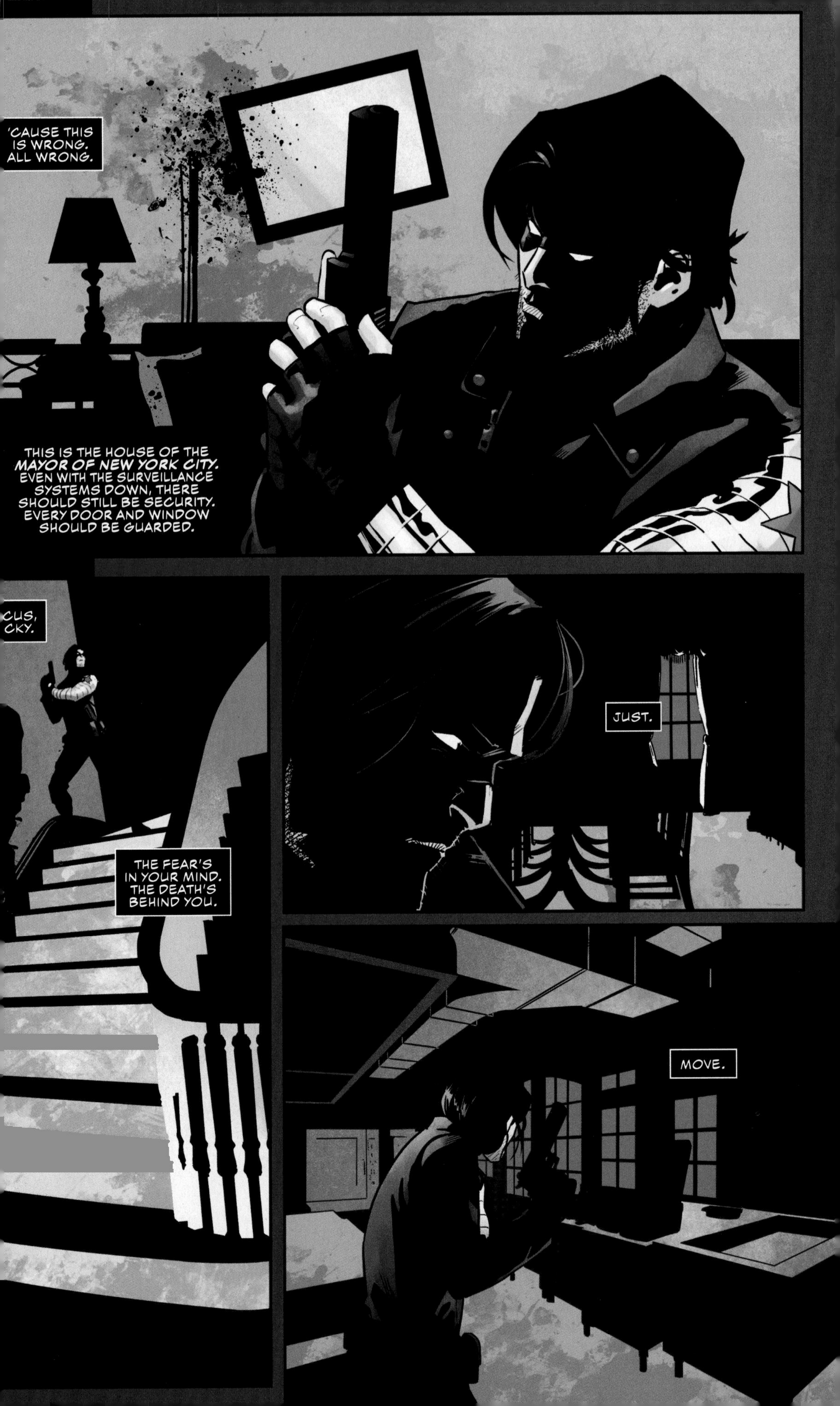

'CAUSE THIS IS WRONG. ALL WRONG.
THIS IS THE HOUSE OF THE ***MAYOR OF NEW YORK CITY.*** EVEN WITH THE SURVEILLANCE SYSTEMS DOWN, THERE SHOULD STILL BE SECURITY. EVERY DOOR AND WINDOW SHOULD BE GUARDED.
CUS, CKY.
THE FEAR'S IN YOUR MIND. THE DEATH'S BEHIND YOU.
JUST.
MOVE.

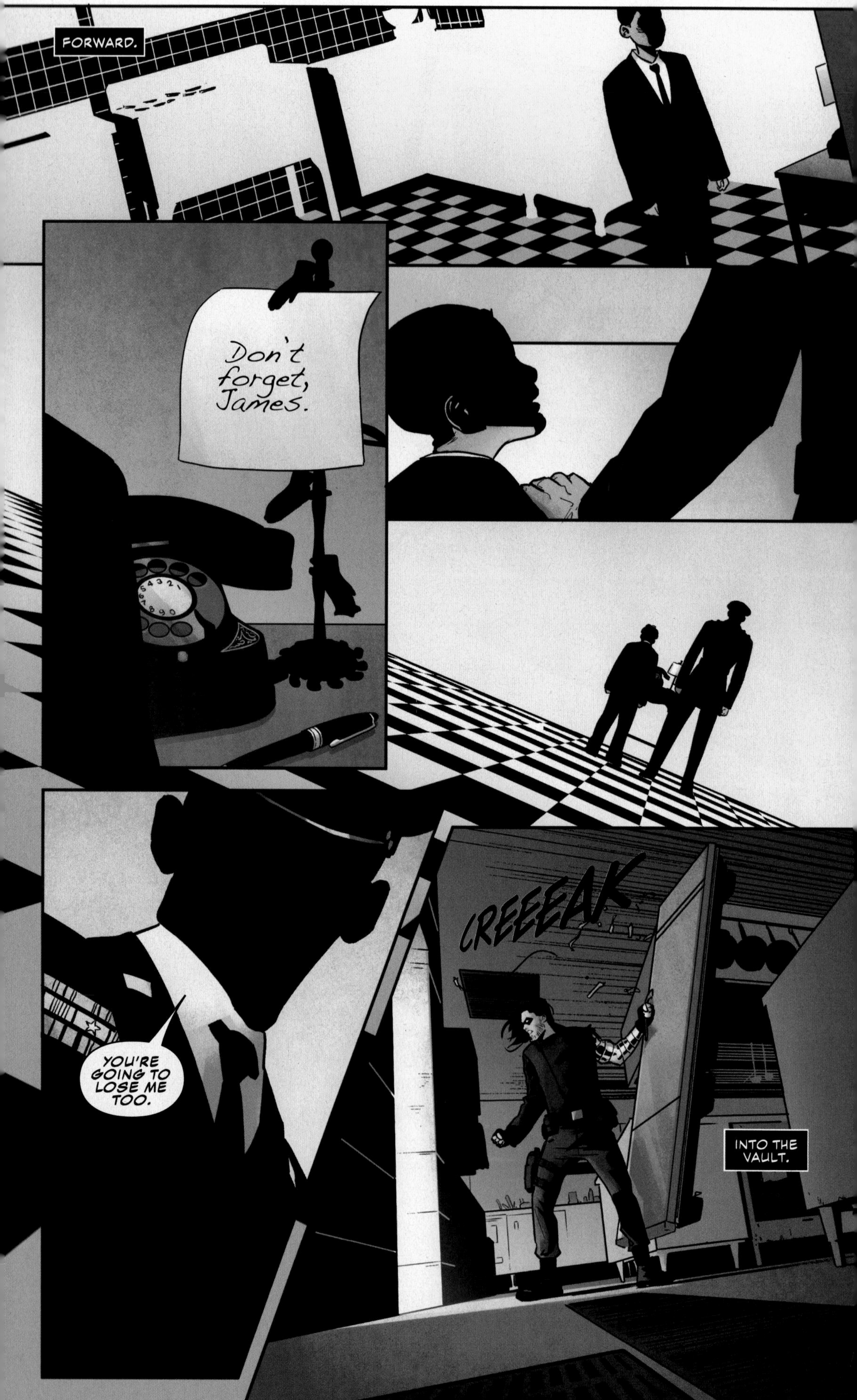
FORWARD.
Don't forget, James.
YOU'RE GOING TO LOSE ME TOO.
CREEEAK
INTO THE VAULT.

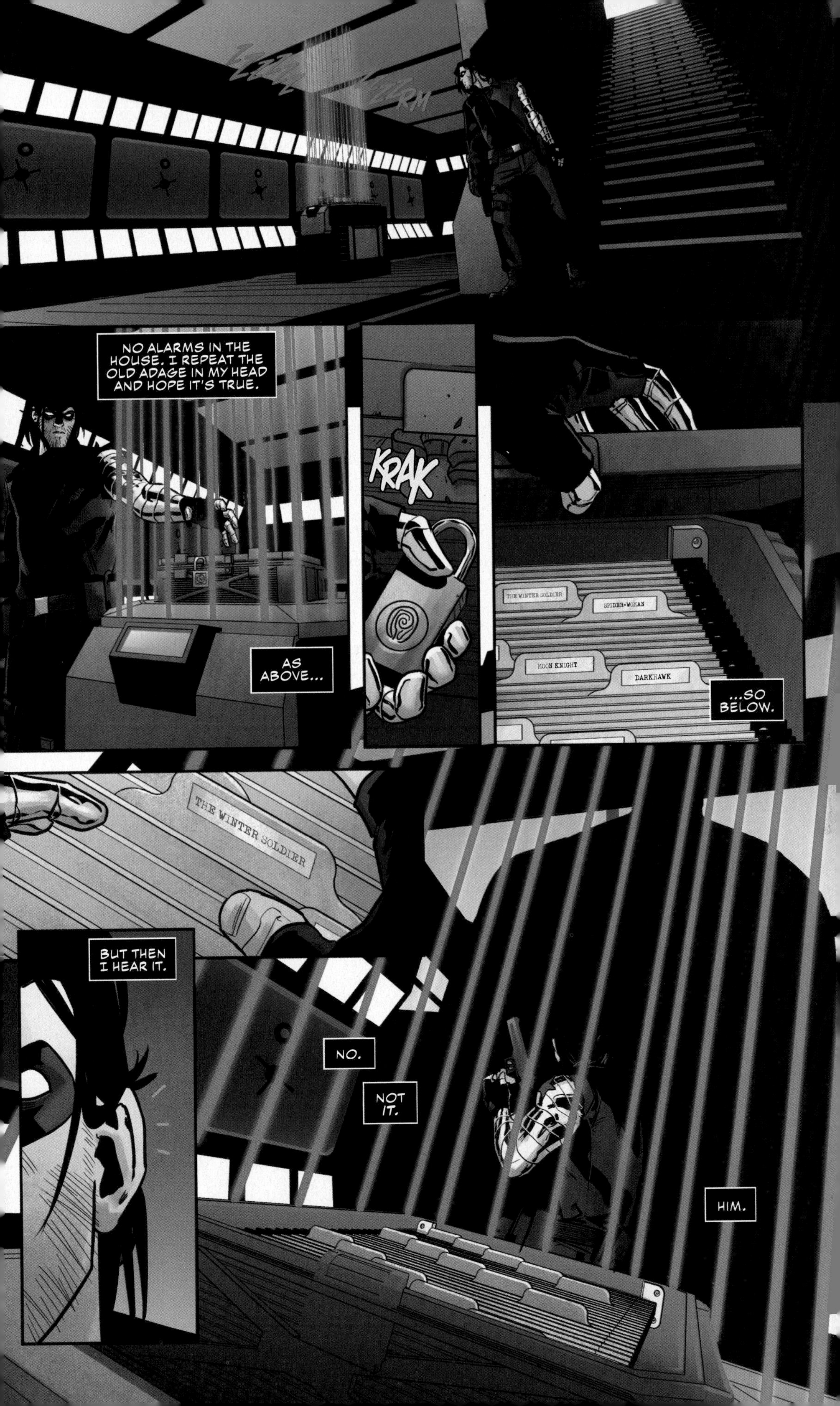

NO ALARMS IN THE HOUSE. I REPEAT THE OLD ADAGE IN MY HEAD AND HOPE IT'S TRUE.
AS ABOVE...
KRAK
THE WINTER SOLDIER
SPIDER-WOMAN
MOON KNIGHT
DARKHAWK
...SO BELOW.
THE WINTER SOLDIER
BUT THEN I HEAR IT.
NO.
NOT IT.
HIM.

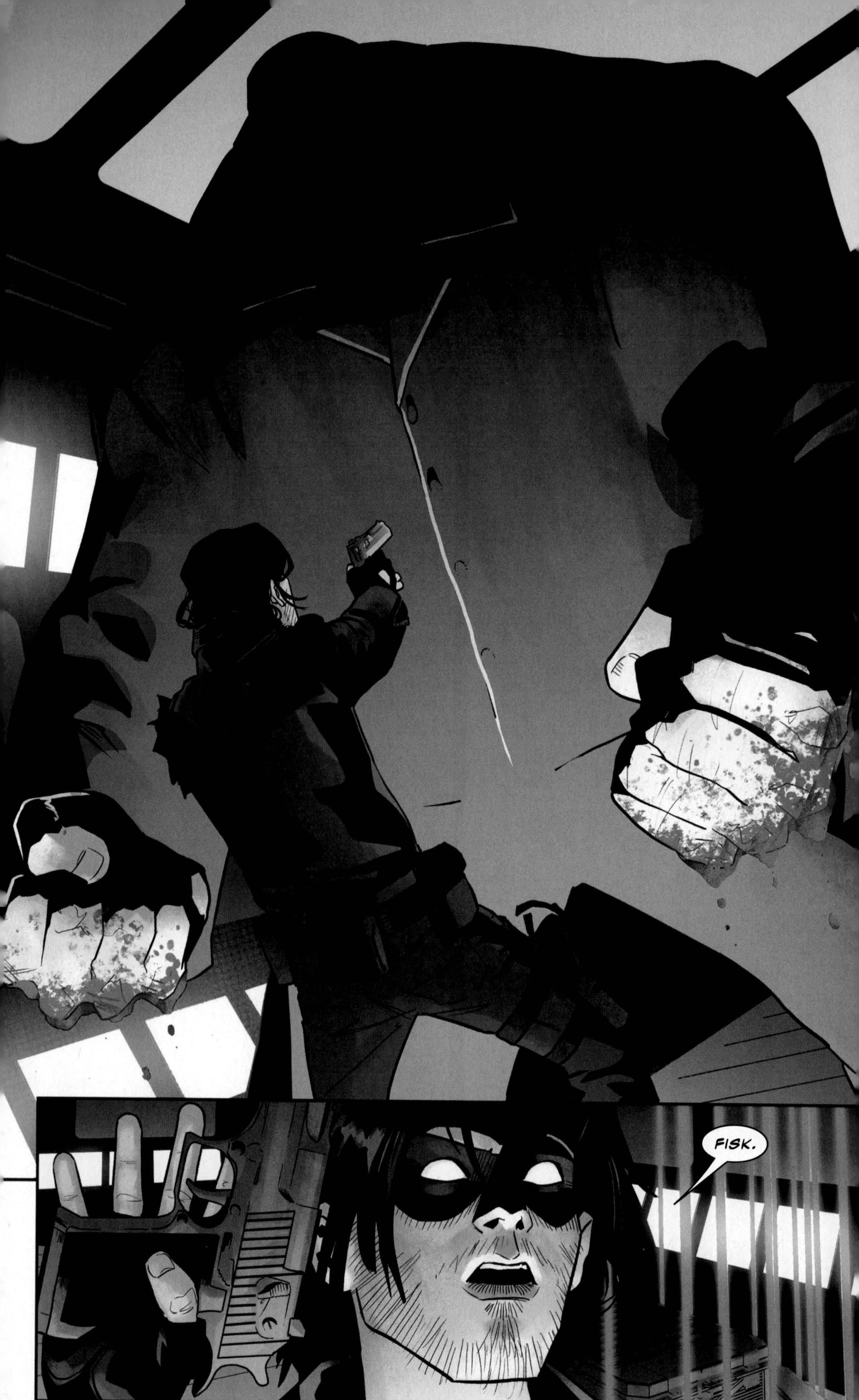
FISK.

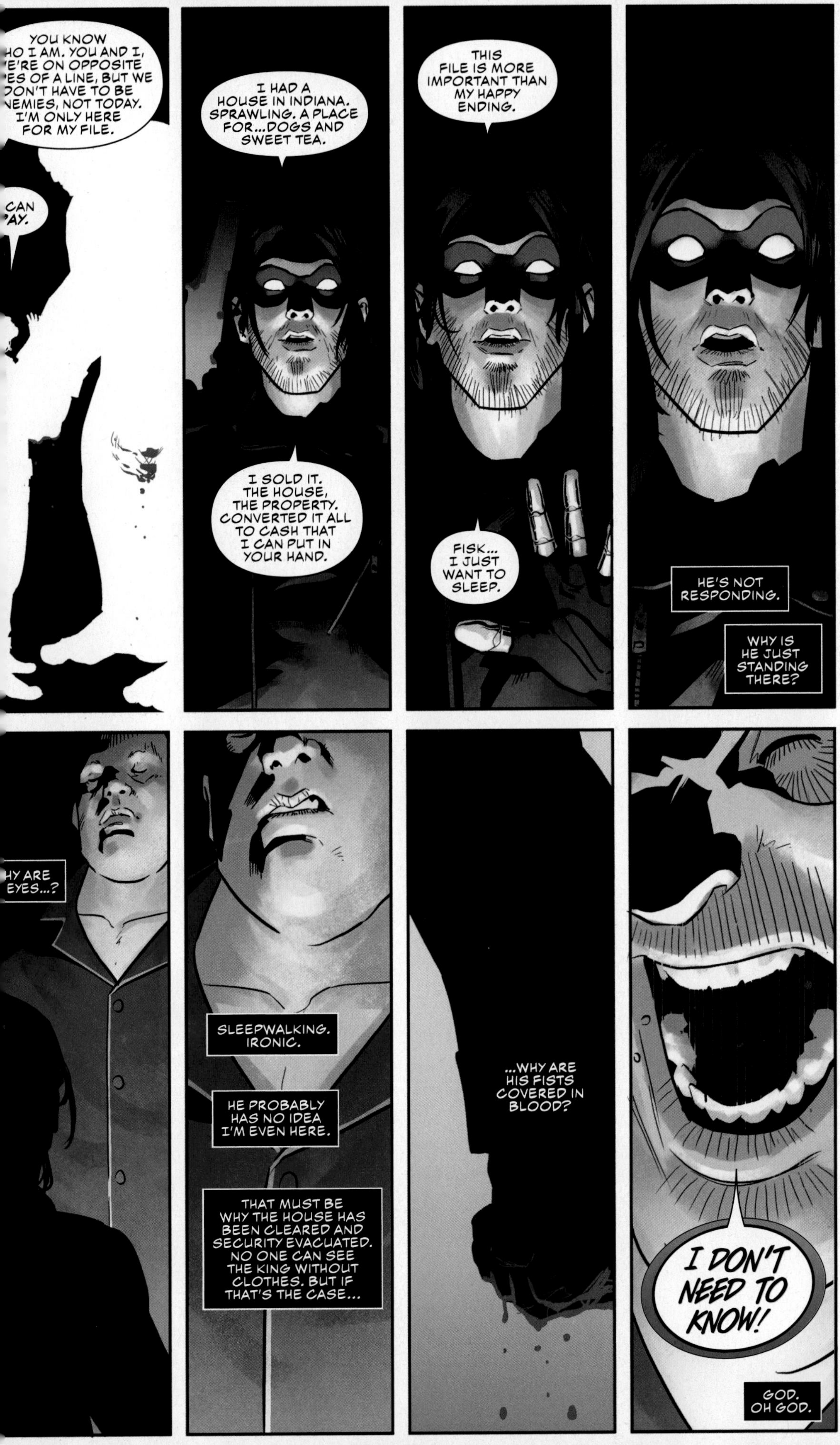
YOU KNOW
HO I AM. YOU AND I,
E'RE ON OPPOSITE
ES OF A LINE, BUT WE
ON'T HAVE TO BE
NEMIES, NOT TODAY.
I'M ONLY HERE
FOR MY FILE.
CAN
AY.
I HAD A HOUSE IN INDIANA. SPRAWLING. A PLACE FOR...DOGS AND SWEET TEA.
I SOLD IT. THE HOUSE, THE PROPERTY. CONVERTED IT ALL TO CASH THAT I CAN PUT IN YOUR HAND.
THIS FILE IS MORE IMPORTANT THAN MY HAPPY ENDING.
FISK... I JUST WANT TO SLEEP.
HE'S NOT RESPONDING.
WHY IS HE JUST STANDING THERE?
HY ARE
EYES...?
SLEEPWALKING. IRONIC.
HE PROBABLY HAS NO IDEA I'M EVEN HERE.
THAT MUST BE WHY THE HOUSE HAS BEEN CLEARED AND SECURITY EVACUATED. NO ONE CAN SEE THE KING WITHOUT CLOTHES. BUT IF THAT'S THE CASE...
...WHY ARE HIS FISTS COVERED IN BLOOD?
I DON'T NEED TO KNOW!
GOD. OH GOD.

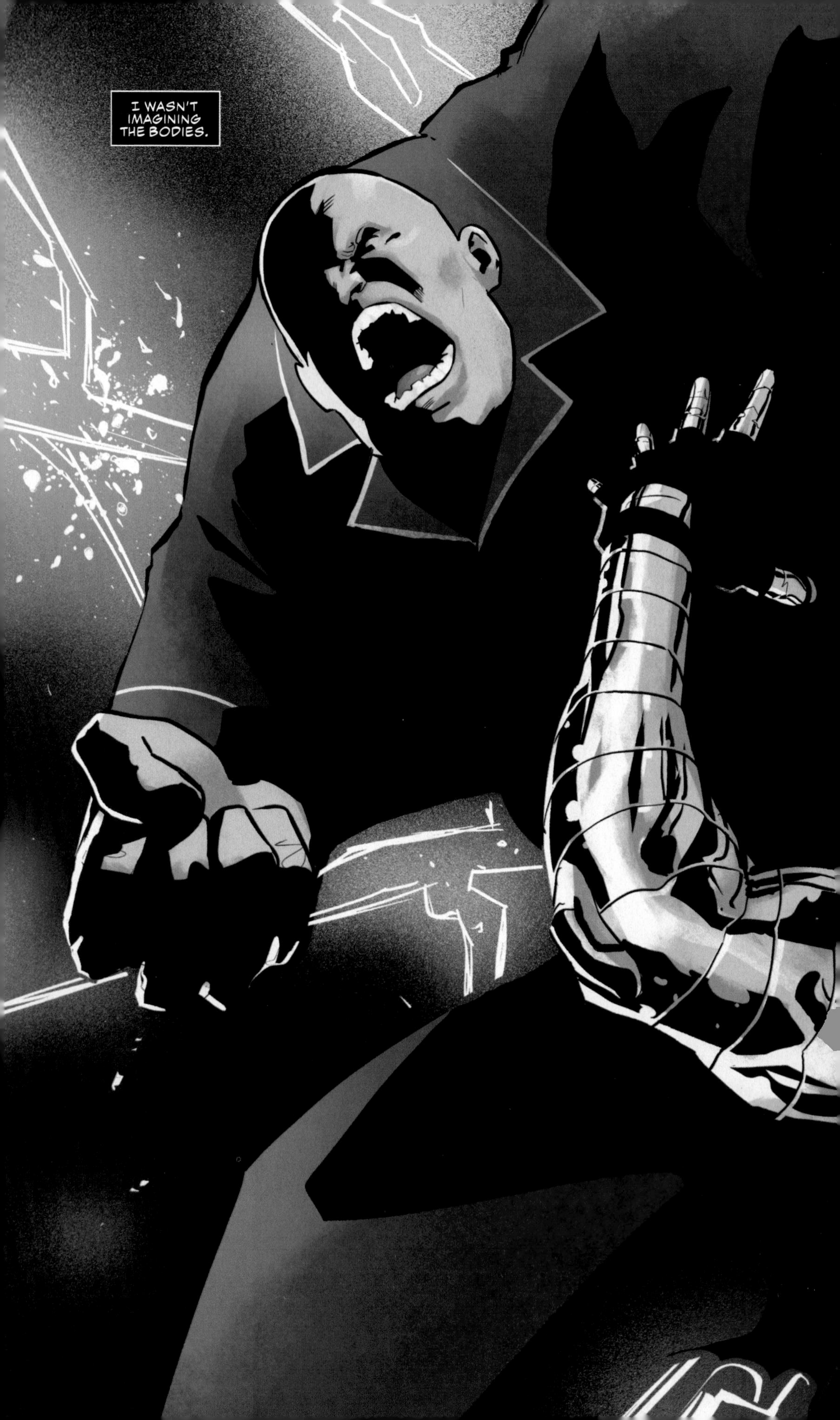
I WASN'T IMAGINING THE BODIES.

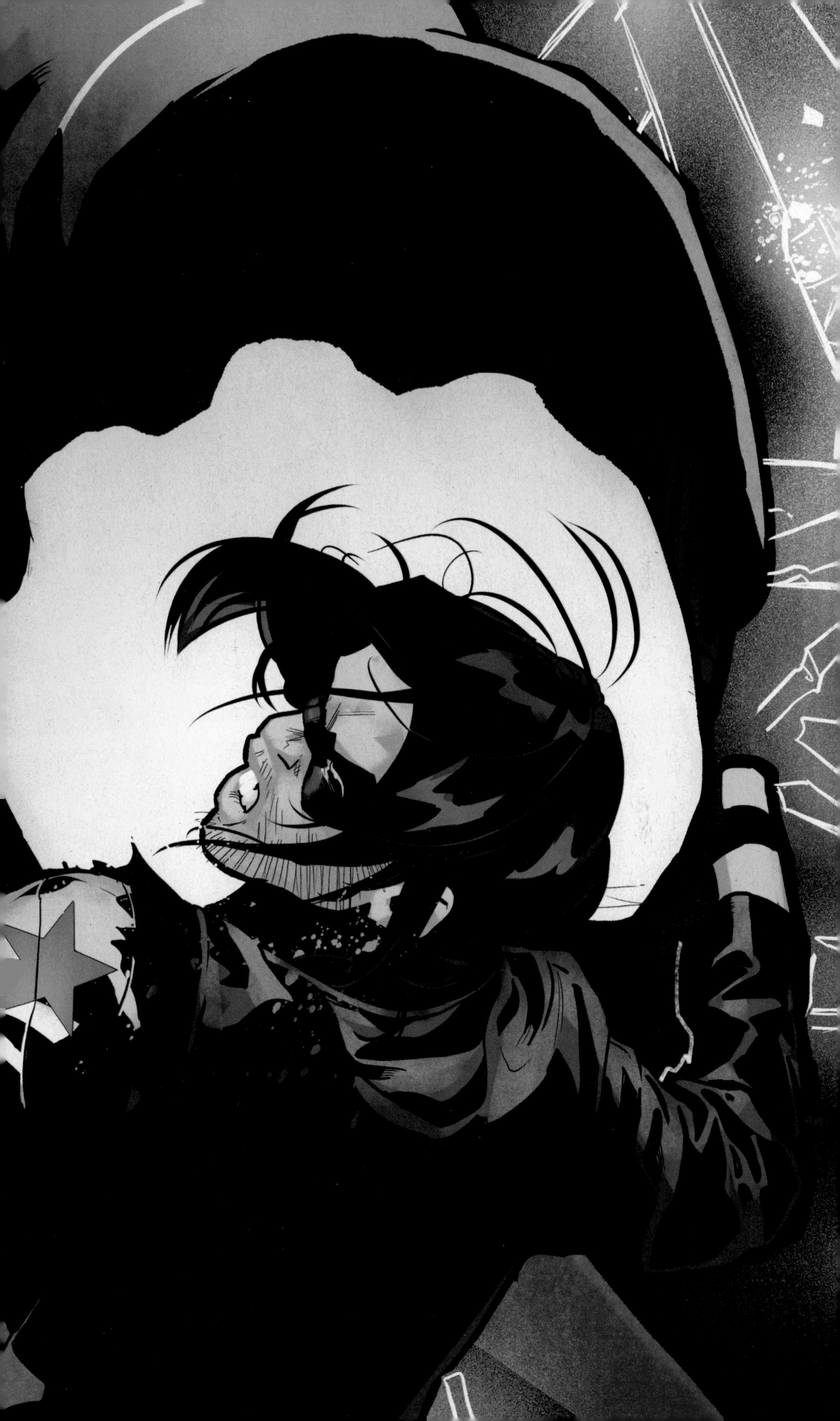

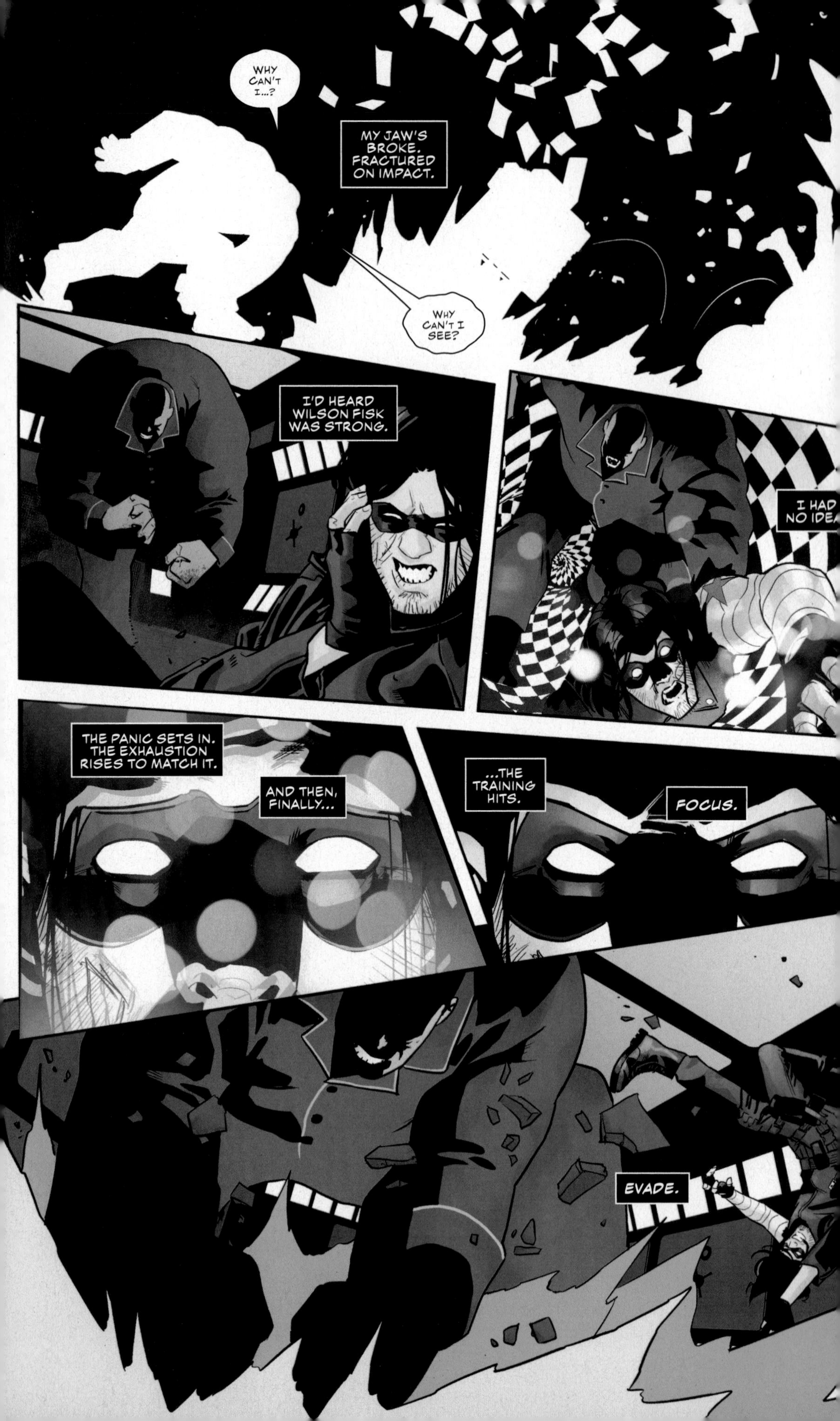
WHY CAN'T I...?
MY JAW'S BROKE. FRACTURED ON IMPACT.
WHY CAN'T I SEE?
I'D HEARD WILSON FISK WAS STRONG.
I HAD NO IDEA
THE PANIC SETS IN. THE EXHAUSTION RISES TO MATCH IT.
AND THEN, FINALLY...
...THE TRAINING HITS.
FOCUS.
EVADE.

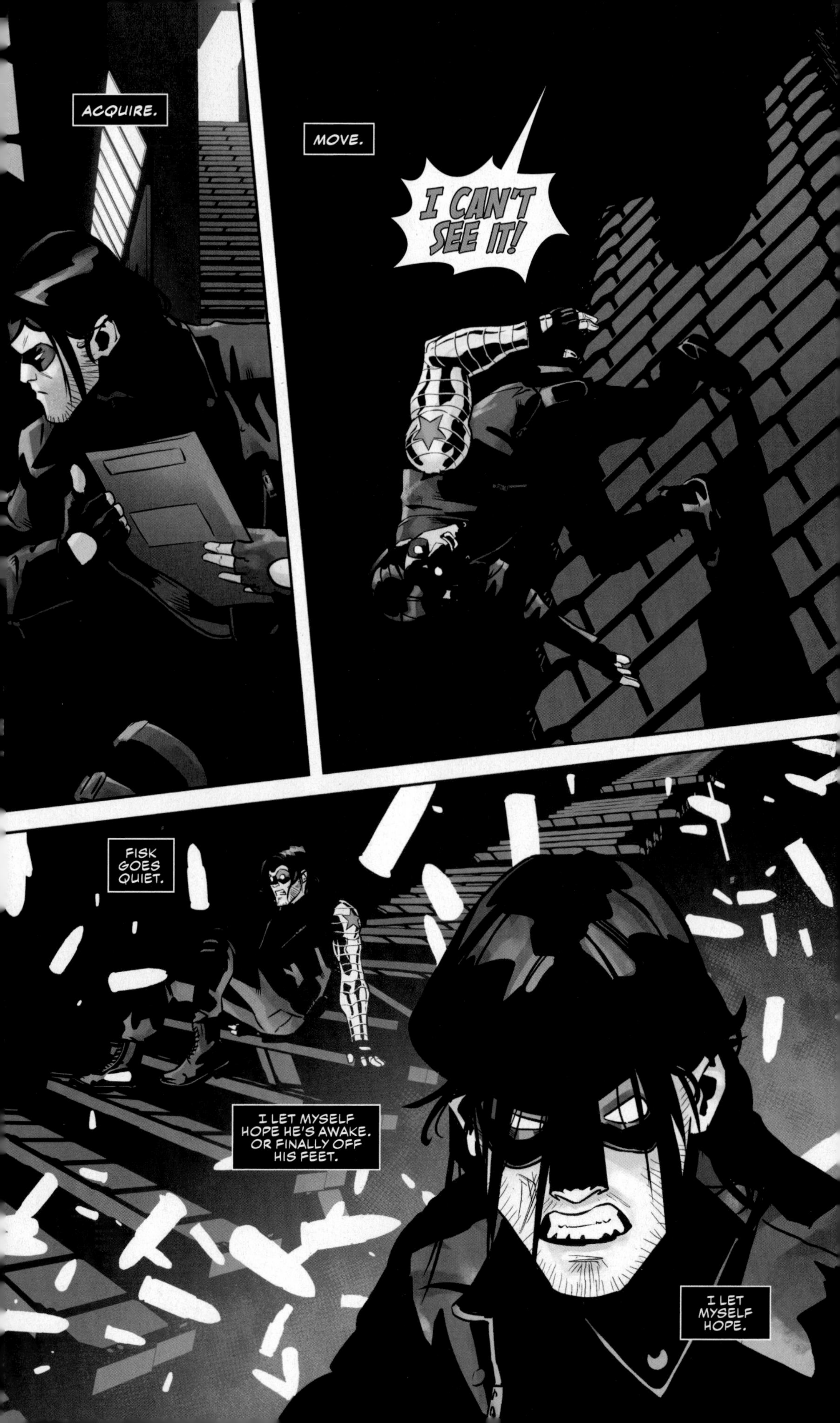

ACQUIRE.
MOVE.
I CAN'T SEE IT!
FISK GOES QUIET.
I LET MYSELF HOPE HE'S AWAKE. OR FINALLY OFF HIS FEET.
I LET MYSELF HOPE.

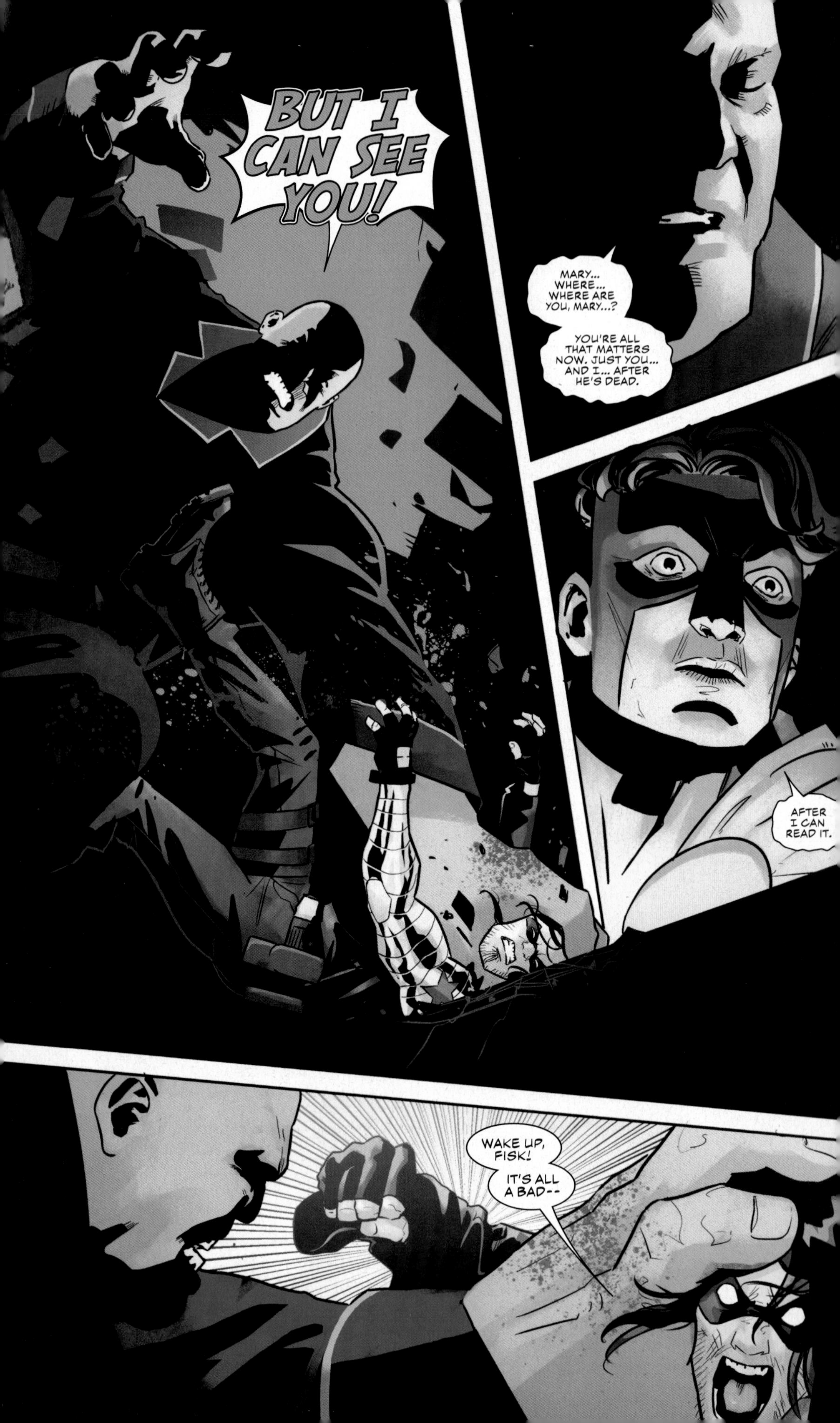
BUT I CAN SEE YOU!
MARY... WHERE... WHERE ARE YOU, MARY...?
YOU'RE ALL THAT MATTERS NOW. JUST YOU... AND I... AFTER HE'S DEAD.
AFTER I CAN READ IT.
WAKE UP, FISK!
IT'S ALL A BAD--

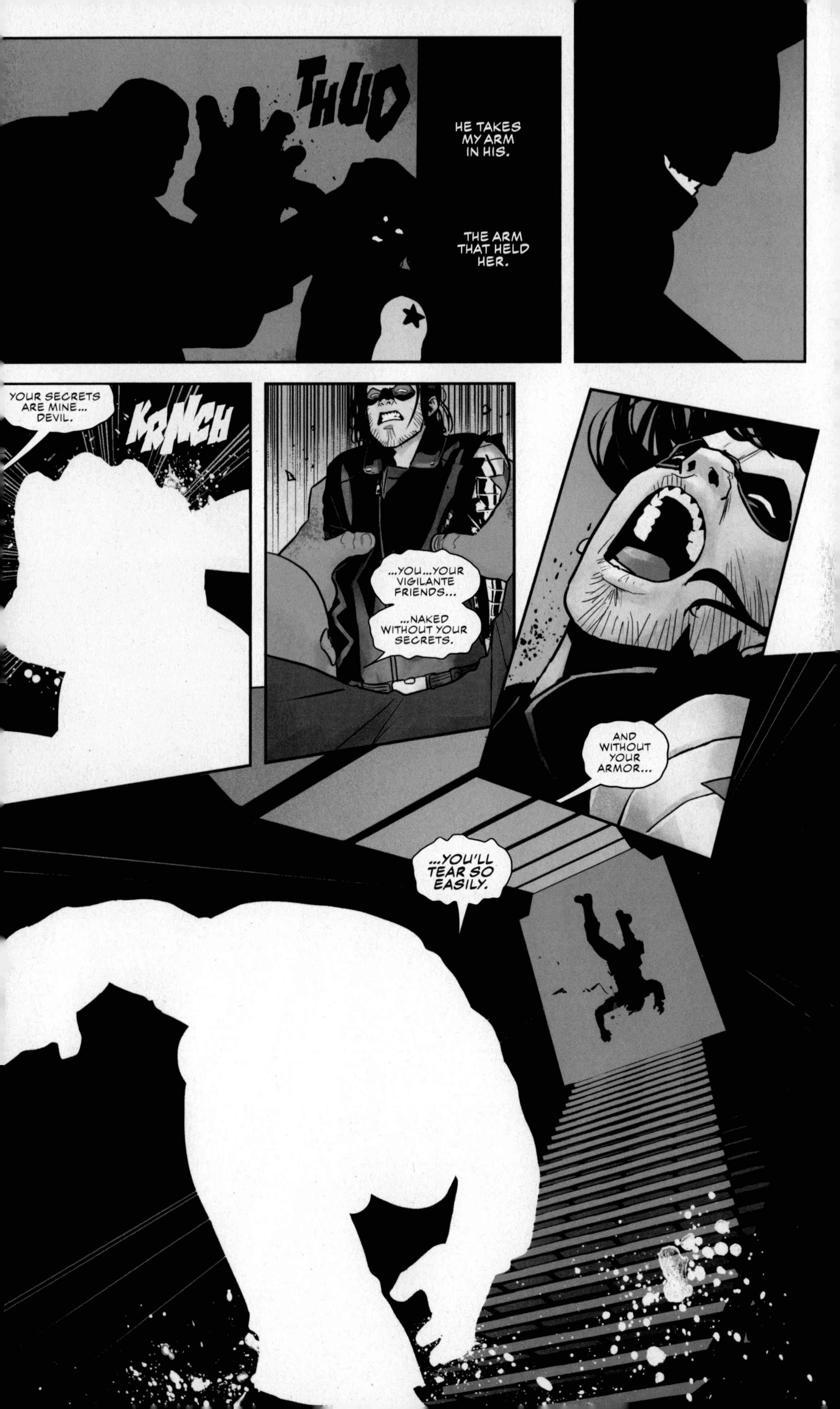
THUD
HE TAKES MY ARM IN HIS.
THE ARM THAT HELD HER.
YOUR SECRETS ARE MINE... DEVIL.
KRNCH
...YOU...YOUR VIGILANTE FRIENDS...
...NAKED WITHOUT YOUR SECRETS.
AND WITHOUT YOUR ARMOR...
...YOU'LL TEAR SO EASILY.

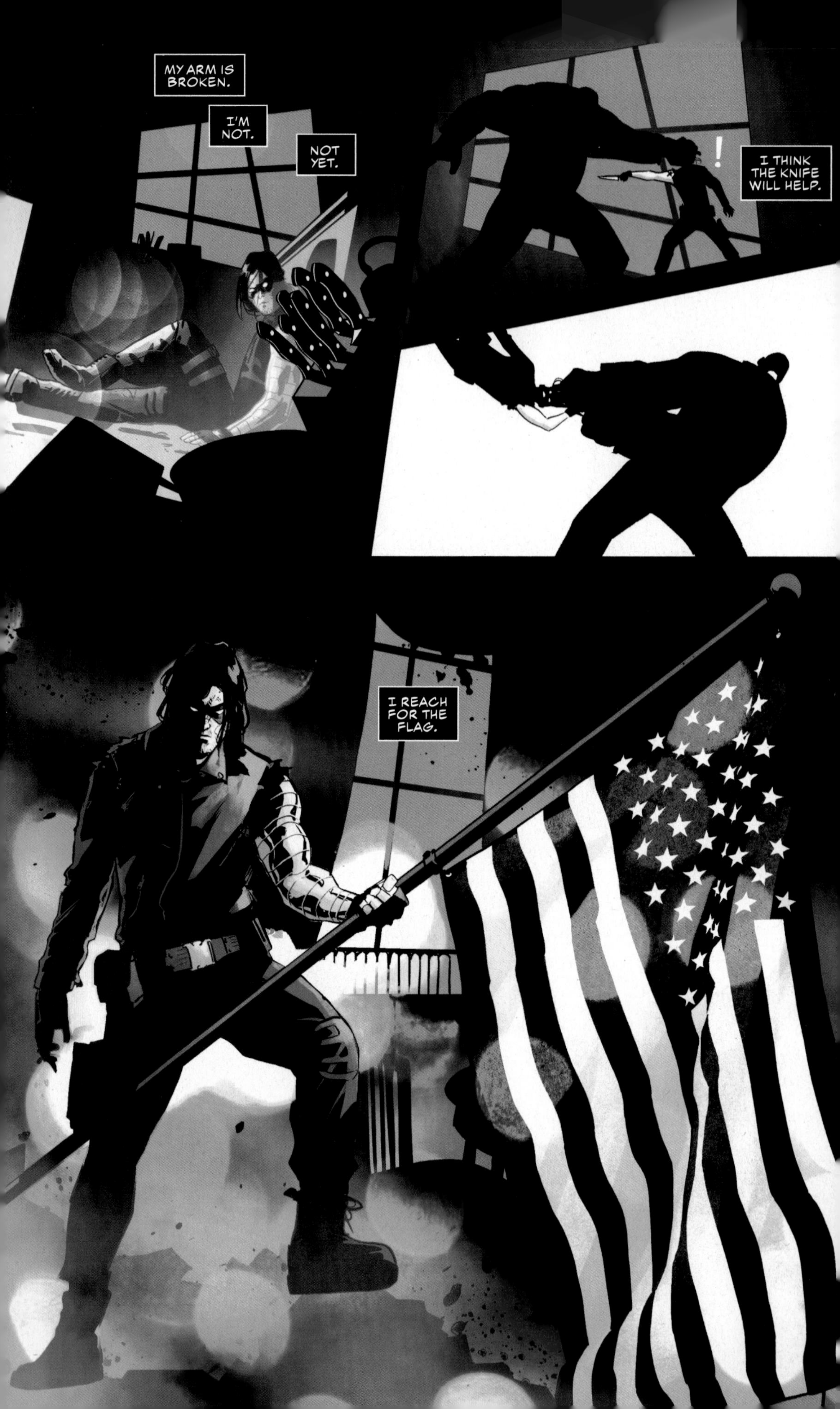
MY ARM IS BROKEN.
I'M NOT.
NOT YET.
I THINK THE KNIFE WILL HELP.
I REACH FOR THE FLAG.

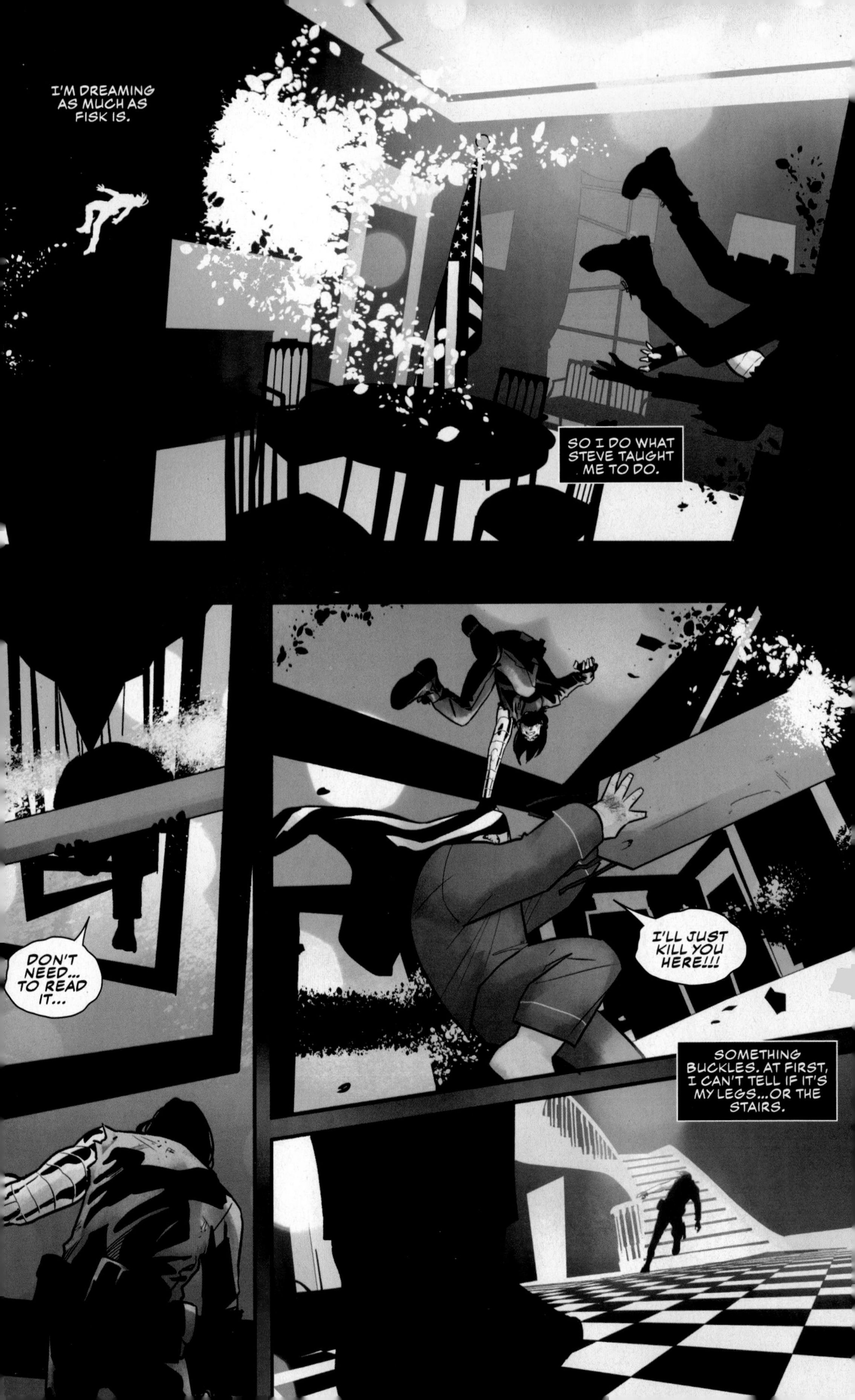
I'M DREAMING AS MUCH AS FISK IS.
SO I DO WHAT STEVE TAUGHT ME TO DO.
DON'T NEED... TO READ IT...
I'LL JUST KILL YOU HERE!!!
SOMETHING BUCKLES. AT FIRST, I CAN'T TELL IF IT'S MY LEGS...OR THE STAIRS.

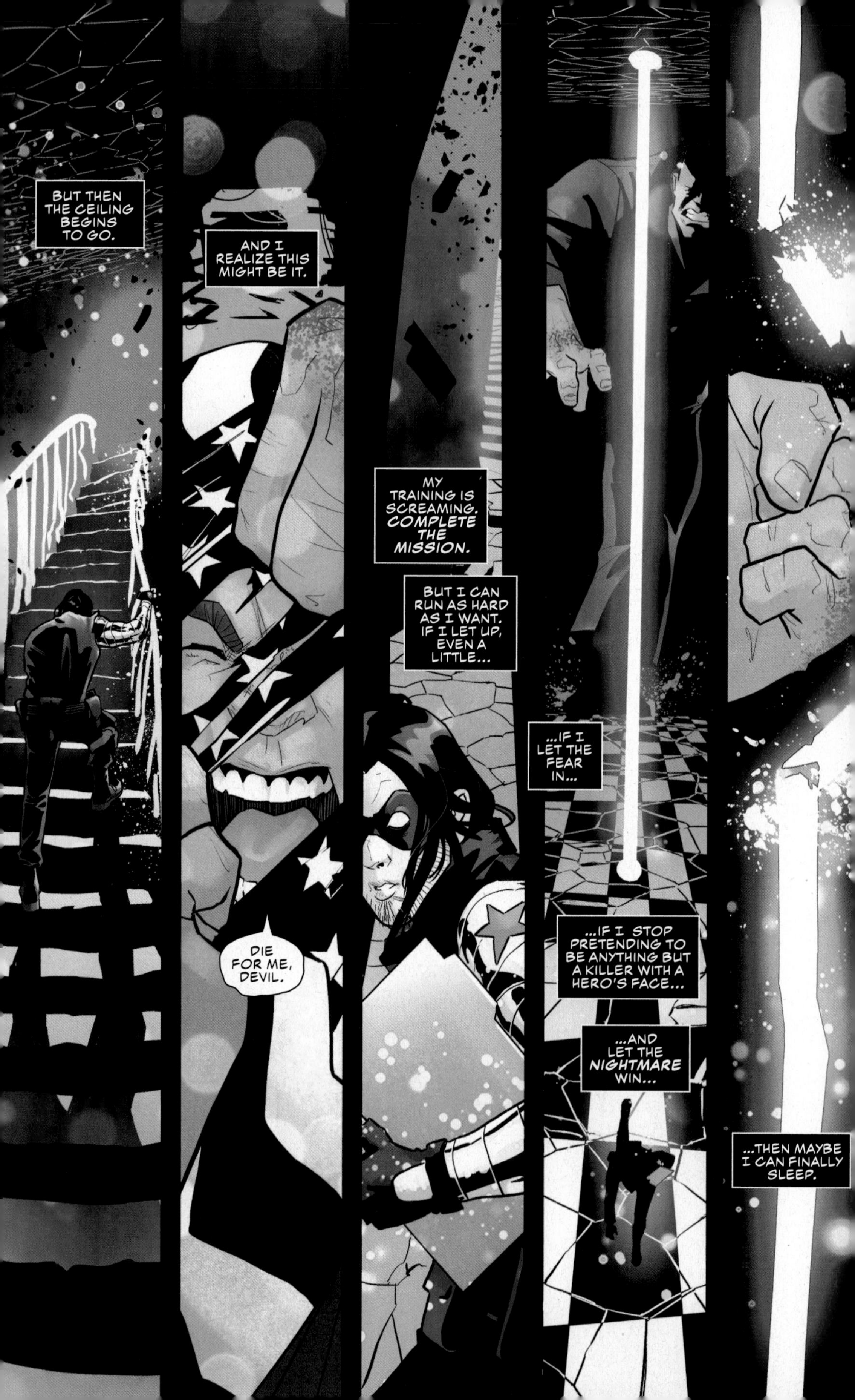
BUT THEN THE CEILING BEGINS TO GO.
AND I REALIZE THIS MIGHT BE IT.
DIE FOR ME, DEVIL.
MY TRAINING IS SCREAMING. COMPLETE THE MISSION.
BUT I CAN RUN AS HARD AS I WANT. IF I LET UP, EVEN A LITTLE...
...IF I LET THE FEAR IN...
...IF I STOP PRETENDING TO BE ANYTHING BUT A KILLER WITH A HERO'S FACE...
...AND LET THE NIGHTMARE WIN...
...THEN MAYBE I CAN FINALLY SLEEP.

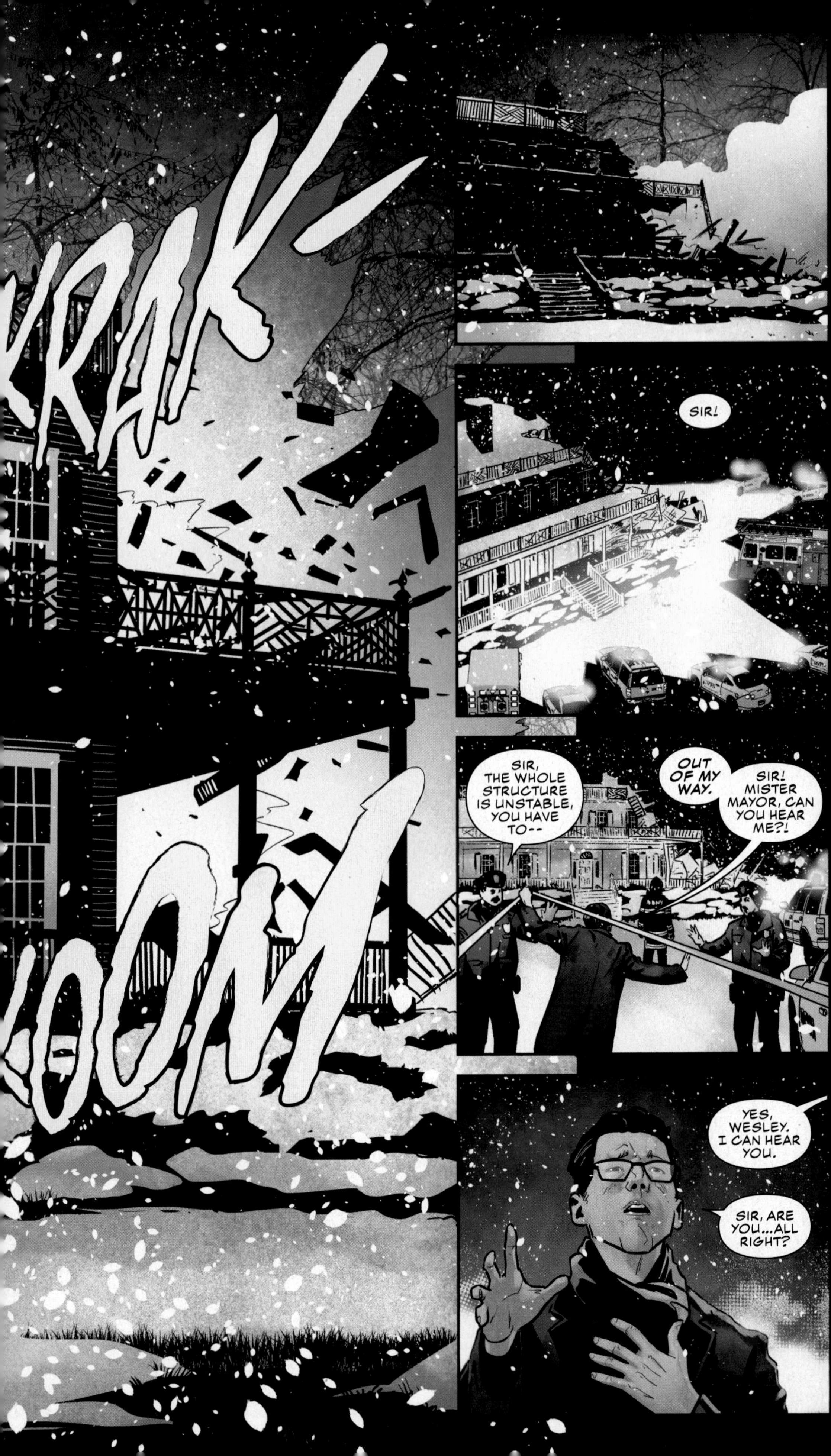
KRAK
BOOM
SIR!
SIR, THE WHOLE STRUCTURE IS UNSTABLE, YOU HAVE TO--
OUT OF MY WAY.
SIR! MISTER MAYOR, CAN YOU HEAR ME?!
YES, WESLEY. I CAN HEAR YOU.
SIR, ARE YOU...ALL RIGHT?

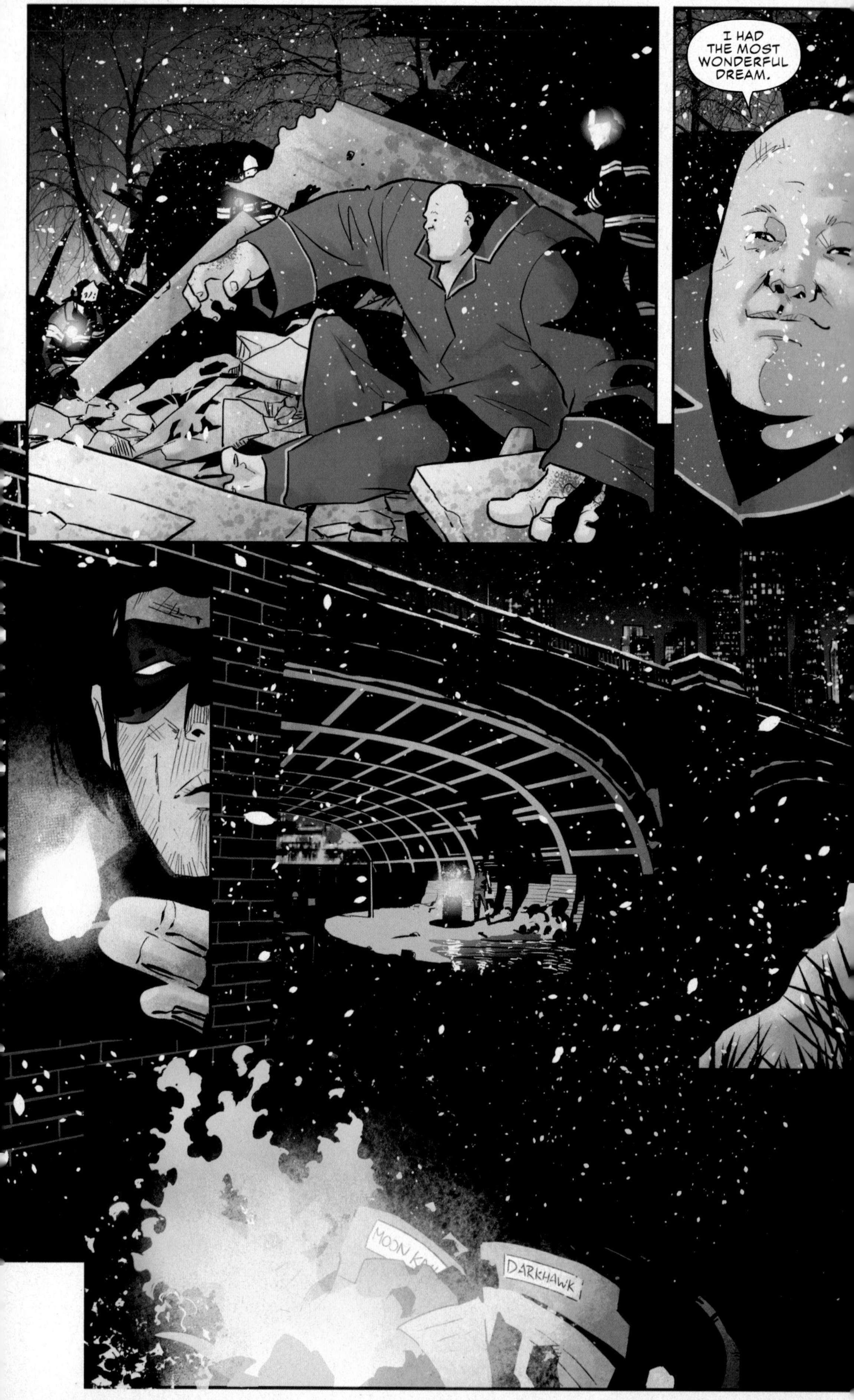
I HAD THE MOST WONDERFUL DREAM.
MOON KN
DARKHAWK

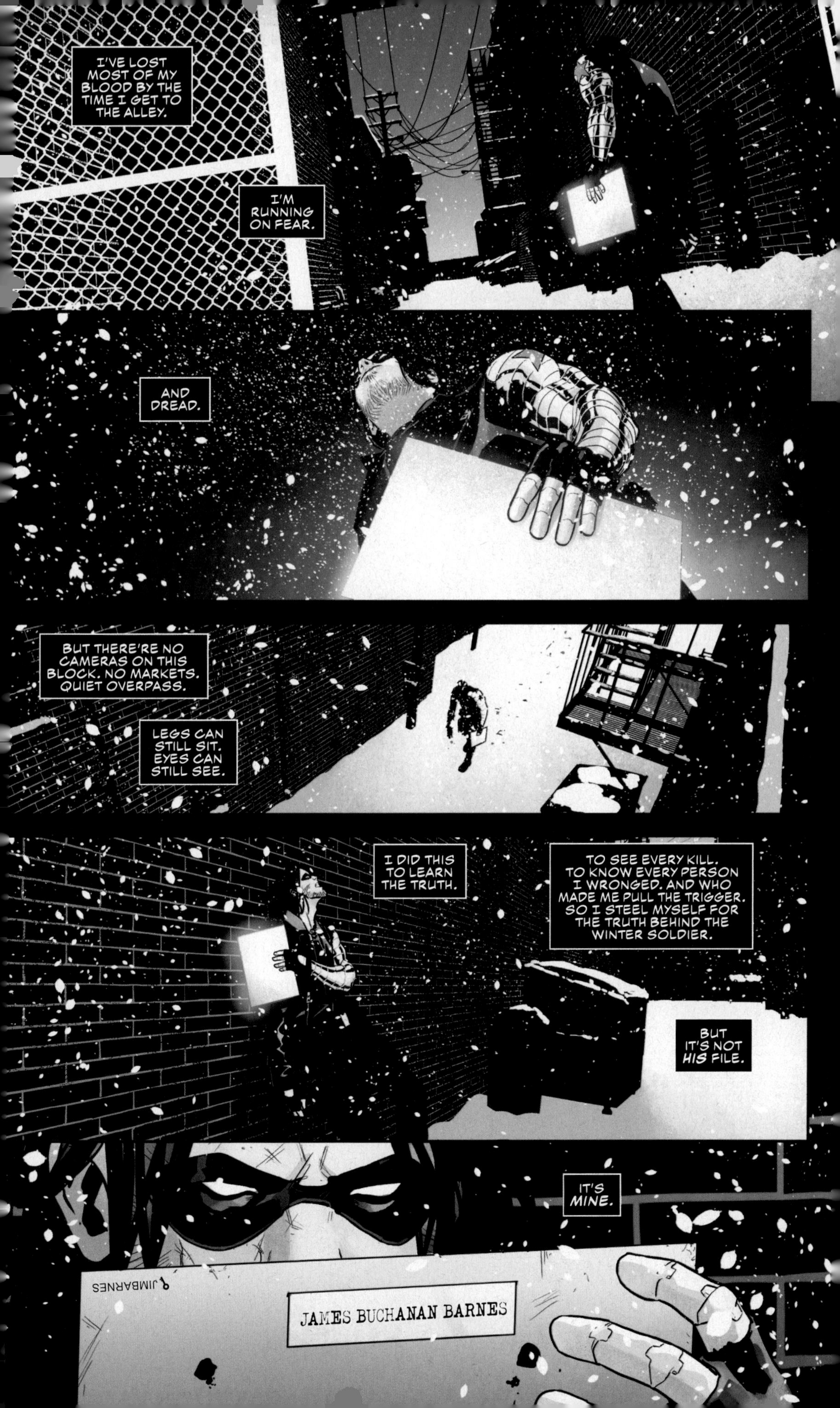

I'VE LOST MOST OF MY BLOOD BY THE TIME I GET TO THE ALLEY.
I'M RUNNING ON FEAR.
AND DREAD.
BUT THERE'RE NO CAMERAS ON THIS BLOCK. NO MARKETS. QUIET OVERPASS.
LEGS CAN STILL SIT. EYES CAN STILL SEE.
I DID THIS TO LEARN THE TRUTH.
TO SEE EVERY KILL. TO KNOW EVERY PERSON I WRONGED. AND WHO MADE ME PULL THE TRIGGER. SO I STEEL MYSELF FOR THE TRUTH BEHIND THE WINTER SOLDIER.
BUT IT'S NOT *HIS* FILE.
IT'S *MINE.*
JAMES BUCHANAN BARNES

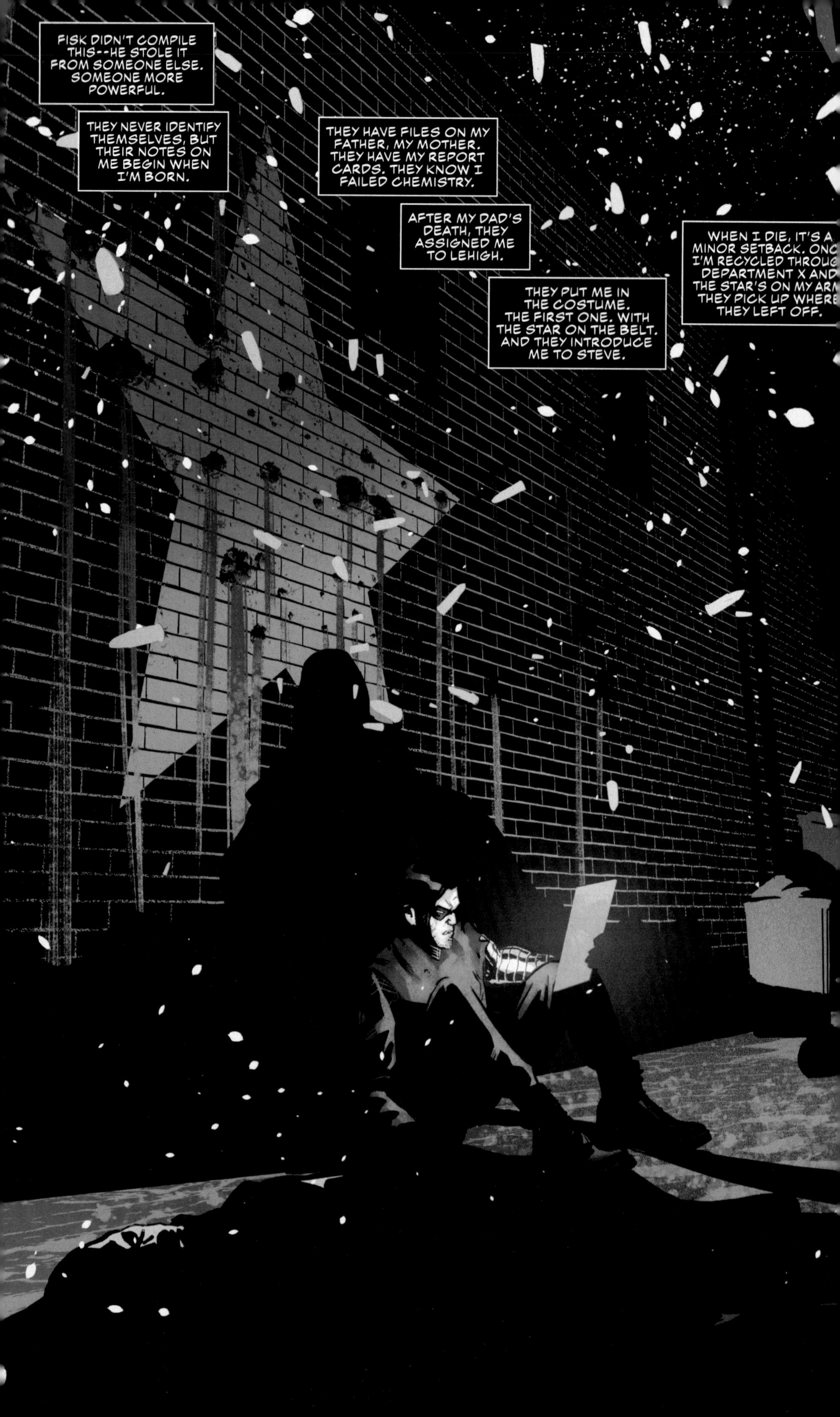
FISK DIDN'T COMPILE THIS--HE STOLE IT FROM SOMEONE ELSE. SOMEONE MORE POWERFUL.
THEY NEVER IDENTIFY THEMSELVES, BUT THEIR NOTES ON ME BEGIN WHEN I'M BORN.
THEY HAVE FILES ON MY FATHER, MY MOTHER. THEY HAVE MY REPORT CARDS. THEY KNOW I FAILED CHEMISTRY.
AFTER MY DAD'S DEATH, THEY ASSIGNED ME TO LEHIGH.
THEY PUT ME IN THE COSTUME. THE FIRST ONE. WITH THE STAR ON THE BELT. AND THEY INTRODUCE ME TO STEVE.
WHEN I DIE, IT'S A MINOR SETBACK. ONC I'M RECYCLED THROUG DEPARTMENT X AND THE STAR'S ON MY ARM THEY PICK UP WHERE THEY LEFT OFF.

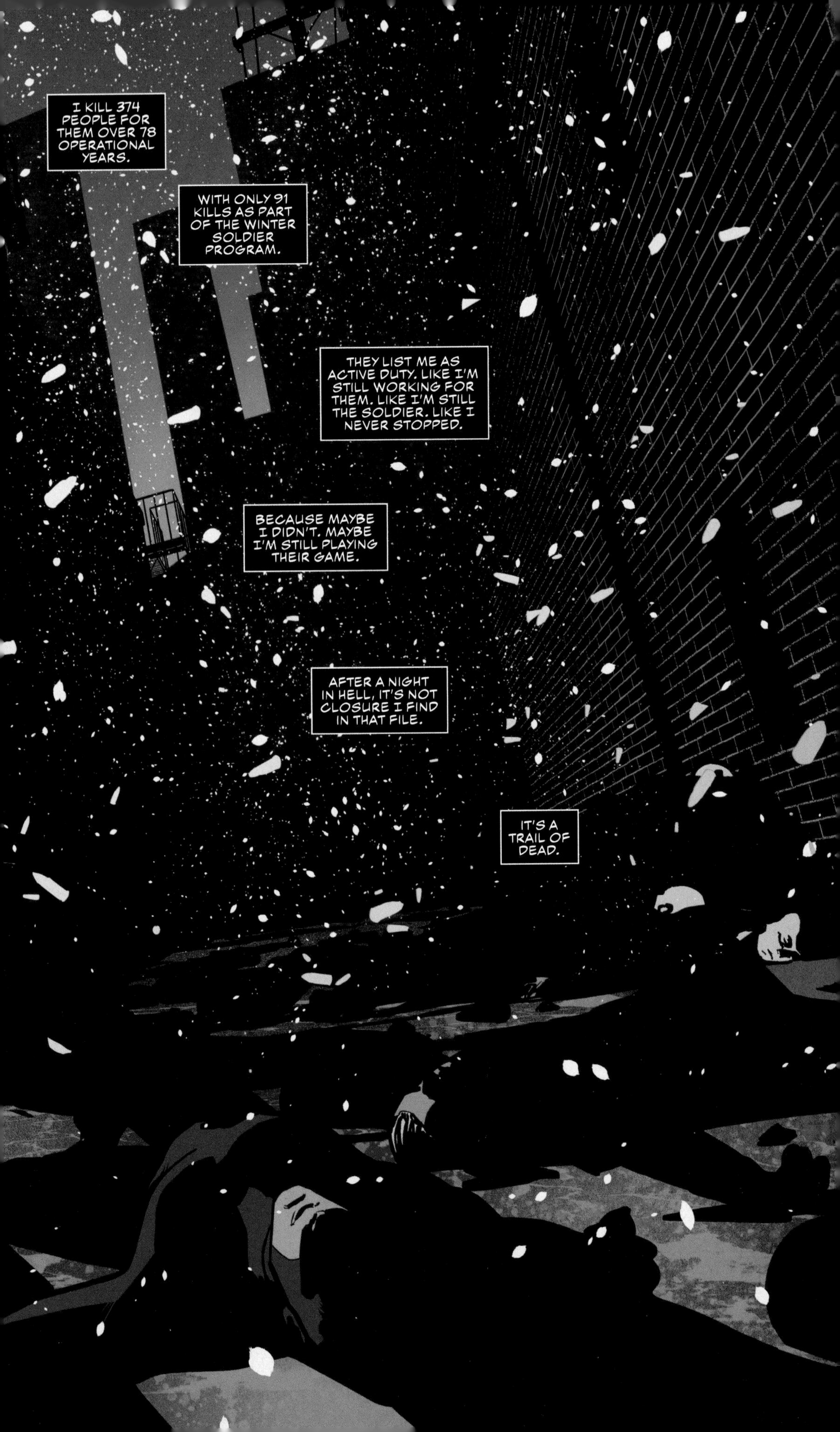
I KILL 374 PEOPLE FOR THEM OVER 78 OPERATIONAL YEARS.
WITH ONLY 91 KILLS AS PART OF THE WINTER SOLDIER PROGRAM.
THEY LIST ME AS ACTIVE DUTY. LIKE I'M STILL WORKING FOR THEM. LIKE I'M STILL THE SOLDIER. LIKE I NEVER STOPPED.
BECAUSE MAYBE I DIDN'T. MAYBE I'M STILL PLAYING THEIR GAME.
AFTER A NIGHT IN HELL, IT'S NOT CLOSURE I FIND IN THAT FILE.
IT'S A TRAIL OF DEAD.

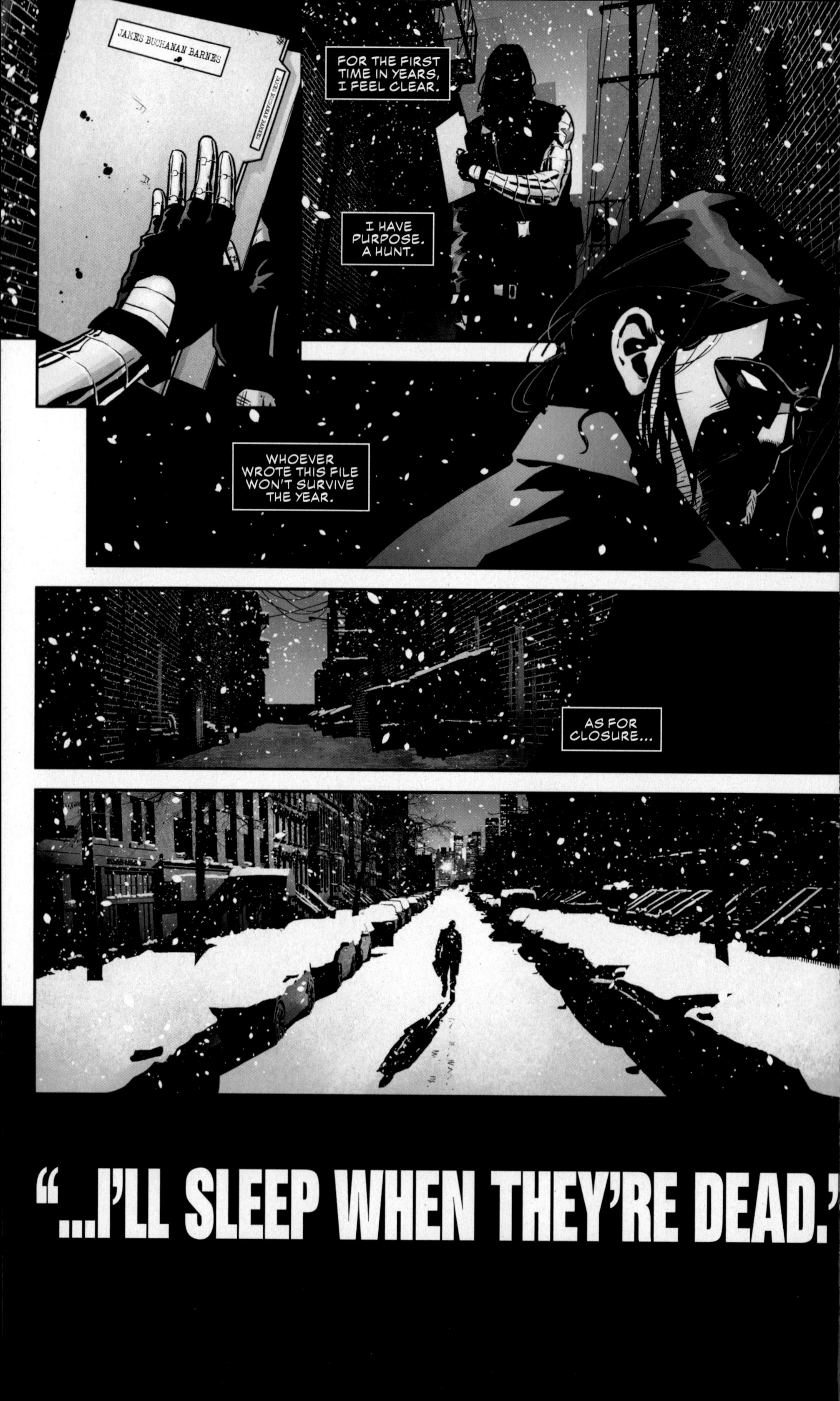
JAMES BUCHANAN BARNES
FOR THE FIRST TIME IN YEARS, I FEEL CLEAR.
I HAVE PURPOSE. A HUNT.
WHOEVER WROTE THIS FILE WON'T SURVIVE THE YEAR.
AS FOR CLOSURE...
"...I'LL SLEEP WHEN THEY'RE DEAD."

CONTINUED IN

CAPTAIN AMERICA: SENTINEL OF LIBERY!

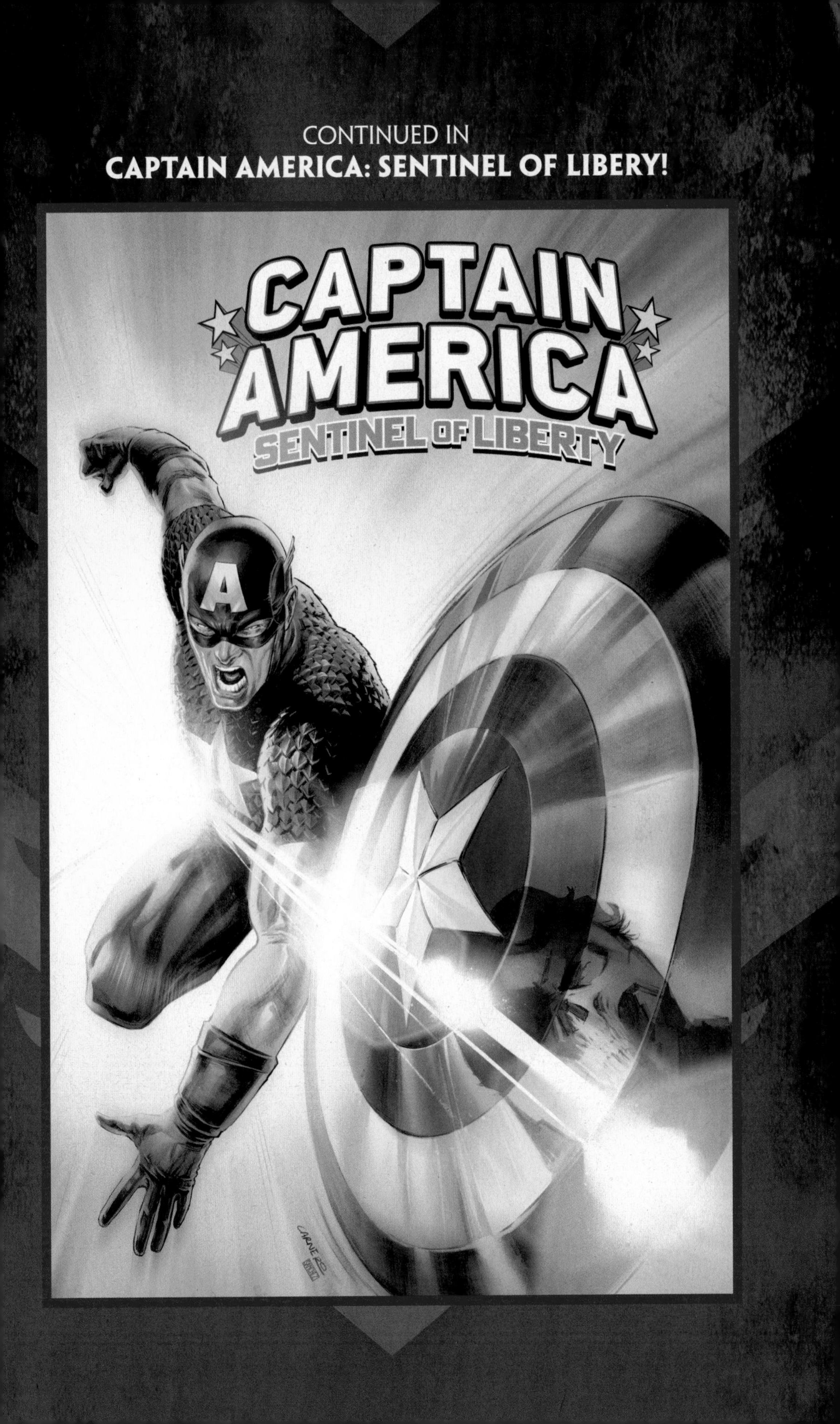
CAPTAIN AMERICA
SENTINEL OF LIBERTY

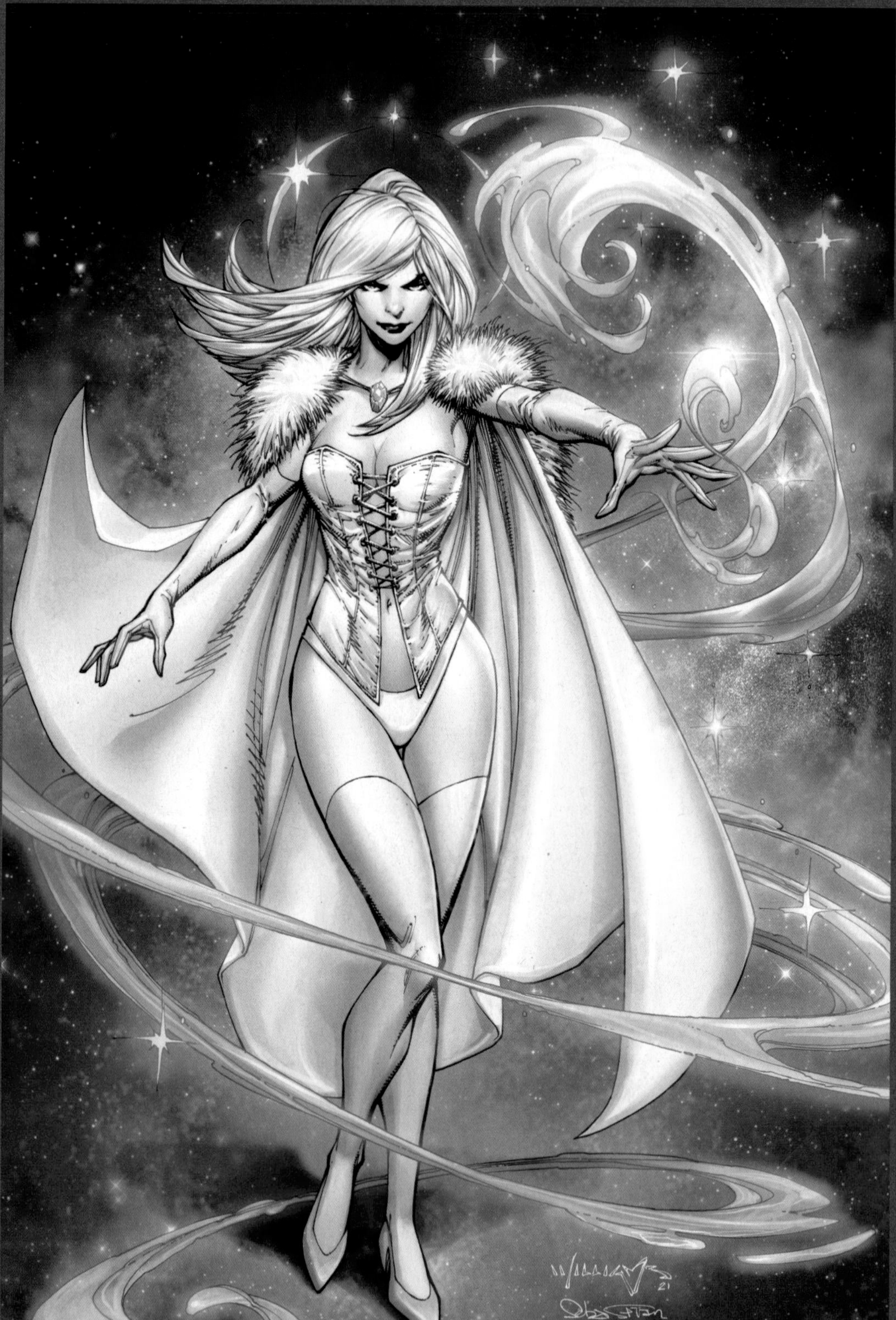

DEVIL'S REIGN: X-MEN #1 VARIANT BY **SCOTT WILLIAMS** & **SEBASTIAN CHENG**

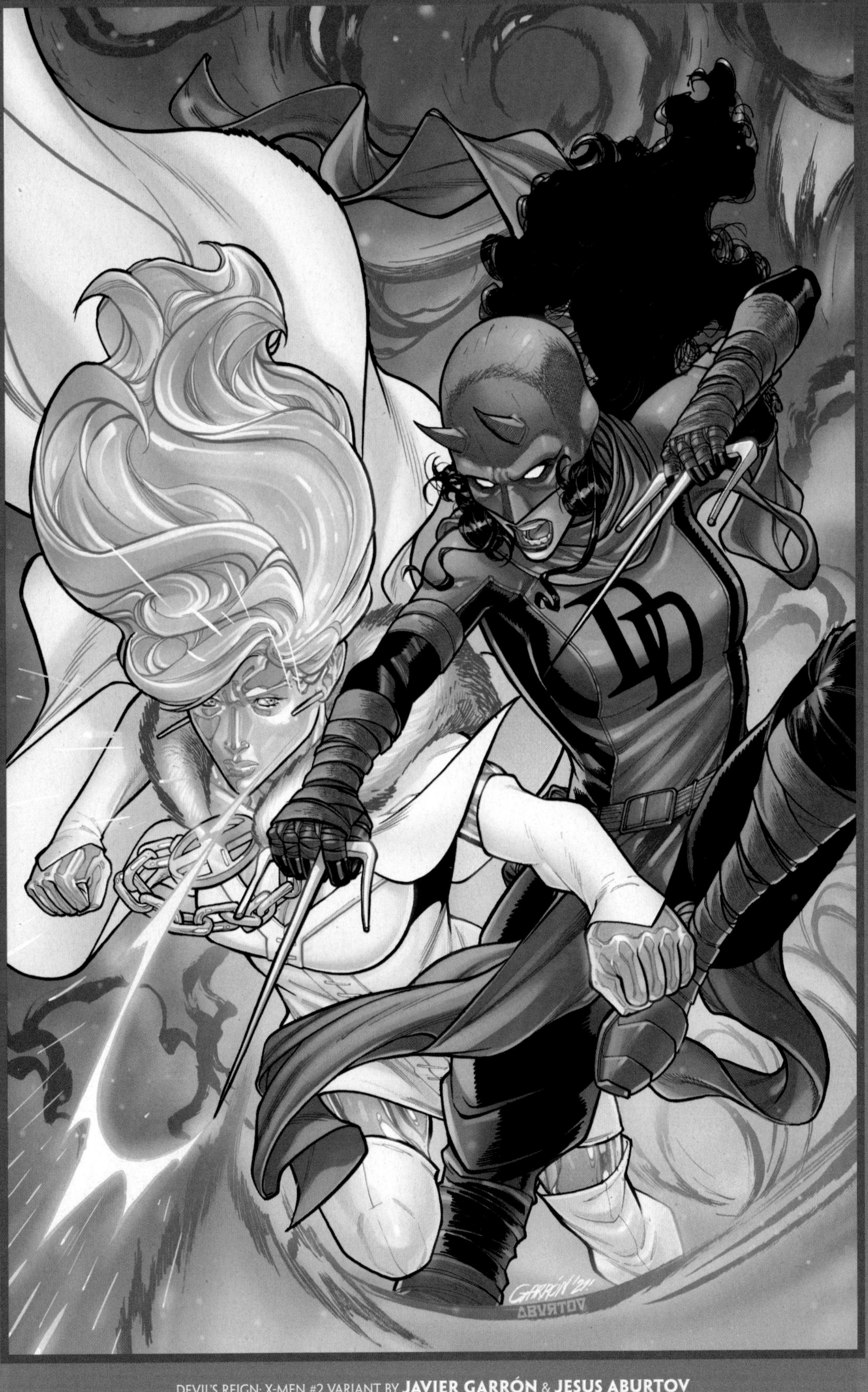
GARRÓN '21
ABURTOV

DEVIL'S REIGN: X-MEN #2 VARIANT BY **JAVIER GARRÓN** & **JESUS ABURTOV**

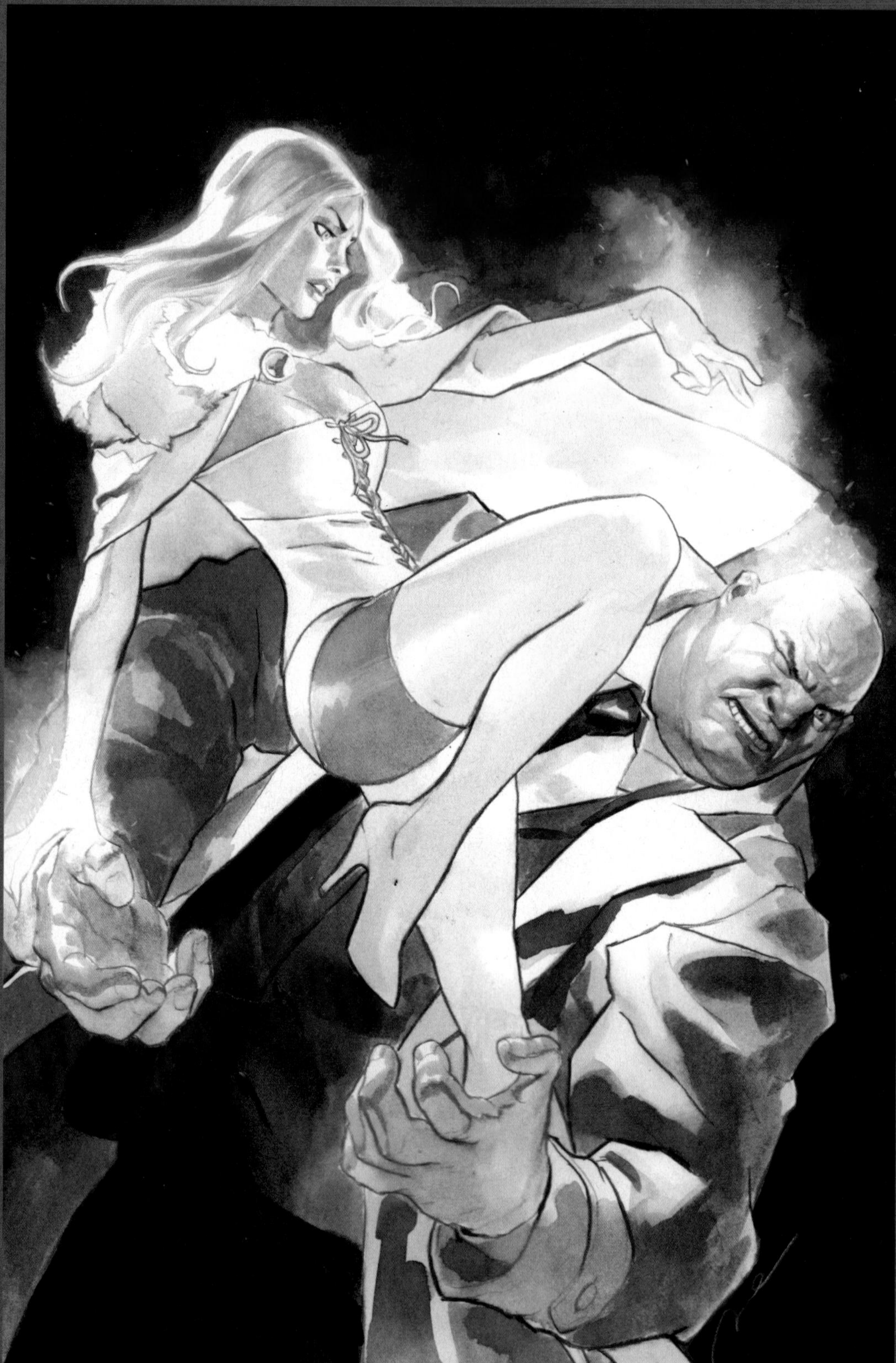

DEVIL'S REIGN: X-MEN #3 VARIANT BY **GERALD PAREL**

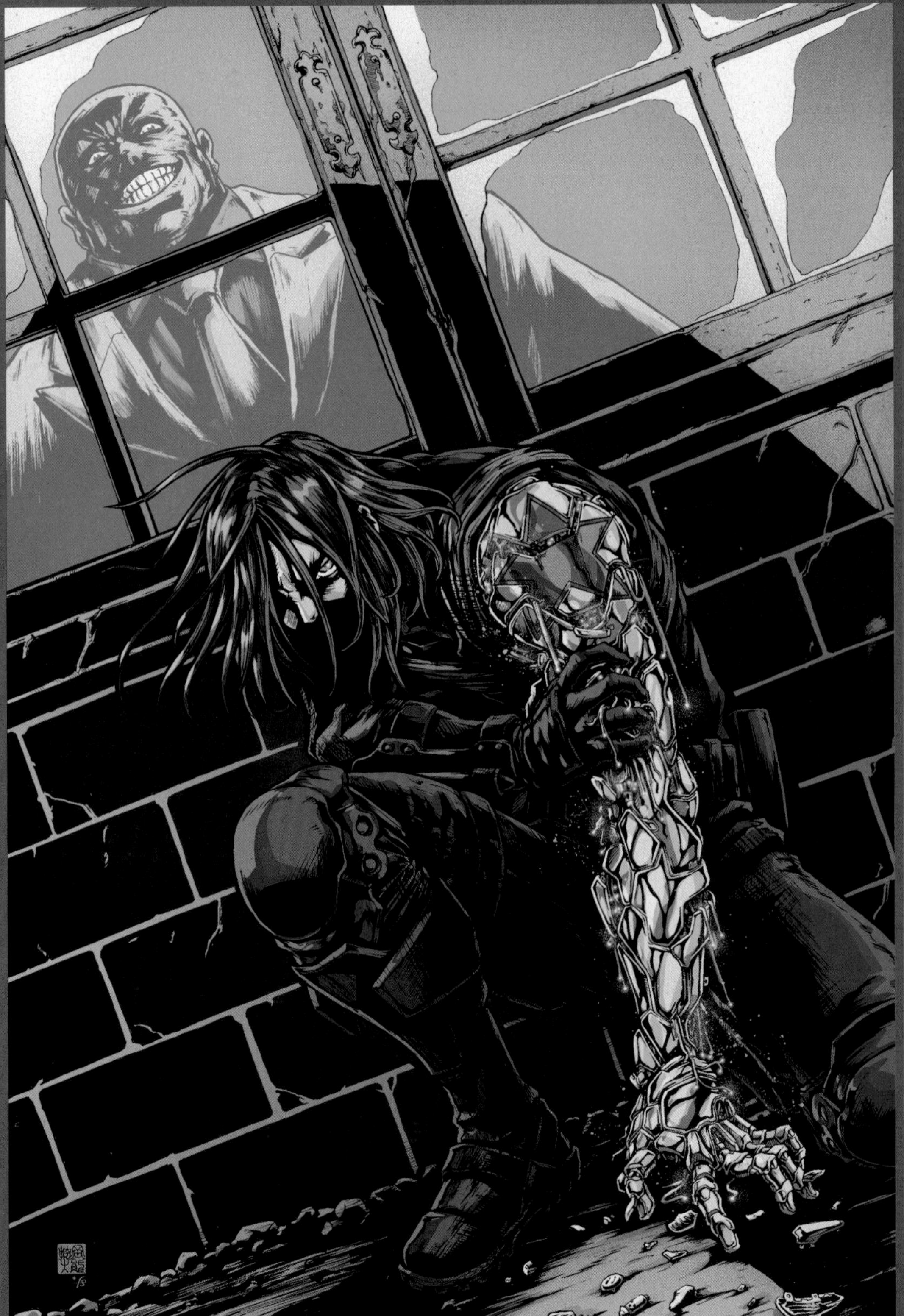

DEVIL'S REIGN: WINTER SOLDIER VARIANT BY **TAKASHI OKAZAKI** & **FELIPE SOBREIRO**